A DIRECTORY OF

BRITISH PEERAGES

A DIRECTORY OF
BRITISH PEERAGES

From the Earliest Times to the Present Day

Compiled by
FRANCIS L. LEESON, F.S.G.
(Editor, Genealogists' Magazine)

Assisted by
COLIN J. PARRY
(Compiler of 'Index of Baronetage Creations')

Baltimore
GENEALOGICAL PUBLISHING CO., INC.
1986

First published by the
Society of Genealogists, London, 1984.
Copyright © by the Society of
Genealogists and the Compiler, 1984.
All Rights Reserved.
Reprinted, with additions and corrections,
by Genealogical Publishing Co., Inc.
Baltimore, Maryland 1985, 1986
Library of Congress Catalogue Card Number 85-70013
International Standard Book Number 0-8063-1121-5
Made in the United States of America

CONTENTS

PREFACE

One of the most difficult tasks in the final editing of this directory
has been to achieve and maintain consistency in the method of presentation
of the peerages and surnames. In this respect, new patents of titles in
the same rank and surname have generally been ignored, particularly where
there has been no break of continuity in time, and no forfeiture has been
involved. Changes in the surname of a family holding a peerage have not
generally been noted, so that the present-day incumbent - and sometimes
intervening holders - may bear a different surname from that of the initial
grantee shown in this directory.

An exception has been made in the case of the Royal Family, where under
its present surname of Windsor adopted in 1917, all the peerages that have
been reserved over the centuries for its exclusive use are assembled with
their most recent years of creation. By referring back to the entry for
the TITLE the original year and surname of creation may be found. Sovereigns
themselves, with Princes of Wales and other royal princes and princesses
are not treated in this volume except insofar as their lesser titles are
concerned. An excellent article on the titles of the Royal Family and a
discussion of the controversial subject of its surnames over the centuries
by Patrick Montague-Smith appeared in Debrett's 'Peerage and Baronetage',
1980.

In putting the whole of this work into a word-processor for the second
edition it is hoped that provision can be made for changes of surname in
order to increase its usefulness. The addenda at the back of this book
can then be incorporated, errors and omission made good, and the latest
creations and extinctions added. In this edition entries may be found
slightly out of order or sequence as a result of manual typewriting.

One other problem of editing is worth mentioning here. This is the question
of the territorial suffix which is sometimes granted as an integral part of
a title, sometimes as a subsidiary part, and sometimes adopted informally to
distinguish one similar-sounding title from another. As a result of these
varying factors, sources are not always consistent in the usage of territorial suffixes, and I have been inclined to accept a suffix rather than
attempt to arbitrate.

My indebtedness to the assistance of Colin Parry is described in the Introduction, but I must here thank Mrs Estelle Leeson for scanning the press for
news of extinctions and supplying me with cuttings over the period of prod-
uction. Needless to say, I will welcome information enabling me to make
corrections and additions to the next edition.

108 Sea Lane   Francis L. Leeson
Ferring
West Sussex BN12 5HB   April 1984

INTRODUCTION

1. This directory of British titles of nobility and the surnames of families or individuals who bear or have borne them is arranged in one continuous alphabetical run with only the minimum of cross-referencing. It is therefore not intended as a work of expertise but as a ready-reference compilation for those wishing to find out quickly whether or when a certain peerage existed, with its rank(s), nationality, ownership, approximate period and fate. Hitherto it has been necessary to find a copy of a rare century-old work ('An Index of Hereditary English, Scottish and Irish Titles of Honour' by Edward Solly, originally published in 1880 and unrevised since then) arranged by titles only, or a wide range of other works, each limited in scope or time, to discover this information.

2. I am indebted to these same works, however, for providing the basis of this directory and in them, of course, the enquirer will find the detailed information that it is not possible to provide here. That much of the resulting condensation is vague and sometimes contradictory is one of the hazards of such a project as this, and it might be said that 'genealogists rush in where heralds fear to tread'. To verify every fact in a work such as this would mean that it could never be accomplished.

3. It will be noted that this directory does not cover the non-noble ranks of Baronet and Knight, which usually go under their own surnames anyway and are adequately covered elsewhere - most recently, in the case of the former, in Colin Parry's 'Index of Baronetage Creations' (1967). Also excluded are what one may call 'ex officio' Lords Spiritual, Lords Justices of Appeal and, in Scotland, Lords of Session, together with Lords of Manors and, in Scotland, territorial Lairds.

4. The 'new' edition of George Edward Cokayne's 'Complete Peerage' (13 volumes under various editors, 1910-59) is, of course, still the definitive work on our subject and in 1981 it was republished in a 6-volume microform edition at a cost of several hundred pounds. The layout of the 'Complete Peerage' (abbreviated CP), typographically impressive though it is, does not lend itself to rapid extraction of primary detail, so for this purpose recourse was had to the indexes in the two main editions of the Burkes' 'Extinct Peerages' (abbreviated BEP): 1831, which gives years of both creation and conclusion, and 1883, which, while failing to give concluding years and the destinations, provides the nationality of the titles; also various editions of Debrett's 'Peerage' for subsequent lists of extinct, dormant, abeyant, or disclaimed peerages (e.g. 1902 for such in 1884-99, 1958 for 1900-50, and 1980 for those since 1950). Whitaker's 'Almanack' and a scrutiny of the daily press have accounted for the very latest information in regard to extinctions.

5. For extant peerages, the well-presented information in the 1980
Debrett and the latest Whitaker's has again been relied on, and due
thanks and acknowledgements are here recorded. The slips written from
all the above sources have been checked against the manuscript updated
copy of Solly held by Colin Parry, compiler of the baronetage index to
which reference has already been made, and, in cases of further doubt,
the 1975 edition of Burke's 'Peerage'. One result of this policy has
been to include baronies by tenure as well as by writ, whereas G.E.C.
decided after letter 'A' of his CP to discontinue their inclusion in
his work. Thanks to Colin Parry's efforts, many errors have been corr-
ected at outset and omissions made good, but there must still remain
many others, so vast and complex is the field, and the compiler will
welcome any information which can enable him to improve the next
edition.

6. Arrangement of the Entries
    This is by one alphabetical sequence of both TITLES and Surnames,
the former printed in upper case (CAPITALS) succeeded by the latter in
lower case (smalls) where they are identically spelt. The arrangement
within the entries is as follows:
  a. TITLES
    i. TITLE-NAME as heading (including territorial suffix where this
       forms an integral part of the creation - e.g. HOWARD DE WALDEN),
       then on each successive line each creation or promotion
       comprising:
   ii. Abbreviated rank, viz.
       D   Duke   Dss   Duchess
       M   Marquis   Mss   Marchioness
       E   Earl   Css   Countess
       V   Viscount   Vss   Viscountess
       B   Baron   Bss   Baroness
       L   Lord (Scotland only)
       B(L) Life Baron   Bss(L) Life Baroness
       followed immediately, in brackets, by the nationality of the
       title where this is not of England, Great Britain, or the
       United Kingdom, viz. (I) Ireland; (S) Scotland. This
       'nationality' may sometimes but not invariably provide a
       clue to the home country of the original peer.
  iii. Period covered by peerage, beginning with the year or reign
       of creation, whether by summons or writ, divided by a
       hyphen from the year or reign of conclusion, or, if this is
       unknown or the title is still extant (even in a more senior
       rank), a blank space. Peerages are shown in chronological
       order of creation but promotions in the same title and
       surname follow on one another, interrupting this sequence.
       Where only the reign rather than the year of an event is
       known this is indicated by the monarch's reign-span, its
       first and last year being divided by an oblique stroke.
   iv. 'Destination' of peerage if not promotion or still extant
       represented by a code letter or sign, viz.
       A In abeyance   P Passed to a different sur-
       C Conveyed to another peerage   name (e.g. on marriage)
       D Dormant   R Resigned
       F Forfeited   S Surrendered or suspended
       L Lapsed or unclaimed   X Extinct
       M Merged in the Crown or   ? Unknown or doubtful
         another peerage   vi

v. Family name, or personal name only in medieval times before
    surnames became established and hereditary. This is, of
    course, frequently the same as the title, while in the case
    of royalty may be a 'house' name.

b. Surnames
    Rather than employ an extensive and complex system of cross-referenc-
    ing, the information given under the TITLE entries is repeated, but
    in alphabetical order of titles rather than chronologically, each
    line comprising:
    i.   Period covered by peerage (see a.iii above)
    ii. 'Destination' of peerage (see a.iv. above)
    iii. TITLE (see a.i. above)
    iv. Abbreviated rank (see a.ii. above)

c. 'Double-barrel' titles or surnames are treated under the first component
    with - as an exception to the above rule - cross-references from the
    other components.

7. How to Find Further Information
    Paragraphs 1., 4., and 5. above described briefly the sources used for
    this directory. There are so many other peerage works by different editors
    and publishers available in most reference libraries that there is not
    space here to list them all. However a summary of where to look may be
    keyed to the year of conclusion and/or destination or the lack of same in
    this directory (see paragraph 6.a.iii. above) as suggested by the following
    chart:

Years of Creation	Year of Conclusion	Destin- ation	Nationality England, G.B.or U.K.	Scot- land	Ireland
Any	None	None	Current editions of Burke's, Debrett's Peerages , Whit- aker's Almanack, or Vacher's Parliamentary Companion		
Pre-1824	None, or post-1823*	Any	'Synopsis of the Peerage of England' by Sir Nich- olas H. Nic- olas (1825)	-	-
Pre-1856	None, or post-1855	Any	'Historic Peerage of England' by Sir N.H.Nic- olas, ed. Wm. Courthope (1857)	-	-

*All these years are perforce approximate, depending on the 'deadline' for
publication of the work concerned, from which two years have in any case
here been deducted.

Years of Creation	Year of Conclusion	Destination	Nationality England, G.B. or U.K.	Scotland	Ireland
Pre-1886 to 1897	None, or post-1885 to 1896	Any	'The Complete Peerage' by G(eorge) E(dward) C(okayne), 8 volumes (1887-98) (Confined to peers themselves, spouses, and original parentage. Baronies by tenure not usually included after initial 'A')		
Pre-1901	None, or post- Titles Ab-Basi 1908 Bass-Cann 1910 Cano-Cutt 1911 D 1914 E-Goo 1924 Gor-Hur 1924 Hus-Linc 1927 Lind-Moa 1930 Moe-N 1934 O-Rich 1943 Rick-Si 1947 Sk-To 1951 Tr-Z 1957	Any	CP above, revised and updated by various editors as follows: Vol.I (1910) Vol.II (1912) Vol.III (1913) Vol.IV (1916) Vol.V (1926) Vol.VI (1926) Vol.VII (1929) Vol.VIII (1932) Vol.IX (1936) Vol.X (1945) Vol.XI (1949) Vol.XII, Part 1 (1953) Vol.XII, Part 2 (1959)		
1901-38	None, or post-1938	Any	CP Vol.XIII (1940) (Peers created 1901-38)		
1939-80	None, or post-1980	Any	CP Vol.XIV (1982) (Addenda and Corrigenda)		
Pre-1830	Pre-1830	All except extant	'Extinct Peerages'* by John Burke (1831). (Arranged by surnames with index of titles - see paragraph 4. above)		
Pre-1880	None, or post-1880	All	'An Index of Hereditary English, Scottish and Irish Titles of Honour' by Edward Solly (1880). (Arranged by titles only with information similar to that in this directory - see paragraph 1. above)		
Pre-1883	Pre-1883	Not extant	'Extinct Peerages' by Sir Bernard Burke (1883). As 1831 Ed.		
Pre-1971	Between 1884 & 1971	All except extant	'New Extinct Peerage' by L.G. Pine (1973). (Arranged by titles with index of surnames).		

*The wordy titles of some 19th century reference works have here been given their popular present-day abbreviated titles.

viii

8. Other Sources

In the past, peerage dictionaries have appeared frequently, not only from the publishers of Burke and Debrett, but under such editorial names as Collins, Dod, Foster, Lodge and Whitaker, and any of these will include details of peerages extant at the time of their publication; however, the Second World War brought all but the first famous pair to an end, and even Burke and Debrett appear on an occasional rather than an annual basis nowadays. Apart from these two, the editors of the great 'Complete Peerage' make reference to a number of other printed peerage works which, in view of this usage, might be considered of more than average authenticity:

a. Collins' 'Peerage of England' edited by Sir E. Brydges, 9 volumes (1812). (The first edition, edited by Arthur Collins, was published in one volume in 1709).

b. Compendium English Peerage, 1718-69 (13 editions); Compendium Scottish Peerage, 1720-64 (7 editions); Compendium Irish Peerage, 1722*-56 (5 editions).

c. Crawfurd's 'Peerage of Scotland' (1716*) (with 2nd and 3rd editions in 1719)

d. Crossley's 'Peerage of Ireland' (1725)

e. Douglas's 'Peerage of Scotland', 2nd edition, ed. J.P. Wood, 2 vols. (1813). (The 1st edition, in one volume, was published in 1764)

f. Dugdale's 'Baronage of England', 2 vols. (1675-76*).

g. Hewlett's 'Dignities in the Peerage of Scotland which are dormant or forfeited' (1882)

h. Lodge's 'Peerage of Ireland', 2nd edition, ed. M. Archdall, 7 vols. (1789). (The 1st edition, in 4 vols., was published in 1754)

j. Selden's 'Titles of Honour', 3rd edition (1672). (The 1st edition was published in 1614)

9. A Note on Name Forms

In early medieval times even peers mostly lacked surnames and their baptismal names have perforce been used in this directory. Both titles and surnames were later frequently formed from place-names and therefore 'De', 'De La' and 'D'' may be found preceding them in reference works, but here the listing is under the proper name (unless it happens to be a D' which forms part of the name-sound), with the prefix following, as a multitude of names would never otherwise be found other than by looking through all the De's and De La's. Ancient surnames generally are a problem in any directory as their spelling was always capricious. Here, the generally recognized modern form has been selected in order to assist the layman rather than the savant in tracing entries.

Royalty has posed particular problems in relation to surnames, not the least of these the Stuarts or Stewarts, a puzzle here shared with the 'rank and file' of the nobility. Mary Queen of Scots adopted the French form of Stuart, but the British Dictionary of National Biography still prefers to lead with Stewart. The editor of this directory has not attempted to arbitrate but has used the two spellings as adopted by various families.

---

*The first printed peerages of the respective nationalities.

10. Conclusion

It is worth mentioning that the decision to include Life Peerages has offered special problems. Most holders adopt their own surnames as titles but in some cases, particularly where the surname is a common one or has been used before as a title, a territorial suffix has been added. It has not always been possible to discover this with recent creations and in the absence of information the surname alone has been used here, possibly incorrectly, as the title. In a few cases Life Peers have died soon after having been ennobled and chosen an obscure title which has failed to reach the reference books because of their decease; a particularly difficult instance was that of Miss Betty Harvie-Anderson who was ennobled and died in 1979 having chosen the title of Baroness Skrimshire of Quarter.

Disclaimers of hereditary peerages, being for the lifetime of the disclaimant only, have not been noted; they may be found listed in both Whitaker and Vacher.

Conjoinments of titles (e.g. Eglinton and Winton, Egremont and Leconfield) have not always been entered, but conversely some titles have been found and listed only in a conjoined form, particularly Scottish ones, the latter sometimes also appearing singly.

Courtesy titles may sometimes cause difficulty in tracing. The three senior ranks of Dukes, Marquesses and Earls usually have lesser titles, either created simultaneously or later acquired or inherited, and the highest of these is taken by the eldest son as his courtesy title until such time as he may inherit the senior peerage. In a few cases, where there is no secondary title, the family name, preceded by the appropriate more junior rank, is used as a courtesy title. Probably the simplest explanation both of normal and courtesy titles is to be found in the latest edition (the first being of 1918) of Adam & Charles Black's 'Titles and Forms of Address: A Guide to Their Correct Use'.

A DIRECTORY OF BRITISH PEERAGES
From the Earliest Times to the Present Day

Each Title is shown in CAPITALS,
  then in Year Order of Creations,
  preceded by Rank and followed by
  Surname

Each Surname is shown in Smalls,
  then in Alphabetical Order of
  TITLES, preceded by Year and
  followed by Rank

SEE PAGE vi OF INTRODUCTION FOR
  ABBREVIATIONS

Abbot
  1817-1819X COLCHESTER B
Abbott
  1827-1939X TENTERDEN B
ABERBROTHWICK
  L(S) 1608-1649D Hamilton
ABERCONWAY
  B   1911-   McLaren
ABERCORN
  L(S) 1603-   Hamilton
  E(S) 1606-   Hamilton
  M   1790-   Hamilton
  D(I) 1868-   Hamilton
ABERCROMBY
  L(S) 1647-1681X Sandilands
  B   1801-1924X Abercromby
Abercromby
  1801-1924X ABERCROMBY B
  1839-1868X DUNFERMLINE B
  1685-1703X GLASFOORD L(S)
ABERDARE
  B   1873-   Bruce
ABERDEEN
  E(S) 1682-   Gordon
  V   1814-   Gordon
ABERDEEN & TEMAIR
  M   1916-   Gordon
ABERDOUR
  L(S) 1351-1458M Douglas
  L(S) 1638-   Douglas
ABERGAVENNY
  B   1240-1272X Cantelupe
  B   1272-1391X Hastings
  B   1392-1422X Beauchamp
  B   1450-   Nevill
  E   1784-   Nevill
  M   1876-   Nevill
ABERNETHY
  L(S) 1292-1312X Abernethy
  M(S) 1703-1761X Douglas
Abernethy
  1292-1312X ABERNETHY L(S)
ABERNETHY & JEDBURGH FOREST
  L(S) 1633-   Douglas
ABERNETHY & STRATHEARN
  L(S) 1562-   Stuart
ABERUTHVEN, MUGDOCK & FINTRIE
  L(S) 1707-   Graham
ABERTAY
  B   1940-1940X Barrie
ABINGDON
  E   1682-   Bertie
ABINGER
  B   1835-   Scarlett
Abney-Hastings
  See BOTREAUX, HASTINGS, STANLEY

ABOYNE
  V(S) 1632-1643F Gordon
ABRINCIS
  B   1070-1235X Abrincis
Abrincis
  1070-1235X ABRINCIS B
  1070-1119P CHESTER E
ACHESON
  B   1847-   Acheson
Acheson
  1847-   ACHESON B
  1776-   GOSFORD B(I)
  1785-   GOSFORD V(I)
  1806-   GOSFORD E(I)
  1835-   WORLINGHAM B
Acland: See Fuller-Acland-Hood
A COURT: See HOLMES A COURT
ACTON
  B   1869-   Acton
Adair
  1873-1886X WAVENEY B
ADAMS
  B   1949-1960X Adams
Adams
  1949-1960X ADAMS B
ADARE
  B(I) 1800-   Quin
  V(I) 1822-   Quin
ADBASTON
  B   1815-1825X Whitworth
Adderley
  1878-   NORTON B
ADDINGTON
  B   1887-   Hubbard
Addington
  1805-   SIDMOUTH V
ADDISON
  B   1937-   Addison
  V   1945-   Addison
Addison
  1937-   ADDISON B
  1945-   ADDISON V
ADEANE
  B(L) 1972-1984X Adeane
Adeane
  1972-1984X ADEANE B(L)
ADRIAN
  B   1955-   Adrian
Adrian
  1955-   ADRIAN B
Agar
  1758-1789X BRANDON Css(I)
  1790-1815X CALLAN B(I)
  1795-   SOMERTON B(I)
  1800-   SOMERTON V(I)
  1873-   SOMERTON B

1

Agar (cont'd)
1806-   NORMANTON E(I)
1920-1932P FURNIVAL B
Agar-Ellis
1831-1899X DOVER B
Agar-Robartes
1776-1974X CLIFDEN B(I)
1781-1974X CLIFDEN V(I)
1869-1974X ROBARTES B
AILESBURY
  E   1664-1747X Bruce
  E   1776-   Bruce
  M   1821   Bruce
AILSA
  B   1806-   Kennedy
  M   1831-   Kennedy
AILWYN
  B   1921-   Fellowes
AIR
  V(S) 1622-   Crichton
AIREDALE
  B   1907-   Kitson
AIREY   *
  B   1876-1881X Airey
Airey
1876-1881X AIREY B
AIRLIE
  E(S) 1639-   Ogilvy
AIRTH: See MONTEITH & AIRTH
AIRTH & MONTEITH
  E(S) 1633-1694D Graham
AITHRIE
  V(S) 1703-   Hope
Aitken
1917-   BEAVERBROOK B
Akers-Douglas
1911-   DOUGLAS OF BAADS B
1911-   VHILSTON V
Alan, or Fergaunt
1066/87-1230P RICHMOND E
ALANBROOKE
  Ct   1100/35-? Le Gros
  Ct   1190-1216/72X Fortibus
  B   1945-   Brooke
  V   1946-   Brooke
Aland, Fortescue- : See Fortescue-
ALBANY
  D(S) 1398-1425F Stewart
  D(S) 1452-1523X Stewart
  D(S) 1565-1567X Stewart
  D(S) 1600-1649F Stewart
  D(S) 1660-1685M Stewart
  D   1881-1919S Guelph

ALBEMARLE
  E   1212-1273X Fortibus
  D   1385-1397X Plantagenet
  D   1397-1399F Plantagenet
  E   1411-1421X Plantagenet
  E(L)   1423-1439X Beauchamp
  D   1660-1688X Monk
  E   1696-   Keppel
Alberic, or Aubrey
1080-1081R NORTHUMBERLAND E
ALBINI of Belvoir
  B   1087/1100-1285X Albini, De
ALBINI
  B   1139-   ? Albini, De
ALBINI of Cainho
  B   1154/89-1233X Albini, De
Albini, De
1087/1100-1285X ALBINI of Belvoir B
1139-   ? ALBINI B
1154/89-1233X ALBINI of Cainho B
1139-1243P ARUNDEL E
1066/87-1216/72P MOWBRAY B

1155-1243M SUSSEX E
ALCESTER
  B   1882-1895X Seymour
ALDBOROUGH   *
  V(I) 1776-1875X Stratford
  E(I) 1777-1875X Stratford
ALDEBURGH
  B   1371-1391A Aldeburgh
Aldeburgh
1371-1391A ALDEBURGH B
ALDENHAM
  B   1896-   Gibbs
ALDERNEY   *
  V   1917-   Mountbatten
ALDINGTON
  B   1962-   Low
Aldithley or Audley
1313-1392C AUDLEY B
ALEXANDER
  L(S) 1630-1739? Alexander
ALEXANDER OF HILLSBOROUGH
  V   1950-1965X Alexander
  E   1963-1965X Alexander
ALEXANDER OF TUNIS
  V   1946-   Alexander
  E   1952-   Alexander
ALEXANDER OF POTTERHILL
  B(L) 1974-   Alexander
Alexander
1630-1739? ALEXANDER L(S)

2   * See also Addenda

Alexander (cont'd)
1950-1965X ALEXANDER OF
          HILLSBOROUGH V
1963-1965X ALEXANDER OF
          HILLSBOROUGH E
1946-   ALEXANDER OF TUNIS V
1952-   ALEXANDER OF TUNIS E
1974-   ALEXANDER OF POTTER-
          HILL B(L)
1790-   CALEDON B(I)
1797-   CALEDON V(I)
1800-   CALEDON E(I)
1633-1739? CANADA V(S)
1313-1951A COBHAM B
1952-   RIDEAU B
1630-1739? STIRLING V(S)
1633-1739? STIRLING E(S)
1963-1965X WESTON-SUPER-MARE B
ALFORD
  B   1698-1754X Nassau, de
  V   1815-1921X Cust
ALINGTON
  B(I) 1642-1722X Alington
  B   1682-1691X Alington
  B   1876-1940X Sturt
Alington
  1642-1722X ALINGTON B(I)
  1682-1691X ALINGTON B
ALLAN OF KILMAHEW
  B(L) 1973-1979 Allan
Allan
  1973-1979X ALLAN OF KILMAHEW B(L)
ALLANSON & WINN
  B(I) 1797-   Winn
Allanson-Winn
  1797-   HEADLEY B(I)
ALLEN
  V(I) 1717-1845X Allen
ALLEN OF HURTWOOD
  B   1932-1939X Allen
ALLEN OF FALLOWFIELD
  B(L) 1974-1985 Allen
ALLEN OF ABBEYDALE
  B(L) 1976-   Allen
Allen
  1717-1845X ALLEN V(I)
  1976-   ALLEN OF ABBEYDALE B(L)
  1974-1985X ALLEN OF FALLOWFIELD
            B(L)
  1932-1939X ALLEN OF HURTWOOD B
  1977-   CROHAM B(L)
ALLENBY
  V   1919-   Allenby
Allenby
  1919-   ALLENBY V

ALLENDALE
  B   1906-   Beaumont
  V   1911   Beaumont
ALLERTON
  B   1902-   Jackson
ALLINGTON
  B   1682-1691X Allington
Allington
  1682-1691X ALLINGTON B
Allsopp
  1886-   HINDLIP B
ALNESS
  B   1934-1955X Munro
ALNWICK: See LOVAINE
ALPORT
  B(L) 1961-   Alport
Alport
  1961-   ALPORT B(L)
ALTAMONT
  E(I) 1771-   Browne
ALTHAM
  B(I) 1680-1844X Annesley
ALTHORP
  V(GB)1765-   Spencer
  V(UK)1905-   Spencer
ALTON
  M   1694-1718X Talbot
ALTRIE
  L(S) 1587-1593X Keith
ALTRINCHAM
  B   1945-   Grigg
ALVANLEY
  B   1801-1857X Arden
ALVERSTONE
  B   1900-1915X Webster
  V   1913-1915X Webster
ALVINGHAM
  B   1929-   Yerburgh
Aman
  1930-   MARLEY B
AMBERLEY
  V   1861-   Russell
AMESBURY
  B   1832-1832X Dundas
AMHERST
  B   1776-1797X Amherst
  B   1788-   Amherst
  E   1826-   Amherst
AMHERST OF HACKNEY
  B   1892-   Cecil
Amherst
  1776-1797X AMHERST B
  1788-   AMHERST B
  1826-   AMHERST E
  1826-   HOLMESDALE V

3

AMIENS
V(I) 1777-   Stratford
AMMON
   B   1944-1960X Ammon
Ammon
   1944-1960X AMMON B
AMPTHILL
   B   1881-   Russell
AMORY
   V   1960-1981X Heathcoat-Amory
Amory, Heathcoat-
   1960-1981X AMORY V
AMULREE
   B   1929-1983X Mackenzie
AMWELL
   B   1947-   Montague
ANCASTER
   E   1892-   Heathcote-Drummond-
                       Willoughby
ANCASTER & KESTEVEN
   D   1715-1809X Bertie
ANCRAM
   E(S) 1633-   Kerr
Anderson
   1952-   WAVERLEY V
Anderson: See Harvie-Anderson
Anderson-Pelham
   1926-1948A FAUCONBERG B
   1837-   WORSLEY B
   1794-   YARBOROUGH B
   1837-   YARBOROUGH E
ANDOVER
   V   1625-   Howard
ANGLESEY
   E   1623-1659X Villiers
   E   1661-1761X Annesley
   M   1815-   Paget
ANGUS
   E(S) 1120-1343 Gilchrist
   E(S) 1297-1381X Umfraville
   E(S) 1330-   Stuart
   E(S) 1389-   Douglas
   M(S) 1703-1761X Douglas
Angus
   1130-1130X MORAY E(S)
ANNALY
   B(I) 1766-1784X Gore
   B(I) 1789-1793 Gore
   B(I) 1863-   White
ANNAN
   B(L) 1965-   Annan
Annan
   1965-   ANNAN B(L)
ANNAND
   V(S) 1622-1658X Murray
   V(S) 1661-1792X Johnstone

ANNANDALE
   E(S) 1624-1658X Murray
   M(S) 1701-1792A Johnstone
ANNESLEY
   B(I) 1758-   Annesley
   E(I) 1789-   Annesley
   B   1917-1949X Annesley
Annesley
   1680-1844X ALTHAM B(I)
   1661-1761X ANGLESEY E
   1758-   ANNESLEY B(I)
   1789-   ANNESLEY B(I)
   1917-1949X ANNESLEY B
   1766-   GLERAWLY V(I)
   1628-   MOUNTNORRIS B(I)
   1793-1844X MOUNTNORRIS E(I)
   1622-   VALENTIA V(I)
ANSLOW
   B   1916-1933X Mosley
ANSON
   B   1747-1762X Anson
   V   1806-   Anson
Anson
   1747-1762X ANSON B
   1806-   ANSON V
   1831-   LICHFIELD E
   1806-   SOBERTON B
Anstruther-Gray
   1966-   KILMANY B(L)
ANTRIM
   E(I) 1620-1791X McDonnell
   M(I) 1644-1682X McDonnell
   E(S) 1785-   McDonnell
   M(I) 1789-1791X McDonnell
AP-ADAM
   B   1299-1330X Ap-Adam
Ap-Adam
   1299-1330X AP-ADAM B
APSLEY
   B   1771-   Bathurst
AQUILA
   B   1100/35-1231F Aquila, De
Aquila, De
   1100/35-1231F AQUILA B
ARASE
   L(S) 1706-1761X Campbell
ARBUTHNOTT
   V(S) 1641-   Arbuthnott
Arbuthnott
   1641-   ARBUTHNOTT V(S)
   1641-   INVERBERVIE L(S)
ARCHDEKNE
   B   1321-1400A Archdekne
Archdekne
   1321-1400A ARCHDEKNE B

4

ARCHER
    B   1747-1778X Archer
Archer
    1747-1778X ARCHER B
ARCHIBALD
    B   1949-   Archibald
Archibald
    1949-   ARCHIBALD B
ARDEE
    B(I) 1616-   Brabazon
ARDEN
    B(I) 1770-   Perceval
Arden
    1801-1857X ALVANLEY B
ARDGLASS
    E(I) 1645-1687X Cromwell
ARDILAUN
    B   1880-1915X Guinness
ARDMANACH
    L(S) 1481-1504X Stewart
ARDROSSAN
    B   1806-   Montgomerie
ARDWICK
    B(L) 1970-   Beavan
ARGENTINE
    B   1297-1383A Argentine
Argentine
    1297-1383A ARGENTINE B
ARGYLL
    E(S) 1457-1701   Campbell
    M(S) 1641-1701   Campbell
    D(S) 1701-   Campbell
    D   1892-   Campbell
ARKLOW
    B(I) 1801-1843X Guelph
    B(I) 1825-   Butler
ARLINGTON
    B   1664-1936A FitzRoy
    E   1672-1936A FitzRoy
ARMAGH
    E(I) 1799-1919F Guelph
ARMAGHDALE
    B   1918-1924X Lonsdale
ARMITSTEAD
    B   1906-1915X Armitstead
Armitstead
    1906-1915X ARMITSTEAD B
ARMSTRONG
    B   1887-1900X Armstrong
    B   1903-   Watson-Armstrong
ARMSTRONG OF SANDERSTEAD
    B(L) 1975-   Armstrong
Armstrong
    1887-1900X ARMSTRONG B
    1975-   ARMSTRONG OF SANDER-
                 STEAD B(L)

Armstrong-Jones
    1961-   LINLEY V
    1961-   SNOWDON E
ARNOLD
    B   1924-1945X Arnold
Arnold
    1924-1945X ARNOLD B
ARRAN
    E(S) 1467-1469F Boyd
    E(S) 1503-   ? Hamilton
    E(S) 1581-1585F Stewart
    E(I) 1662-1685X Butler
    E(I) 1693-1759X Butler
    E(I) 1762-   Gore
ARRAN, LANARK & CAMBRIDGE
    E(S) 1643-   Hamilton
ARRASS
    L(S) 1660-1680X Macdonell
    See also MACDONELL & ARRASS
Arthur
    1918-   GLENARTHUR B
ARUNDEL
    B   1139-1243P Albini
    E   1289-1326F Fitz-Alan
    E   1331-1347F Fitz-Alan
    E   1400-1580   Fitz-Alan
    B   1377-1435A Arundel, De
    E   1433-   Fitzalan
Arundel, De
    1377-1435A ARUNDEL B
ARUNDELL OF TRERICE
    B   1664-1768X Arundell
ARUNDELL OF WARDOUR
    B   1605-1944X Arundell
Arundell
    1664-1768X ARUNDELL OF TRERICE B
    1605-1944X ARUNDELL OF WARDOUR B
    See also Monckton-Arundell
ARWYN
    B(L) 1964-1978X Arwyn
Arwyn
    1964-1978X ARWYN B(L)
ASCOTT
    V   1628-1709X Dormer
ASHBOURNE
    B   1885-   Gibson
ASHBROOK
    V(I) 1751-   Flower
ASHBURNHAM
    B   1689-1924X Ashburnham
    E   1730-1924X Ashburnham
Ashburnham
    1689-1924X ASHBURNHAM B
    1730-1924X ASHBURNHAM E
    1730-1924X ST ASAPH V

5

ASHBURTON
  B   1782-1823X Dunning
  B   1835-   Baring
ASHBY
  B(L) 1973-   Ashby
Ashby
  1973-   ASHBY B(L)
ASHBY ST LEDGERS
  B   1910-   Guest
ASHCOMBE
  B   1892-   Cubitt
ASHDOWN
  B(L) 1974-1977X Silverstone
ASHFIELD
  B   1920-1948 Stanley
ASHFORD
  B   1696-   Keppel
ASHLEY
  B   1661-   Ashley-Cooper
Ashley
  1932-1939X MOUNT TEMPLE B
Ashley-Cooper
  1661-   ASHLEY B
  1672-   COOPER B
  1672-   SHAFTESBURY E
ASHTON
  B   1895-1930X Williamson
Ashton
  1911-   ASHTON OF HYDE B
ASHTON OF HYDE
  B   1911-   Ashton
ASHTOWN
  B(I) 1800-   Trench
ASKWITH
  B   1919-1942X Askwith
Askwith
  1919-1942X ASKWITH B
ASQUITH
  V   1925-   Asquith
ASQUITH OF BISHOPSTONE
  B(L) 1951-1954X Asquith
ASQUITH OF YARNBURY
  Bss(L) 1964-1969X Bonham Carter
Asquith
  1925-   ASQUITH V
  1951-1954X ASQUITH OF BISHOPSTONE
             B(L)
  1925-   OXFORD & ASQUITH E
Assheton
  1955-   CLITHEROE B
ASTLEY
  B   1295-1554F Astley
ASTLEY OF READING
  B   1644-1688X Astley

Astley
  1295-1554F ASTLEY B
  1644-1688X ASTLEY OF READING B
  1290-   HASTINGS B
ASTON
  B   1627-1845X Aston
Aston
  1627-1845X ASTON B
ASTOR
  B   1916-   Astor
  V   1917-   Astor
ASTOR OF HEVER
  B   1856   Astor
Astor
  1916-   ASTOR B
  1917-   ASTOR V
  1956-   ASTOR OF HEVER B
ATHENRY
  B(I) 1759-1799S Bermingham, De
ATHLONE
  V(I) 1620-1681X Wilmot
  E   1692-1844X Ginkel
  B   1881-1919S Guelph
  E   1890-1892X Guelph
  E   1917-1957X Cambridge
ATHLUMNEY
  B   1863-1929X Somerville
ATHOLL
  E(S) 1115-1375A Strathbogie
  E(S) 1314-1333R Campbell
  E(S) 1341-1371M Douglas
  E(S) 1457-1595R Stewart
  E(S) 1596-1625R Stewart
  E(S) 1629-   Murray
  M(S) 1676-   Murray
  D(S) 1703-   Murray
ATHOLSTAN
  B   1917-1938X Graham
ATKIN
  B(L) 1928-1944X Atkin
Atkin
  1928-1944X ATKIN B(L)
ATKINSON
  B(L) 1905-1932X Atkinson
Atkinson
  1905-1932X ATKINSON B(L)
ATON
  B   1324-1373A Aton
Aton
  1324-1373A ATON B
ATTLEE
  E   1955-   Attlee
Attlee
  1955-   ATTLEE E

6

```
AUBERVILL                                      AVONDALE
   B    1066/87-1199-1216X Aubervill, De         E(S) 1437-1456F Douglas
Aubervill, De                                    L(S) 1459-1543R Stewart
   1066/87-1199/1216X AUBERVILL B                L(S) 1500-1543R Stewart
AUBIGNY                                           See also CLARENCE & AVONDALE
   L(S) 1580-1672X Stewart                     AVONMORE
AUCHTERHOOSE                                      B(I) 1795-1910D Yelverton
   L(S) 1469-         Stewart                     V(I) 1800-1910D Yelverton
AUCKLAND                                        AYLESBURY: See AILESBURY
   B(I) 1789-         Eden                      AYLESFORD
   B    1793-         Eden                        E    1714-         Finch
   E    1839-1849X Eden                         AYLESTONE
AUDLEY                                            B(L) 1967-         Bowden
   B    1313-         Souter                    AYLMER
   B    1321-1521F Audley                          B(I) 1718-         Aylmer
   B    1405-1631F Touchet                      Aylmer
AUDLEY OF WALDEN                                     1718-      AYLMER B(I)
   B    1538-1544X Audley                       AYR
Audley                                             V(S) 1622-         Stuart
   1321-1521F AUDLEY B
   1538-1544X AUDLEY OF WALDEN B
   1337-1347X GLOUCESTER E
AUGHRIM
   B(I) 1676-1677X Butler
AUNGIER
   B(I) 1621-1704X Aungier
   V(I) 1675-1704X Aungier
   E(I) 1677-1704X Aungier
Aungier
   1621-1704X AUNGIER B(I)
   1675-1704X AUNGIER V(I)
   1621-1704X LONGFORD B(I)
   1675-1704X LONGFORD V(I)
   1677-1704X AUNGIER E(I)
   1677-1704X LONGFORD E(I)
AUSTIN
   B    1936-1941X Austin
Austin
   1936-1941X AUSTIN B
AVA
   E    1888-         Hamilton-Temple-
                        Blackwood
   See also DUFFERIN & AVA
AVANE
   L(S) 1581-1585F Stewart
AVEBURY
   B    1900-         Lubbock
AVELAND
   B    1856-         Heathcote
AVEN & INNERDALE
   L(S) 1643-         Hamilton
AVON                                           (TITLES are in CAPITALS
   E    1961-         Eden                       Surnames in smalls)
```

7

BAALUN
  B   1066/87-1216/72X Baalun, De
Baalun, De
  1066/87-1216/72X BAALUN B
BACON
  Bss(L) 1970-
Bacon
  1621-1626X ST ALBANS V
  1618-1626X VERULAM B
  1970-   BACON Bss(L)
BADELEY
  B   1949-1951X Badeley
Badeley
  1949-1951X BADELEY B
BADEN-POWELL
  B   1929-   Baden-Powell
Baden-Powell
  1929-   BADEN-POWELL B
BADENOCH
  L(S) 1240-1306X Cummin
BADLESMERE
  B   1309-1338A Badlesmere
Badlesmere
  1309-1338A BADLESMERE B
BAGOT
  B   1780-   Bagot
Bagot
  1780-   BAGOT B
Bailey
  1899-   GLANUSK B
Baillie
  1897-1931P BURTON B
  1962-   BURTON B
  See also Cochrane-Baillie
Baillie-Hamilton
  1619-   HADDINGTON E(S)
BAILLIEU
  B   1953-   Baillieu
Baillieu
  1953-   BAILLIEU B
Baird
  1925-   STONEHAVEN B
  1938-   STONEHAVEN V
BAKER
  B(L) 1977-   Baker
Baker
  1977-   BAKER B(L)
  See also Noel-Baker
BALCARRES
  E(S) 1651-   Lindsay
  See also CRAWFORD & BALCARRES
BALDWIN OF BEWDLEY
  E   1937-   Baldwin
Baldwin
  1937-   BALDWIN OF BEWDLEY B

BALERNO
  B(L) 1963-   Buchanan-Smith
BALFOUR
  B(I) 1619-1636X Balfour
  E   1922-   Balfour
BALFOUR OF BURLEIGH
  L(S) 1607-1716F Bruce
  L(S) 1869-   Bruce
BALFOUR OF INCHRYE
  B   1945-   Balfour
Balfour
  1619-1636X BALFOUR B(I)
  1922-   BALFOUR E
  1945-   BALFOUR OF INCHRYE B
  1614-1636X KILWINNING L(S)
  1902-   KINROSS B
  1935-   RIVERDALE B
  1922-   TRAPRAIN V
BALGONIE
  L(S) 1641-   Leslie
BALINHARD
  B   1869-   Carnegie
BALIOL
  B   1066/87-1216/72X Baliol, De
BALIOL OF CAVERS
  B   1272/1307-1307/27X Baliol, De
Baliol, De
  1066/87-1216/72X BALIOL B
  1272/1307-1307/27X BALIOL OF CAVERS B
BALLANTRAE
  B(L) 1972-   Fergusson
BALLENBREICH: See LESLIE
BALLYANE
  B(I) 1554-1555X Kavanagh
BALLYMOTE
  B   1628-1919F Taaffe
BALMERINO
  L(S) 1603-1746F Elphinstone
BALNIEL: See LINDSAY & BALNIEL
BALOGH
  B(L) 1968-   Balogh
Balogh
  1968-   BALOGH B(L)
BALTIMORE
  B(I) 1624-1771X Calvert
BALTINGLASS
  V(I) 1541-1585F Eustace
  V(I) 1627-1676X Roper
  V(I) 1685-1691F Talbot
  B(I) 1763-1875X Stratford
BALVENIE: See MURRAY, BALVENIE & GASK
BALVAIRD
  L(S) 1641-1776C Murray
BALWEARIE: See RAITH, MONYMAILL &
  BALWEARIE

BALWHIDDER, GLENALMOND & GLENLYON
V(S) 1703-   Murray
Bampfylde
1831-   POLTIMORE B
BANBURY
E   1626-1632D Knollys
BANBURY OF SOTHAM
B   1924-   Banbury
Banbury
1924-   BANBURY OF SOTHAM B
BANCROFT
B(L) 1982-   Bancroft
Bancroft
1982-   BANCROFT B(L)
BANDON
B(I) 1793-1979X Bernard
V(I) 1795-1979X Bernard
E(I) 1800-1979X Bernard
BANDON BRIDGE
B(I) 1627-   Boyle
BANFF
L(S) 1642-1803D Ogilvy
BANGOR
E(I) 1691-1719X Schomberg
B(I) 1770-   Ward
V(I) 1781-   Ward
BANKS
B(L) 1974-   Banks
Banks
1974-   BANKS B(L)
BANNERMAN OF KILDONAN
B(L) 1967-1969X Bannerman
Bannerman
1967-1969X BANNERMAN OF KILDONAN
          B(L)
BANTRY
B(I) 1627-1676X Roper
B(I) 1797-1891X White
V(I) 1800-1891X White
E(I) 1816-1891X White
BANYARD
B   1313-1331X Banyard, De
Banyard, De
1313-1331X BANYARD B
BARBER
B(L) 1974-   Barber
Barber
1974-   BARBER B(L)
BARD
B(I) 1646-1660X Bard
Bard
1646-1660X BARD B(I)
1646-1680X BELMONT V(I)
BARDOLF
B   1299-1406F Bardolf

BARDOLF OF HOO
B   1154/89-1199/1216X Bardolf
Bardolf
1154/89-1199/1216X BARDOLF OF HOO B
1299-1406F BARDOLF B
BARFLEUR
V   1697-1727X Russell
BARGENY
L(S) 1639-1736D Hamilton
BARHAM
B   1805-1813P Middleton
B   1813-   Noel
BARING
V   1876-1929X Baring
Baring
1835-   ASHBURTON B
1876-1929X BARING V
1892-   CROMER B
1899-   CROMER V
1901-   CROMER E
1901-   ERRINGTON V
1960-   HOWICK OF GLENDALE B
1866-   NORTHBROOK B
1876-1929X NORTHBROOK E
1885-   REVELSTOKE B
Barker
1980-   TRUMPINGTON Bss(L)
BARNARD
V   1754-1891X Powlett
B   1698-   Vane
V   1754-   Vane
BARNBY
B   1922-1982 Willey
Barnes
1909-   GORELL B
BARNETSON
B(L) 1975-   Barnetson
Barnetson
1975-   BARNETSON B(L)
BARNEWALL OF KINGSLAND   *
V(I) 1646-1833D Barnewall
Barnewall
1646-1833D BARNEWALL OF KINGSLAND
          V(I)
1646-1833D KINGSLAND V
1461-   TRIMLESTOWN B(I)
1646-1833D TURVEY B(I)
BARRELLS
V   1762-1772X Knight
BARRET
L(S) 1627-1644X Barret
Barret
1627-1644X BARRET L(S)
Barrie
1940-1940X ABERTAY B

9   * See Addenda

BARRINGTON
  B(I) 1720-   Barrington
  V(I) 1720-   Barrington
Barrington
  1720-   BARRINGTON B(I)
  1720-   BARRINGTON V(I)
  1880-   SHUTE B
BARROGILL
  B   1866-1889X Sinclair
BARRY OF BARRYSCOURT
  B(I) 1250-1557X Barry
BARRY OF SANTRY
  B(I) 1661-1751X Barry
Barry
  1250-1557X BARRY OF BARRYSCOURT B(I)
  1661-1751X BARRY OF SANTRY B(I)
  1628-1824X BARRYMORE E(I)
  1902-1925X BARRYMORE B
  1661-1751X SANTRY B(I)
BARRYMORE
  E(I) 1628-1824X Barry
  B   1902-1925X Barry
BASING
  B   1887-   Sclater-Booth
Bass
  1886-1909X BAILLIE B
  1886-1909X BURTON B
BASSET OF DRAYTON
  B   1264-1390A Basset
BASSET OF HEDENDON
  B   1154/89-1154/89A Basset
BASSET OF SAPCOATE
  B   1264-1378A Basset
BASSET OF STRATTON
  B   1797-1855X Basset
BASSET OF WELDEN
  B   1299-1314X Basset
Basset
  1264-1390A BASSET OF DRAYTON B
  1154/89-1154/89A BASSET OF HEDENDON B
  1264-1378A BASSET OF SAPCOATE B
  1797-1855X BASSET OF STRATTON B
  1299-1314X BASSET OF WELDEN B
  1796-1835X DUNSTANVILLE B
BASSINGBOURN OF ABINGTON (Cambs)
  B 1307/27-1307/27X Bassingbourn, De
Bassingbourn, De
  1307/27-1307/27X BASSINGBOURN OF
                 ABINGTON B
BASSINGBOURNE OF ABINGTON (Northants)
  B 1154/89-1272/1307X Bassingbourne, De
Bassingbourne, De
  1154/89-1272/1307X BASSINGBOURNE OF
                 ABINGTON B

BATEMAN
  V(I) 1725-1802X Bateman
  B   1837-1931X Bateman-Hanbury
Bateman
  1725-1802X BATEMAN V(I)
  1725-1802X CULMORE B(I)
Bateman-Hanbury
  1837-1931X BATEMAN B
Bateson: See Yarburgh-Bateson, De
BATH
  E   1485-15..X Shaunde, De
  E   1536-1645X Bourchier
  E   1661-1711X Granville
  E   1742-1764X Pulteney
  Bss 1792-1808X Pulteney
  Css 1803-1808X Pulteney
  M   1789-   Thynne
BATHURST
  B   1711-   Bathurst
  E   1772-   Bathurst
Bathurst
  1771-   APSLEY B
  1711-   BATHURST B
  1772-   BATHURST E
  1918-   BLEDISLOE B
  1935-   BLEDISLOE V
BATTERSEA
  B   1892-1907X Flower
BAUER
  B(L) 1982-   Bauer
Bauer
  1982-   BAUER B(L)
BAVENT
  B   1313-1370A Bavent
Bavent
  1313-1370A BAVENT B
BAYEUX
  B   1100/35-1216/72X Bayeux, De
Bayeux, De
  1100/35-1216/72X BAYEUX B
BAYFORD
  B   1929-1940X Sanders
BAYHAM
  V   1786-   Pratt
BAYNING
  B   1627-1638X Bayning
  V   1627-1638X Bayning
  B   1797-1866X Powlett
  Vss 1674-1698X Murray
Bayning
  1627-1638X BAYNING B
  1627-1638X BAYNING V
  1680-1686X SHEPEY Css(L)
Beach: See Hicks-Beach

BEACONSFIELD
  Vss 1868-1872X Disraeli
  E   1876-1881X Disraeli
Beamish
  1974-   CHELWOOD B(L)
Beardmore
  1921-1936X INVERNAIRN B
BEARSTED
  B   1921-   Samuel
  V   1925-   Samuel
BEATTY
  B   1919-   Beatty
  E   1919-   Beatty
Beatty
  1919-   BEATTY B
  1919-   BEATTY E
  1919-   BORODALE V
BEAUCHAMP
  V   1536-1552F Seymour
  B   1660-1688X Monk
  Vss 1674-1698X Murray
  V   1750-   Seymour
  B   1797-1810X Powlett
  B   1810-1866X Townshend
  E   1815-1979X Lygon
BEAUCHAMP OF BEDFORD
  B   1066/87-1265X Beauchamp, De
BEAUCHAMP OF BLETSHO
  B   1363-1836A Beauchamp
BEAUCHAMP OF EATON
  B   1154/89-1272/1307X Beauchamp,
                          De
BEAUCHAMP OF ELMLEY
  B   1100/35-1272/1307X Beauchamp,
                          De
BEAUCHAMP OF HACCHE
  B   1299-1360A Beauchamp
  B   1559-1750X Seymour
BEAUCHAMP OF KYDERMINSTER
  B   1387-1420X Beauchamp
BEAUCHAMP OF POWYK
  B   1447-1496X Beauchamp
  B   1806-1979X Lygon
BEAUCHAMP OF WARWICK
  B   1350-1360X Beauchamp
Beauchamp
  1392-1422X ABERGAVENNY B
  1423-1439X ALBEMARLE E(L)
  1363-1836A BEAUCHAMP OF BLETSHO B
  1299-1360A BEAUCHAMP OF HACCHE B
  1387-1420X BEAUCHAMP OF KYDER-
             MINSTER B
  1447-1496X BEAUCHAMP OF POWYK B
  1350-1360X BEAUCHAMP OF WARWICK B
  1313-1508A ST AMAND B

Beauchamp (Cont'd)
  1268-1445X WARWICK E
  1444-1445X WARWICK D
  1445-1449X WARWICK Css
  1420-1431X WORCESTER E
Beauchamp, De
  1066/87-1265X BEAUCHAMP OF BEDFORD B
  1154/89-1272/1307X BEAUCHAMP OF
                     EATON B
  1100/35-1272/1307X BEAUCHAMP OF
                     ELMLEY B
Beauclerk
  1676-   BURFORD E
  1676-   HEDINGTON B
  1684-   ST ALBANS D
  1750-   VERE OF HANWORTH B
BEAUFORT
  D   1682-   Somerset
Beaufort
  1416-1426X EXETER D
  1411-1426X DORSET E
  1397-1463F DORSET E
  1442-1471F DORSET M
  1418-1509X KENDAL E
  1397-1471X SOMERSET E
  1397-1471X SOMERSET M
  1443-1444X SOMERSET D
  1448-1471F SOMERSET D
BEAULIEU
  B   1762-1802X Hussey Montagu
  E   1784-1802X Hussey Montagu
BEAUMARIS
  B   1784-1822X Bulkeley
BEAUMONT
  B   1309-1507A Beaumont
  V   1432-1507X Beaumont
  V(I) 1622-1702X Beaumont
  B   1840-   Stapleton
BEAUMONT OF WHITLEY
  B(L) 1967-   Beaumont
Beaumont
  1906-   ALLENDALE B
  1911-   ALLENDALE V
  1309-1507A BEAUMONT B
  1432-1507X BEAUMONT V
  1622-1702X BEAUMONT V(I)
  1967-   BEAUMONT OF WHITLEY B(L)
  1103-1204X LEICESTER E
  1622-1702X SWORDS V(I)
BEAUVALE
  B   1839-1853X Lamb
Beavan
  1970-   ARDWICK B(L)
BEAVERBROOK
  B   1917-   Aitken

11

BECHE
B   1342-1347X Beche
Beche
1342-1347X BECHE B
BECHE, DE LA
B   1342-1342X Beche, De la
Beche, de la
1342-1342X BECHE,DE LA B
Beckett
1886-   GRIMTHORPE B
BECTIVE
E(I) 1766-   Taylour
BEDFORD
E   1150-....X Bellomont
E   1366-1397X Courcy, De
D   1414-1435X Plantagenet
D   1469-1477F Nevill
D   1485-1495X Tudor
E   1550-   Russell
D   1694-   Russell
BEECHING
B(L) 1965-   Beeching
Beeching
1965-   BEECHING B(L)
BEKE OF ERESBY
B   1295-1310A Beke
Beke
1295-1310A BEKE OF ERESBY B
BELASYSE
B   1644-1692X Belasyse
BELASYSE OF OSGODBY
Bss 1674-1713X Belasyse
Belasyse
1644-1692X BELASYSE B
1674-1713X BELASYSE OF OSGODBY Bss
1627-1815X FAUCONBERG OF YARM B
1643-1815X FAUCONBERG V
1689-1700X FAUCONBERG E
BELET
B   1135/54-1216/72X Belet
Belet
1135/54-1216/72X BELET B
BELFAST
B(I) 1625-   Chichester
E(I) 1791-   Chichester
BELGRAVE V
V   1784-   Grosvenor
BELHAVEN
V(S) 1633-1639X Douglas
BELHAVEN & STENTON
L(S) 1647-   Hamilton
BELLA AQUA
B   1272/1307-....X Bella Aqua
Bella Aqua
1272/1307-....X BELLA AQUA B

Belisha: See Hore-Belisha
BELLAMONT
E   1680-1683X Kirckhoven
E(I) 1689-1766X Coote
E(I) 1767-1800X Coote
BELLEISLE
V(I) 1768-1802X Gore
BELLENDEN
L(S) 1661-1671C Bellenden
Bellenden
1661-1671C BELLENDEN L(S)
BELLEW
B(I) 1848-   Bellew
BELLEW OF DULEEK
B(I) 1686-1770X Bellew
Bellew
1686-1770X BELLEW OF DULEEK B(I)
1848-   BELLEW B(I)
BELLFIELD
B(I) 1737-1814X Rochfort
V(I) 1751-1814X Rochfort
BELLOMONT
E(I) 1680-1683X Wotton
Bellomont
1150-....X BEDFORD E
Bellomont, de
1135/54-1166X WORCESTER E
Bellow
1979-   BELLWIN B(L)
BELLWIN
B(L) 1979-   Bellow
BELMONT
V(I) 1646-1660X Bard
BELMORE
B(I) 1781-   Lowry-Corry
V(I) 1789-   Lowry-Corry
E(I) 1797-   Lowry-Corry
BELOFF
B(L) 1981-   Beloff
Beloff
1981-   BELOFF B(L)
BELPER
B   1856-   Strutt
BELSTEAD
B   1938-   Ganzoni
BELVEDERE
E(I) 1756-1814X Rochfort
Bempde: See Vanden-Bempde-Johnson
BENEDARALOCH: See GLENORCHY, BENED-
ARALOCH, ORMELIE & WEICK
BENHALE
B   1360-1369X Benhale
Benhale
1360-1369X BENHALE B

12

Benn
1936-1937X GLENRAVEL B
1942-   STANSGATE V
BENNETT
V   1941-1947X Bennett
BENNETT OF EDGBASTON
B   1953-1957X Bennett
Bennett
1941-1947X BENNETT V
1953-1957X BENNETT OF EDGBASTON B
1682-   OSSULSTON E
1714-   TANKERVILLE E
BENSON
B(L) 1981-   Benson
Benson
1713-1730X BINGLEY B
1911-1955X CHARNWOOD B
1981-   BENSON B(L)
Bentinck
1689-   CIRENCESTER B
1689-   PORTLAND E
1716-   PORTLAND D
1716-   TITCHFIELD M
1689-   WOODSTOCK V
BERESFORD
B(I) 1720-   Beresford
B   1916-1919X Beresford
V   1823-1854X Beresford
B   1814-1854X Beresford
Beresford
1720-   BERESFORD B(I)
1814-1854X BERESFORD B
1823-1854X BERESFORD V
1916-1919X BERESFORD B
1720-   TYRONE V(I)
1746-   TYRONE E(I)
1786-   TYRONE B
1789-   WATERFORD M(I)
See also Poer and De La Poer
Beresford
BERGAVENNY: See ABERGAVENNY
BERKELEY
B   1066/87-1281C Berkeley, de
B   1295-1417A Berkeley, de
B   1421-   Berkeley
V   1481-1492X Berkeley
M   1488-1492X Berkeley
E   1679-1942D Berkeley

BERKELEY OF RATHDOWN
B(I) 1661-1712X Berkeley
BERKELEY OF STRATTON
B   1658-1773X Berkeley

Berkeley, De
1066/87-1281C BERKELEY B
1295-1417A   BERKELEY B
Berkeley
1481-1492X BERKELEY V
1488-1492X BEREKELY M
1658-1773X BERKELEY OF STRATTON B
1661-1712X BERKELEY OF RATHDOWN
    B(I)
1679-1942D BERKELEY E
1664-1665X BOTETOURT B
1764-1776A BOTETOURT B
1679-1942D DURSLEY V
1664-1665X FALMOUTH E
1661-1712X FITZHARDING V(I)
1841-1857X FITZHARDINGE E
1861-1916X FITZHARDINGE B
1483-1491X NOTTINGHAM E
1831-1857X SEGRAVE B

BERKHAMSTEAD
M   1726-1765X Guelph
E   1917-1960X Mountbatten
BERKSHIRE
E   1620-1623X Norris
E   1626-   Howard
BERMINGHAM
B   1326-1509/47S Bermingham, De
Bermingham,(De)
1759-1799S ATHENRY B(I)
1326-1509/47S BERMINGHAM
1541-....X CARBERY B(I)
1319-1329X LOUTH E(I)
1759-1799X LOUTH E(I)
BERNARD
V(I) 1800-1800M Bernard
Bernard
1800-1800M BERNARD V(I)
1800-1979X BANDON B(I)
1800-1979X BANDON V(I)
1800-1979X BANDON E(I)
BERNERS
B   1455-1743A Bourchier
B   1832-1871P Wilson
B   1871-   Tyrwhitt
E   1455-   Williams
BERNSTEIN
B(L) 1969-   Bernstein
Bernstein
1969-   BERNSTEIN B(L)
BERRIEDALE
L(S) 1592-   Sinclair

13

Berry
  1926-1928X BUCKLAND B
  1929-   CAMROSE B
  1941-   CAMROSE V
  1968-   HARTWELL B(L)
  1936-   KEMSLEY B
  1945-   KEMSLEY V
BERTIE
  B   1675-1682M Bertie
BERTIE OF THAME
  B   1915-1954X Bertie
  V   1918-1954X Bertie
Bertie
  1682-   ABINGDON E
  1715-1809X ANCASTER & KESTEVEN D
  1675-1682M BERTIE B
  1915-1954X BERTIE OF THAME B
  1918-1954X BERTIE OF THAME V
  1626-   LINDSEY E
  1706-1809X LINDSEY M
  1572-   NORREYS OF RYCOTE B
BERTRAM OF BOTHALL
  B   1154/89-1364X Bertram
BERTRAM OF MITFORD
  B   1264-1311A Bertram
Bertram
  1154/89-1364X BERTRAM OF BOTHALL B
  1264-1311A BERTRAM OF MITFORD B
BERWICK

  D   1687-1695F Fitz-James
  B   1784-1953X Hill
BESSBOROUGH
  B(I) 1721-   Ponsonby
  E(I) 1739-   Ponsonby
  E   1937-   Ponsonby
Best
  1829-   WYNFORD B
BESWICK
  B(L) 1964-   Beswick
Beswick   BESWICK B(L)
  1964-
BETHELL
  B   1922-   Bethell
Bethell
  1922-   BETHELL B
  1861-   WESTBURY B
Bethune
  1440-   LINDSAY L(S)
  See also Lindesay-Bethune
Betterton
  1935-1949X RUSHCLIFFE B
Bevan
  1970-   LEE Bss(L)

BEVERER, DE
  B   1066/87-....X Beverer, De
Beverer, De
  1066/87-....X BEVERER, De
BEVERIDGE
  B   1946-1963X Beveridge
Beveridge
  1946-1963X BEVERIDGE B
BEVERLEY
  M   1708-1778M Douglas
  E   1790-   Percy
Bewicke-Copley: See Cromwell
BEWLIE
  L(S) 1609-1660X Hay
BEXLEY
  B   1823-1851X Vansittart
BICESTER
  B   1938-   Smith
Bickersteth
  1836-1851X LANGDALE B
BIDDULPH
  B   1903-   Biddulph
Biddulph
  1903-   BIDDULPH B
BIDUN
  B   1100/35-1154/89X Bidun, De
Bidun, De
  1100/35-1154/89X BIDUN B
Bigge
  1911-1931X STAMFORDHAM B
BIGGS: See EWART-BIGGS
Bigham
  1910-   MERSEY B
  1916-   MERSEY V
  See also Nairne
Bigod
  1135-1307X NORFOLK E
  1154-1177X NORWICH E
BILSLAND
  B   1950-1970X Bilsland
Bilsland
  1950-1970X BILSLAND B
BINDON
  V   1559-1691X Howard
  E   1706-1722X Howard
BINGHAM
  B   1934-   Bingham
Bingham
  1934-   BINGHAM B
  1800-   CLANMORRIS B(I)
  1776-   LUCAN B(I)
  1795-   LUCAN E(I)

14

BINGLEY
  B   1713-1730X Benson
  B   1762-1763X Lane-Fox
  B   1933-1947X Lane-Fox
BINNING: See BYRES & BINNING
Birch
  1970-1981X RHYL B(L)
BIRDWOOD
  B   1938-   Birdwood
Birdwood
  1938-   BIRDWOOD B
BIRK
  Bss(L) 1967-   Birk
Birk
  1967-   BIRK Bss(L)
BIRKENHEAD
  B   1919-   Smith
  V   1921-   Smith
  E   1922-   Smith
BIRKETT
  B   1958-   Birkett
Birkett
  1958-   BIRKETT B
Bishop
  1981-1984X BISHOPSTON B(L)
BISHOPSTON
  B(L) 1981-1984X Bishop
BLACHFORD
  B   1871-1889X Rogers
BLACK
  B(L) 1968-   Black
Black
  1968-   BLACK B(L)
BLACKBURN
  B(L) 1876-1896X Blackburn
Blackburn
  1876-1896X BLACKBURN B(L)
BLACKETT
  B(L) 1969-1974X Blackett
Blackett
  1969-1974X BLACKETT B(L)
BLACKFORD
  B   1935-   Mason
Blackwood
  1800-   DUFFERIN & CLANDEBOYE
              B(I)
  See also Hamilton-Blackwood
Blades
  1928-   EBBISHAM B
BLAKE
  B(L) 1971-   Blake
Blake
  1800-1920X WALLSCOURT B(I)
  1971-   BLAKE B(L)

BLAKENHAM
  V   1963-   Hare
BLAKENEY
  B(I) 1756-1761X Blakeney
Blakeney
  1756-1761X BLAKENEY B(I)
BLANDFORD   *
  M   1702-   Churchill
BLANESBURGH
  B(L) 1923-1946X Younger
BLANTYRE
  L(S) 1606-   Stewart
BLAQUIERE, DE
  B   1800-1920X Blaquiere, De
Blaquiere, De
  1800-1920X BLAQUIERE, DE B
BLARNEY
  B   1628-1691F MacCarthy
BLAYNEY
  B   1621-1874X Blayney
Blayney
  1621-1874X BLAYNEY B
BLEASE
  B(L) 1978-   Blease
Blease
  1978-   BLEASE B(L)
BLEDISLOE
  B   1918-   Bathurst
  V   1935-   Bathurst
BLESSINGTON
  E(I) 1816-1829X Gardiner
BLESINTON
  E(I) 1745-1769X Stewart
  V(I) 1673-1732X Boyle
BLETCHLEY
  B   1616-1687X Villiers
Bligh
  1608-   CLIFTON OF LEIGHTON
              BROMSWOLD B
  1721-   CLIFTON OF RATHMORE B(I)
  1723-   DARNLEY V(I)
  1725-   DARNLEY E(I)
Blois
  1148-1160P SURREY E
BLOOMFIELD
  B(I) 1825-1879X Bloomfield
  B   1871-1879X Bloomfield
Bloomfield
  1825-1879X BLOOMFIELD B(I)
  1871-1879X BLOOMFIELD B
BLOUNT
  B   1326-1337X Blount
Blount
  1326-1337X BLOUNT B

15   * See Addenda

Blount (Cont'd)
1603-1606X DEVON E
1465-1606X MONTJOY B
1616-1681X MONTJOY B(I)
1627-1681X MONTJOY B
1628-1681X NEWPORT E
BLUNDELL
V(I) 1720-1756X Blundell
Blundell
1720-1756X BLUNDELL V(I)
1720-1756X EDENDERRY B(I)
Blundevil, De
1217-1232P LINCOLN E
BLYTH
B 1907- Blyth
Blyth
1907- BLYTH B
BLYTHSWOOD
B 1892-1940X Campbell
BLYTON
B(L) 1964- Blyton
Blyton
1964- BLYTON B(L)
BOARDMAN
B(L) 1980- Boardman
Boardman
1980- BOARDMAN B(L)
BOCLAND
B 1154/89-1199/1216X Bocland, De
Bocland,
1154/89-1199/1216X BOCLAND B
BODMIN
V 1679-1757X Robartes
BODRIGAN
B 1309-....S Bodrigan, De
Bodrigan, De
1309-....S BODRIGAN B
BOHUN
B 1066/87-1199M Bohun, De
BOHUN OF MIDHURST
B 1363-1367S Bohun, De
Bohun, de
1066/87-1199M BOHUN B
1363-1367S BOHUN OF MIDHURST B
1239-1372X ESSEX E
1199-1372X HEREFORD E
1337-1372X NORTHAMPTON E
See also Fitz-Piers
BOLEBEC OF BUCKINGHAMSHIRE
B 1066/87-1154/89M Bolebec, De
BOLEBEC OF NORTHUMBERLAND
B 1100/35-1216/72X Bolebec, De
Bolebec, De
1066/87-1154/89M BOLEBEC OF BUCKING-
HAMSHIRE B

Bolebec, De (Cont'd)
1100/35-1216/72X BOLEBEC OF
NORTHUMBERLAND B
BOLEBROOKE
B 1782-1843X Sackville
Boleyn
1527-1538A ORMONDE E(I)
1532-1533M PEMBROKE Mss
1525-1538X ROCHFORD V
1529-1533X WILTSHIRE E
BOLINGBROKE
E 1624-1711X StJohn
V 1712- StJohn
BOLLERS
B 1100/35-1209X Bollers, De
Bollers, De
1100/35-1209X BOLLERS B
BOLLES OF OSBERTON
Bss(S) 1635-1670X Bolles
Bolles
1635-1670X BOLLES OF OSBERTON
Bss(S)
BOLSOVER
B 1880- Cavendish-Bentinck
BOLTEBY
B 1216/72-1272/1307X Bolteby,
De
Bolteby, De
1216/72-1272/1307X BOLTEBY B
BOLTON
B 1797- Orde-Powlett
D 1689-1794X Paulet
BOLTOUN
L(S) 1624-1624M Maitland
BOLUM
B 1154/89-1154/89X Bolum, De
Bolum, De
1154/89-1154/89X BOLUM B
Bonham Carter
1964-1969X ASQUITH OF YARNBURY
Bss(L)
BONVILE
B 1449-1554F Bonvile
Bonvile
1449-1554F BONVILE B
Boot
1929-1956X TRENT B
Booth
1661-1770X MERE, DE LA B
1690-1758X WARRINGTON E
See also Gore-Booth and
Sclater-Booth
BOOTHBY
B(L) 1958- Boothby

16

Boothby
  1747-1787P COBHAM B
  1958-   BOOTHBY B(L)
Bootle-Wilbraham
  1880-1930X LATHOM E
  1828-   SKELMERSDALE B
BORINGDON
  B   1784-   Parker
  V   1815-   Parker
BORODALE
  V   1919-   Beatty
BORTHWICK
  L(S) 1433-1910D Borthwick
Borthwick
  1433-1910D BORTHWICK L(S)
  1895-1908X GLENESK B
  1912-1967X WHITBURGH B
BORWICK
  B   1922-   Borwick
Borwick
  1922-   BORWICK B
BOSCAWEN
  B   1720-   Boscawen
Boscawen
  1720-   BOSCAWEN B
  1720-   FALMOUTH V
  1808-1852X FALMOUTH E
BOSSOM
  B(L) 1960-1965X Bossom
Bossom
  1960-1965X BOSSOM B(L)
BOSTON
  V   1698-1754X Nassau, De
  B   1761-   Irby
BOSTON OF FAVERSHAM
  B(L) 1976-   Boston
Boston
  1976-   BOSTON OF FAVERSHAM B(L)
BOSWORTH
  B   1687-1695F Fitzjames
BOTELER OF OVERSLEY & WEMME
  B   1100/35-1289A Boteler
  B   1308-1369A Boteler
BOTELER OF WARRINGTON
  B   1216/72-1303X Pincerna
  B   1295-1299X Boteler
BOTELER OF BRAMFIELD
  B   1628-1647X Boteler
Boteler
  1100/35-1289A BOTELER OF OVERSLEY
                 & WEMME B
  1308-1369A BOTELER OF OVERSLEY
                 & WEMME B
  1295-1299X BOTELER OF WARRINGTON B

Boteler (Cont'd)
  1628-1647X BOTELER OF BRAMFIELD B
  1441-1473X SUDELEY B
BOTETOURT
  B   1305-1406A Botetourt
  B   1764-1776A Berkeley
  B   1803-1803M Somerset
BOTETOURT OF LANGPORT
  B   1664-1665X Berkeley
Botetourt
  1305-1406A BOTETOURT B
BOTHWELL
  L(S) 1225-1336A Moray
  L(S) 1486-1500F Ramsay
  E(S) 1488-1567F Hepburn
  E(S) 1587-1624F Stewart
  L(S) 1651-1761X Douglas
Bothwell
  1607-1635D HOLYROODHOUSE L(S)
BOTREAUX
  B   1154/89-1272S Botreaux, De
  B   1368-1960A Botreaux
Botreaux, De
  1154/69-1272S BOTREAUX B
Botreaux
  1368-1960A BOTREAUX B
BOTTESFORD
  B   1835-1941X Manners-Sutton *
Bould
  1468-....X RATOATH B(I)
BOULTON: See THIRLESTANE & BOULTON
BOURCHIER
  B   1342-1646A Bourchier
Bourchier
  1536-1645X BATH E
  1455-1743A BERNERS B
  1342-1646A BOURCHIER B
  1461-1539X ESSEX E
  1292-1636A FITZ-WARINE B
BOURKE OF CASTLECONNEL
  B(I) 1580-1700X Bourke
BOURKE OF MAYO
  V(I) 1628-1767D Bourke
Bourke
  1580-1700X BOURKE OF CASTLECONNEL
                 B(I)
  1628-1767D BOURKE OF MAYO V(I)
  1618-1691F BRITTAS B(I)
  1887-1902X CONNEMARA B
  1628-1767D MAYO V(I)
  1776-   MAYO B(I)
  1781-   MAYO V(I)
  1785-   MAYO E(I)
  1776-   NAAS B(I)

17   * See Addenda

BOURNE
  B(L) 1964-   Bourne
Bourne
  1964-   BOURNE B(L)
Bouverie, de
  1747-   FOLKESTONE V
  1747-   LONGFORD B
  1765-   PLEYDELL-BOUVERIE B
  1765-   RADNOR E
BOWDEN
  B(L) 1963-   Bowden
Bowden
  1967-   AYLESTONE B(L)
  1963-   BOWDEN B(L)
Bowdon: See Butler-Bowdon
BOWEN
  B(L) 1893-1894X Bowen
Bowen
  1893-1894X BOWEN B(L)
BOWES
  B(I) 1758-1767X Bowes
  B   1815-1820X Bowes
  B   1887-   Bowes-Lyon
Bowes
  1758-1767X BOWES B(I)
  1815-1820X BOWES B
Bowes-Lyon
  1887-   BOWES B
  1937-   STRATHMORE & KINGHORNE E
  See also Lyon
BOWLES
  B(L) 1964-1970X Bowles
Bowles
  1964-1970X BOWLES B(L)
BOWMONT & CESSFORD
  M(S) 1707-   Ker
Bowyer
  1937-   DENHAM B
BOYD
  L(S) 1459-1746F Boyd
  L(S) 1536-1746F Boyd
BOYD OF MERTON
  V   1960-   Lennox-Boyd
Boyd
  1467-1469F ARRAN E(S)
  1459-1746F BOYD L(S)
  1536-1746F BOYD L(S)
  1482-1746F KILMARNOCK L(S)
  1661-1746F KILMARNOCK E(S)
  1831-   KILMARNOCK B
  See also Lennox-Boyd
BOYD-CARPENTER
  B(L) 1972-   Boyd-Carpenter
Boyd-Carpenter
  1972-   BOYD-CARPENTER B(L)

BOYD-ORR
  B   1949-1971X Orr
BOYLE
  L(S) 1699-   Boyle
  V(I) 1756-   Boyle
BOYLE OF HANDSWORTH
  B(L) 1970-1981X Boyle
BOYLE OF KINALMEAKY
  V(I) 1627-   Boyle
BOYLE OF MARSTON
  B   1711-   Boyle
BOYLE OF YOUGHAL
  B(I) 1616-   Boyle
Boyle
  1627-   BANDON BRIDGE B(I)
  1673-1732X BLESINTON V(I)
  1699-   BOYLE L(S)
  1756-   BOYLE V(I)
  1970-1981X BOYLE OF HANDSWORTH B(L)
  1627-   BOYLE OF KINALMEAKY V(I)
  1711-   BOYLE OF MARSTON B
  1616-   BOYLE OF YOUGHAL B(I)
  1628-   BROGHILL B(I)
  1664-1753X BURLINGTON E
  1714-1725X CARLETON B
  1786-   CARLETON B
  1714-1725X CARLTON B
  1756-   CASTLE MARTYR B(I)
  1644-1753X CLIFFORD OF LANESBOR-
                OUGH B
  1620-   CORK E(I)
  1616-   DUNGARVAN V(I)
  1897-   FAIRLIE B
  1703-   GLASGOW E(S)
  1660-1673X GUILDFORD Css
  1703-   KELBURN V(S)
  1628-   KINALMEAKY V(I)
  1660-   ORRERY E(I)
  1815-1890X ROSS B
  1660-1740X SHANNON V(I)
  1756-   SHANNON E(I)
BOYNE
  B(I) 1715-   Hamilton
  V(I) 1717-   Hamilton
BRABAZON
  B(I) 1616-   Brabazon
BRABAZON OF TARA
  B   1942-   Moore-Brabazon
Brabazon
  1616-   ARDEE B(I)
  1616-   BRABAZON B(I)
  1831-   CHAWORTH B
  1627-   MEATH E(I)
  See also Moore-Brabazon

18

BRABOURNE
B   1880-   Knatchbull
BRACKEN
V   1952-1958X Bracken
Bracken
1952-1958X BRACKEN V
BRACKLEY
V   1616-1829X Egerton
M   1720-1803X Egerton
V   1846-   Leveson-Gower
BRACO
B(I) 1735-1912D Duff
BRADBURY
B   1925-   Bradbury
Bradbury
1925-   BRADBURY B
BRADESTON
B   1342-1374A Bradeston
Bradeston
1342-1374A BRADESTON B
BRADFORD
E   1694-1762X Newport
B   1794-   Bridgeman
E   1815-   Bridgeman
BRADWELL
B(L) 1975-1976X Driberg
BRAIN
B   1962-   Brain
Brain
1962-   BRAIN B
BRAINTREE
B   1948-1961X Crittall
BRAMPTON
B   1899-1907X Hawkins
BRAMWELL
B   1882-1892X Bramwell
Bramwell
1882-1892X BRAMWELL B
BRANCEPETH
B   1613-1645X Carr
B   1866-   Hamilton-Russell
BRAND
B   1946-1963X Brand
Brand
1946-1963X BRAND B
1884-   HAMPDEN V
BRANDON   *
V   1679-1702M Gerard
D   1711-   Hamilton
Css(I) 1758-1789X Agar
B(I) 1758-1832X Crosbie
Brandon
1525-1545X LINCOLN E
1513-1523S LISLE V
1514-1551X SUFFOLK D

BRAOSE
B   1299-1326A Braose, De
B   1342-1399X Braose, De
BRAOSE OF BRAMBER
B   1066/87-1230X Braose, De
Braose, De
1299-1326A BRAOSE B
1342-1399X BRAOSE B
1066/87-1230X BRAOSE OF BRAMBER B
Brass
1945-1945X CHATTISHAM B
BRASSEY
B   1886-1919X Brassey
E   1911-1919X Brassey
BRASSEY OF APETHORPE
B   1938-   Brassey
Brassey
1886-1919X BRASSEY B
1911-1919X BRASSEY E
1938-   BRASSEY OF APETHORPE B
1911-1919X HYTHE V
BRAYBROOK
B   1199/1216-1257X Braybrook, De
Braybrook, De
1199/1216-1257X BRAYBROOK B
BRAYBROOKE
B   1786-   Griffin
BRAYE
B   1527-1557A Braye
B   1529-   Braye
B   1839-1862A Otway Cave
Braye   *
1527-1557A BRAYE B
BRAYLEY
B(L) 1973-1977X Brayley
Brayley
1973-1977X BRAYLEY B(L)
BREADALBANE
E(S) 1677-   Campbell
B   1806-1862X Campbell
M   1831-1862X Campbell
B   1873-1922X Campbell
M   1885-1922X Campbell
BREADALBANE & HOLLAND
E(S) 1677-   Campbell
BREAUT B
B   1199/1216-1228X Breaut, De
Breaut, De
1199/1216-1228X BREAUT B
BRECHIN
L(S) 1481-1504X Stewart
L(S) 1646-1715F Maule
BRECKNOCK
E   1660-1715F Butler
E   1812-   Pratt

19

* See also Addenda

```
BRECON                                    BRISTOL
   B      1958-1976X Lewis                    E     1622-1698X Digby
BRENTFORD                                     E     1714-      Hervey
   E     1644-1651X Ruthven or Ruthyn         M     1826-      Hervey
   E     1689-1719X Schomberg              BRITANNIA
   Bss(L) 1722-1730X Kielmansegg             B     1305-1333X Britannia, De
   V      1929-      Joynson-Hicks        Britannia, De
BRERETON                                     1305-1333X BRITANNIA B
   B(I) 1624-1722X Brereton               BRITTAS
Brereton                                     B(I) 1618-1691F Bourke
   1624-1722X BRERETON B(I)               BRITTEN
Brett                                        B(L) 1976-1976X Britten
   1885-        ESHER B                   Britten
   1897-        ESHER V                      1976-1976X BRITTEN B(L)
BRIDGE OF HARWICH                          BRIWERE
   B(L) 1980-        Bridge                   B     1199/1216-1232X
Bridge                                     Briwere
   1980-        BRIDGE OF HARWICH B(L)        1199/1216-1232X BRIWERE B
BRIDGEMAN                                  BROADBRIDGE
   V     1929-        Bridgeman              B     1945-        Broadbridge
Bridgeman                                  Broadbridge
   1794-        BRADFORD B                    1945-        BROADBRIDGE B
   1815-        BRADFORD E                 BROCAS
   1929-        BRIDGEMAN V                   V     1925-        Jellicoe
   1815-        NEWPORT V                  BROCK
BRIDGES                                       B(L) 1965-        Brock
   B     1957-        Bridges             Brock
Bridges                                       1965-        BROCK B(L)
   1957-        BRIDGES B                  BROCKET
   1868-1875X FITZ WALTER B                   B     1933-        Nall-Cain
BRIDGEWATER                                Brocklehurst
   E     1538-1548X D'Aubeney                 1914-1921X RANKSBOROUGH B
   E     1617-1829X Egerton               BROCKWAY
   D     1720-1803X Egerton                   B(L) 1964-        Brockway
BRIDPORT                                   Brockway
   B(I) 1794-        Hood                     1964-        BROCKWAY B(L)
   V     1868-        Hood                 BRODRICK
   B     1796-1814X Hood                      B(I) 1715-        Brodrick
   V     1800-1814X Hood                      B     1796-        Brodrick
BRIEN                                      Brodrick
   V(S) 1701-        Kerr                      1715-        BRODRICK B(I)
BRIGGS                                        1796-        BRODRICK B
   B(L) 1976-        Briggs                    1920-        DUNSFORD V
Briggs                                        1717-1979X MIDLETON V(I)
   1976-        BRIGGS B(L)          *        1920-1979X MIDLETON E
BRIGINSHAW                                 BROGHILL
   B(L) 1974-        Briginshaw               B(I) 1628-        Boyle
Briginshaw                                 Bromflete
   1974-        BRIGINSHAW B(L)               1449-1468X VESCI B
BRIMELOW                                   Bromley
   B(L) 1976-        Brimelow                 1741-1851X MONTFORT B
Brimelow                                   Brook
   1976-        BRIMELOW B(L)                 1963-1967X NORMANBROOK B

                        20          * See Addenda
```

BROOKE
 B   1621-   Greville
 E   1746-   Greville
BROOKE OF CUMNOR
 B(L) 1966-1984X Brooke
BROOKE OF OAKLEY
 B(L) 1939-1944X Capell-Brooke
BROOKE OF YSTRADFELLTE
 Bss(L) 1964-   Brooke
Brooke
 1946-   ALANBROOKE B
 1946-   ALANBROOKE V
 1966-1984X BROOKE OF CUMNOR B(L)
 1964-   BROOKE OF YSTRADFELLTE
               Bss(L)
 1952-   BROOKEBOROUGH V
 1445-1607F COBHAM B
 1645-1651X COBHAM B
 See also Capell-Brooke, de
BROOKEBOROUGH
 V   1952-   Brooke
BROOKES
 B(L) 1975-   Brookes
Brookes
 1975-   BROOKES B(L)
BROOKS OF TREMORFA
 B(L) 1979-   Brooks
Brooks
 1979-   BROOKS B(L)
 1892-   CRAWSHAW B
BROOME
 V   1914-   Kitchener
BROTHERTON
 B   1929-1930X Brotherton
Brotherton
 1929-1930X BROTHERTON B
Brougham
 1830-   BROUGHAM & VAUX B
BROUGHAM & VAUX
 B   1830-   Brougham
BROUGHSHANE
 B   1945-   Davison
BROUGHTON DE GYFFORD
 B   1851-1869X Hobhouse
Broughton
 1929-1966X FAIRHAVEN OF LODE B
 1961-   FAIRHAVEN OF ANGLESEY
               ABBEY B
BROUNCKER
 V(I) 1645-1687X Brouncker
Brouncker
 1645-1687X BROUNCKER V(I)
BROWN
 B(L) 1964-   Brown

Brown
 1964-   BROWN B(L)
 1554-1797X MONTAGU V
 1951-1958X RUFFSIDE V
 See also George-Brown
Browne
 1771-   ALTAMONT E(I)
 1798-1952X CASTLEROSSE B(I)
 1801-1952X CASTLEROSSE V(I)
 1959-   CRAIGTON B(L)
 1798-1952X KENMARE V(I)
 1801-1952X KENMARE E(I)   *
 1856-1952X KENMARE B
 1789-   KILMAINE B (I)
 1926-   MEREWORTH B
 1760-   MONTEAGLE B(I)
 1806-   MONTEAGLE B
 1836-   ORANMORE & BROWNE B(I)
 1800-   SLIGO M(I)
 1768-   WESTPORT V(I)
BROWNLOW
 B(I) 1718-1754X Brownlow
 B   1776-1921X Cust
 E   1815-1921X Cust
Brownlow
 1718-1754X BROWNLOW B(I)
 1718-1754X CHARLEVILLE B(I)
 1839-   LURGAN B
 1718-1754X TYRCONNEL V(I)   *
BROXMOUTH
 V(S) 1707-   Ker
BRUCE
 B   1746-   Bruce
 E   1821-   Bruce
BRUCE OF ANNANDALE
 B   1295-1306X Bruce
BRUCE OF DONNINGTON
 B(L) 1974-   Bruce
BRUCE OF KINLOSS
 L(S) 1604-   Bruce
BRUCE OF MELBOURNE
 V   1947-1967X Bruce
BRUCE OF TORRY
 L(S) 1647-   Bruce
BRUCE OF WHORLTON
 B   1640-1747X Bruce   *
Bruce
 1873-   ABERDARE B
 1664-1747X AILESBURY E
 1776-   AILESBURY E
 1821-   AILESBURY M
 1746-   BRUCE B
 1821-   BRUCE E
 1295-1306X BRUCE OF ANNANDALE B

* See Addenda

Bruce (Cont'd)
1607-1716F	BALFOUR OF BURLEIGH	L(S)
1974-	BRUCE OF DONNINGTON	B(L)
1604-	BRUCE OF KINLOSS	L(S)
1947-1967X	BRUCE OF MELBOURNE	V
1647-	BRUCE OF TORRY	L(S)
1640-1747X	BRUCE OF WHORLTON	B
1200-1306M	CARRICK	E(S)
1314-1371X	CARRICK	E(S)
1633-	ELGIN	E(S)
1647-	KINCARDINE	E(S)
1602-	KINLOSS	L(S)
1821-	SAVERNAKE	V

*

BRUDENELL
  B   1628-   Brudenell
Brudenell
  1628-   BRUDENELL B
  1661-   CARDIGAN E
  1766-1790X MONTHERMER M
Bruges
  1472-1499S WINCHESTER E
BRUNTISFIELD
  B   1942-
BRYAN
  B   1350-1456X Bryan
  Bss 1516-....X Bryan
Bryan
  1350-1456X BRYAN B
  1516-....X BRYAN Bss
BRYCE
  V   1914-1922X Bryce
Bryce
  1914-1922X BRYCE V
Brydges
  1714-1789X CARNARVON E
  1719-1789X CARNARVON M
  1554-1789D CHANDOS B
  1719-1789X CHANDOS D
  1714-1789X WILTON V
BUCCLEUCH
  E(S) 1619-   Scott
  D(S) 1663-   Scott
BUCHAN
  E(S) 1221-1320F Cumyn
  E(S) 1374-1425M Stewart
  E(S) 1469-   Stewart
Buchan
  1935-   TWEEDSMUIR B
BUCHANAN: See GRAHAM & BUCHANAN
Buchanan
  1922-1935X WOOLAVINGTON B
Buchan-Hepburn
  1957-1974X HAILES B

Buchanan-Smith
  1963-   BALERNO B(L)
BUCKHURST
  B   1567-1843X Sackville
  Bss 1864-   Sackville
BUCKINGHAM
  E   1066-1166X Giffard
  E   1377-1397X Plantagenet
  E   1403-1521F Stafford
  D   1444-1483F Stafford
  D   1486-1521F Stafford
  E   1616-1687X Villiers
  M   1618-1687X Villiers
  Css 1618-1632X Villiers
  D   1623-1687X Villiers
  D   1703-1735X Sheffield
  M   1784-1889X Grenville
  D   1822-1889X Grenville
BUCKINGHAMSHIRE
  E   1746-   Hobart
BUCKLAND
  B   1926-1928X Berry
Buckley
  1915-   WRENBURY B
BUCKMASTER
  B   1915-   Buckmaster
  V   1933-   Buckmaster
Buckmaster
  1915-   BUCKMASTER B
  1933-   BUCKMASTER V
BUCKTON
  B   1966-1978X Storey
BUISLI
  B   1066/87-1212X Buisli, De
Buisli, De
  1066/87-1212X BUISLI B
BULKELEY
  V(I) 1643-1822X Bulkeley
BULKELEY OF BEAUMARIS
  B   1784-1822X Bulkeley
Bulkeley
  1643-1822X BULKELEY V(I)
  1784-1822X BEAUMARIS B
  1784-1822X BULKELEY OF BEAUMARIS B
Buller: See Manningham-Buller and
          Yarde-Buller
BULLOCK
  B(L) 1976-   Bullock
Bullock
  1976-   BULLOCK B(L)
BULMER
  B   1432-1558A Bulmer
Bulmer
  1432-1558A BULMER B

      * See Addenda

Bulwer
1871-1872X DALLING & BULWER B
Bulwer-Lytton
1866-   LYTTON B
1880-   LYTTON V
1880-   LYTTON E
Bunbury: See M'Clintock
BURDEN
B   1950-   Burden
Burden
1950-   BURDEN B
BURDETT-COUTTS
Bss 1871-1906X Burdett-Coutts
Burdett-Coutts
1871-1906X BURDETT-COUTTS Bss
BURFORD
E   1676-   Beauclerk
BURGH
B   1199/1216-1279X Burgh, De
B   1327-....X Burgh, De
B   1487-1597A Burgh
B   1529-   Leith
B   1784-1802X Lowther
Burgh
1487-1597A BURGH B
1822-1864X DOWNES B
1226-1243X KENT E
1628-1659X ST ALBANS E
1624-1659X SOMERHILL B
1624-1659X TUNBRIDGE V
Burgh, De
1199/1216-1279X BURGH B
1327-....X BURGH B
1800-   CLANRICARDE E(I)
1243-1352P ULSTER E(I)
Burgh-Canning, De
1629-1916X BURKE V(I)
1543-1916X CLANRICARDE E(I)
1825-1916X CLANRICARDE M(I)
1543-1916X DUNKELLIN B(I)
1644-1657X DUNKELLIN M(I)
1785-1797X DUNKELLIN M(I)
1826-1916X SOMERHILL B
BURGHCLERE
B   1895-1921X Gardner
BURGHERSH
B   1303-1369C Burghersh
B   1624-   Fane
Burghersh
1303-1369C BURGHERSH B
BURGHLEY
B   1571-   Cecil
BURKE
V(I) 1629-1916X Burgh-Canning, De

Burke
1687-1691X GALWAY V(I)
1583-1583X LEITRIM B(I)
1687-1691X TYAQUIN B(I)
BURLINGTON
E   1664-1753X Boyle
E   1831-   Cavendish
BURNELL
B   1311-1315X Burnell
B   1350-1420A Handlo
B   1658-1660X Dunch
Burnell
1311-1315X BURNELL B
BURNHAM
B   1903-   Levy-Lawson
V   1919-1933X Lawson
Burns
1897-1957X INVERCLYDE B
BURNTISLAND
L(S) 1672-1685X Wemyss
BURNTWOOD
B(L) 1970-   Snow
Burrell
1796-1915X GWYDYR B
BURTON
B   1711-1769X Paget
B   1886-1909X Bass
B   1897-1931P Baillie
B   1932-1962P Melles
B   1962-   Baillie
BURTON OF COVENTRY
Bss(L) 1962-   Burton
Burton
1962-   BURTON OF COVENTRY Bss(L)
BURY
V   1696-   Keppel
Bury
1800-1875X CHARLEVILLE V(I)
1806-1875X CHARLEVILLE E(I)
1797-   TULLAMORE B(I)
BUSSEL
B   1066/87-1206F Bussel
Bussel
1066/87-1206F BUSSEL B
Butcher
1924-1935X DANESFORT B
BUTE
E(S) 1703-   Stuart
M   1796-   Stuart
BUTLER
V(I) 1603-1613X Butler
B(I) 1607-....M Butler
B   1666-1905A Cowper

23

BUTLER OF BRAMFIELD
  B   1628-1647X Butler
BUTLER OF LANTHONY
  B   1660-1715F Butler
  B   1801-1820X Butler
BUTLER OF MORE PARK
  B   1679-1715F Butler
BUTLER OF MOUNT JULIET
  B   1912-   Butler
BUTLER OF SAFFRON WALDEN
  B(L) 1965-1982X Butler
BUTLER OF WESTON
  B   1673-1685X Butler
  B   1694-1759X Butler
Butler
  1825-   ARKLOW B(I)
  1662-1685X ARRAN E(I)
  1693-1759X ARRAN E(I)
  1676-1677X AUGHRIM B(I)
  1660-1715F BRECKNOCK E
  1603-1613X BUTLER V(I)
  1607-....M BUTLER B(I)
  1628-1647X BUTLER OF BRAMFIELD B
  1660-1715F BUTLER OF LANTHONY B
  1801-1820X BUTLER OF LANTHONY B
  1679-1715F BUTLER OF MORE PARK B
  1912-   BUTLER OF MOUNT JULIET B
  1965-1982X BUTLER OF SAFFRON
           WALDEN B(L)
  1673-1685X BUTLER OF WESTON B
  1693-1759X BUTLER OF WESTON B
  1543-1858X CAHER B(I)
  1583-1858X CAHER B(I)
  1816-1858X CAHER V(I)
  1315-1321X CARRICK E(I)
  1748-   CARRICK E(I)
  1693-1759X CLOGHGRENAN B(I)
  1676-1677X CLONMORE V(I)
  1324-   DUNBOYNE B(I)
  1541-   DUNBOYNE B(I)
  1646-1697F GALMOYE V(I)
  1816-1858X GLENGALL E
  1676-1677X GOWRAN E(I)
  1629-   IKERRIN V(I)
  1793-1846X KILKENNY E
  1728-   LANESBOROUGH V(I)
  1728-   LANESBOROUGH E(I)
  1550-   MOUNTGARRET V(I)
  1911-   MOUNTGARRET B
  1715-   NEWTOWN BUTLER B(I)
  1603-1613X ORMONDE E(I)
  1642-1715F ORMONDE M(I)
  1661-1715F ORMONDE D(I)
  1495-1515A ORMOND OF ROCHFORD B

  1328-   ORMONDE E(I)
  1681-1715F ORMONDE D
  1816-1820X ORMONDE M(I)
  1821-   ORMONDE B
  1825-   ORMONDE M(I)
  1527-   OSSORY E(I)
  1495-1515X ROCHFORD B
  1535-   THURLES V(I)
  1693-1759X TULLOUGH V(I)
  1449-1461X WILTSHIRE E
Butler-Bowdon
  1940-1963A GREY DE RUTHYN B
BUXTON
  V   1914-1934X Buxton
  E   1920-1934X Buxton
BUXTON OF ALSA
  B(L) 1978-   Buxton
Buxton
  1914-1934X BUXTON V
  1920-1934X BUXTON E
  1978-   BUXTON OF ALSA B(L)
  1930-   NOEL-BUXTON B
BYERS
  B(L) 1964-1984X Byers
Byers
  1964-1984X BYERS B(L)
BYNG
  B   1721-   Byng
BYNG OF VIMY
  B   1919-1935X Byng
  V   1928-1935X Byng
Byng
  1919-1935X BYNG B
  1928-1935X BYNG V
  1847-   ENFIELD V
  1835-   STRAFFORD B
  1847-   STRAFFORD E
  1875-   STRAFFORD B
  1721-   TORRINGTON V
BYRES & BINNING
  L(S) 1619-   Hamilton
BYRON
  B   1643-   Byron
Byron
  1643-   BYRON

(TITLES are in CAPITALS
Surnames in smalls)

24

CABARSTOWN: See LINTON & CABARSTOWN
CABLE
B   1921-1927X Cable
Cable
   1921-1927X CABLE B
CACCIA
B(L) 1965-   Caccia
Caccia
   1965-   CACCIA B(L)
CADMAN
B   1937-   Cadman
Cadman
   1937-   CADMAN B
CADOGAN
E   1718-1726X Cadogan
E   1800-   Cadogan
CADOGAN OF OAKLEY
B   1718-   Cadogan
CADOGAN OF READING
B   1716-1726X Cadogan
Cadogan
   1718-1726X CADOGAN E
   1800-   CADOGAN E
   1718-   CADOGAN OF OAKLEY B
   1716-1726X CADOGAN OF READING B
   1718-1726X CAVERSHAM V
   1800-   CHELSEA V
   1831-   OAKLEY B
Cadurcis, De
   1066/87-1272/1307X CHAWORTH B
CAHER
B(I) 1543-1858X Butler
V(I) 1816-1858X Butler
CAILLI
B   1309-1317X Cailli
Cailli
   1309-1317X CAILLI B
Cain: See Nall-Cain
CAIRNS
B   1867-   Cairns
E   1878-   Cairns
Cairns
   1867-   CAIRNS B
   1878-   CAIRNS E
   1878-   GARMOYLE V
CAITHNESS
E(S) 1129-1222X MacWilliam
E(S) 1371-1437F Stewart
E(S) 1450-1455X Crichton
E(S) 1455-   Sinclair
CALDECOTE
V   1939-   Inskip
Calder
   1966-1982X RITCHIE-CALDER B(L)

*See Addenda

CALEDON
B(I) 1790-   Alexander
V(I) 1797-   Alexander
E(I) 1800-   Alexander
CALENDAR
E(S) 1641-1716F Livingston
CALLAN
B(I) 1790-1815X Agar
V(I) 1622-   Feilding
CALNE & CALSTONE
V   1784-   Petty-Fitzmaurice
CALSTONE: See CALNE & CALSTONE
CALTHORPE
B   1796-   Gough-Calthorpe
CALVERLEY
B   1945-   Muff
Calvert
   1624-1771X BALTIMORE B(I)
CAMBRIDGE
E   1139-....X Meschines, De
E   1205-....X Vere, De
E   1340-1361X Juliers, De
E   1362-1461M Plantagenet
E   1619-1651X Hamilton
E   1644-1660X Stuart
D   1661-1661X Stuart
E   1664-1667X Stuart
D   1664-1667X Stuart
D   1667-1671X Stuart
D   1677-1677X Stuart
D   1706-1727M Guelph
D   1801-1904X Guelph
M   1917-1981X Cambridge
   See also: ARRAN, LANARK & CAMBRIDGE
Cambridge
   1917-1957X ATHLONE E
   1917-1981X CAMBRIDGE M
   1917-1981X ELTHAM E
   1917-1981X NORTHALLERTON V
   1917-1957X TREMATON V
CAMDEN
B   1765-   Pratt
E   1786-   Pratt
M   1794-   Pratt
CAMELFORD
B   1784-1804X Pitt
CAMERON OF BALHOUSIE
B(L) 1983-   Cameron   *
Cameron
   1983-   CAMERON OF BALHOUSIE B(L)
CAMOYS
B   1264-1426A Camoys
B   1839-   Stonor
Camoys
   1264-1426A CAMOYS B

25

CAMPBELL
L(S) 1445-   Campbell
B   1841-   Campbell
CAMPBELL OF ALLOWAY
B(L) 1981-   Campbell
CAMPBELL OF CROY
B(L) 1974-   Campbell
CAMPBELL OF ESKAN
B(L) 1966-   Campbell
CAMPBELL OF LOUDOUN
L(S) 1601-   Campbell
CAMPBELL & COWAL
E(S) 1701-   Campbell
Campbell
  1706-1761X ARASE L(S)
  1457-   ARGYLL E(S)
  1641-   ARGYLL M(S)
  1701-   ARGYLL D(S)
  1314-1333R ATHOLL E(S)
  1892-1940X BLYTHSWOOD B
  1677-   BREADALBANE E(S)
  1806-1862X BREADALBANE B
  1831-1862X BREADALBANE M
  1873-1922X BREADALBANE B
  1885-1922X BREADALBANE M
  1677-   BREADALBANE &
            HOLLAND E(S)
  1445-   CAMPBELL L(S)
  1841-   CAMPBELL B
  1981-   CAMPBELL OF
            ALLOWAY B(L)
  1974-   CAMPBELL OF CROY B(L)
  1966-   CAMPBELL OF ESKRAN B(L)
  1701-   CAMPBELL & COWAL E(S)
  1796-   CAWDOR B
  1827-   CAWDOR E
  1705-1743X CHATHAM B
  1858-1863X CLYDE L(S)
  1946-   COLGRAIN B
  1706-1761X DUNOON L(S)
  1827-   EMLYN V
  1921-1984X GLENAVY B
  1677-   GLENORCHY, BENEDARA-
            LOCH, ORMELIE &
            WEICK L(S)
  1705-1743X GREENWICH E
  1719-1743X GREENWICH D
  1776-   HAMILTON B
  1706-1761X ILAY E(S)
  1706-1761X ILAY V(S)
  1701-   INVERARY, MULL, MOR-
            VERN & TIRY L(S)
  1642-1660X IRVINE E(S)
  1626-1660X KINTYRE L(S)

Campbell (Cont'd)
  1701-   KINTYRE & LORNE M(S)
  1701-   LOCHOW & GLENILLA V(S)
  1470-   LORNE L(S)
  1801-   LORNE M(S)
  1601-   LOUDOUN L(S)
  1633-   LOUDOUN E(S)
  1642-1660X LUNDIE L(S)
  1706-   ORANSAY L(S)
  1681-   ORMELIE L(S)
  1831-1862X ORMELIE E
  1885-1922X ORMELIE E
  1677-   SINCLAIR L(S)
  1836-   STRATHEDEN B
  1766-   SUNDRIDGE B
  1633-   TARRINZEAN & MAUCHLIN
            E(S)
  1677-   TAY & PAINTLAND
  1677-   WEIK L(S)
  See also:
  Clifton-Hastings-Campbell
  Hume
Campbell-Gray
  1445-   GRAY L(S)
CAMPDEN   *
  V   1841-   Noel
CAMPERDOWN
  E   1831-1933X Haldane-Duncan
CAMPION
  B   1950-1958X Campion
Campion
  1950-1958X CAMPION B
CAMPSIE
  L(S) 1661-1716F Livingston
CAMROSE
  B   1929-   Berry
  V   1941-   Berry
CAMVILLE
  B   1295-1338A Camville
Camville
  1295-1338A CAMVILLE B
CANADA
  V(S) 1633-1739A Alexander
CANCI
  B   1135/54-1215F Canci, De
Canci, De
  1135/54-1215F CANCI B
CANNING
  Vss 1828-1862X Canning
  E   1859-1862X Canning
Canning
  1828-1862X CANNING Vss
  1859-1862X CANNING E
  1818-   GARVAGH B(I)

* See also Addenda

Canning (Cont'd)
  1852-1880X STRATFORD DE
          REDCLIFFE V
  See also: Burgh-Canning, De
CANTELUPE
  B   1299-1376X Cantelupe
  V   1761-   West
Cantelupe
  1240-1272P ABERGAVENNY B
  1299-1376X CANTELUPE B
CANTERBURY
  V   1835-1941X Manners-Sutton
CAPEL
  B   1641-   Capel
CAPEL OF TEWKESBURY
  B   1692-1696X Capel
Capel
  1641-   CAPEL B
  1692-1696X CAPEL OF TEWKESBURY B
  1661-   ESSEX E
  1661-   MALDEN V
Capell-Brooke, De
  1939-1944X BROOKE OF OAKLEY B
CARADON
  B(L) 1964-   Foot
CARBERY
  B(I) 1541-....X Bermingham
  E(I) 1628-1712X Vaughan
  B(I) 1715-   Evans-Freke
CARDIFF
  B   1766-   Stuart
CARDIGAN
  E   1661-   Brudenell
CARDROSS
  L(S) 1606-   Erskine
CARDWELL
  V   1874-1886X Cardwell
Cardwell
  1874-1886X CARDWELL V
CAREW
  B   1605-1629X Carew
  B(I) 1834-   Conolly-Carew
  B   1838-   Conolly-Carew
Carew
  1605-1629X CAREW B
  1626-1629X TOTNESS E
CAREY
  B   1622-1661X Carey
Carey
  1622-1661X CAREY B
  1628-1677X DOVER E
  1559-1765X HUNSDON B
  1626-1660X MONMOUTH E
  1621-1677X ROCHFORD V

    * See also Addenda

CARHAMPTON
  B(I) 1768-1829X Luttrell
  V(I) 1781-1829X Luttrell
  E(I) 1785-1829X Luttrell
CARISBROOKE
  M   1917-1960X Mountbatten
CARLETON
  B   1714-1725X Boyle
  B   1786-   Boyle
  B(I) 1789-1825X Carleton
  V(I) 1797-1825X Carleton
Carleton
  1789-1825X CARLETON B(I)
  1797-1825X CARLETON V(I)
  1786-1897X DORCHESTER B
  1899-1963X DORCHESTER B
CARLINGFORD
  V(I) 1627-1634X Swift
  E(I) 1662-1738X Taaffe
  V(I) 1761-1853X Carpenter
  B   1874-1898X Parkinson-Fortescue
CARLISLE
  E   1322-1323F Harcla
  E   1622-1660X Hay
  E   1661-   Howard
CARLOW
  V(I) 1776-   Dawson
CARLTON
  B   1626-1631X Carlton
  B   1714-1725X Boyle
  V   1876-   Stuart-Wortley-
                  MacKenzie
Carlton
  1628-1631X CARLTON B
  1628-1631X DORCHESTER B
CARLYLE
  L(S) 1471-1580X Carlyle
  L(S) 1609-1638R Douglas
  L(S) 1620-1716A Maxwell
Carlyle
  1471-1580X CARLYLE L(S)
CARMARTHEN
  M   1689-1964X Osborne
CARMICHAEL   *
  L(S) 1647-1817X Carmichael
  B   1912-1926X Gibson-Carmichael
Carmichael
  1647-1817X CARMICHAEL L(S)
  1701-1817X HYNDFORD E(S)
  1701-1817X INGLISBERRY & NEMPHLAR V(S)
CARNARVON
  E   1628-1709X Dormer
  E   1714-1789X Brydges
  M   1719-1789X Brydges
  E   1793-   Herbert

27

CARNEGIE
L(S) 1616-   Carnegie
Carnegie
1616-   CARNEGIE L(S)
1633-   SOUTHESK E(S)
1639-   INGLISMALDIE L(S)
1639-   LOUR L(S)
1647-   NORTHESK E(S)
1869-   BALINHARD B
1900-   FIFE D
1900-   MACDUFF E
CARNEGY
Bss(L) 1982-   Carnegy
Carnegy
1982-   CARNEGY Bss(L)
CARNOCK
B   1916-   Nicolson
CARNWATH
E(S) 1639-1941D Dalzell
CARPENTER
B   1719-1853X Carpenter
Carpenter
1719-1853X CARPENTER B(I)
1761-1853X CARLINGFORD V(I)
1761-1853X TYRCONNELL E(I)
See also: Boyd-Carpenter
CARR
B   1613-1645X Carr
CARR OF HADLEY
B(L) 1975-   Carr
Carr
1611-1645X ROCHESTER V
1613-1645X SOMERSET E
1613-1645X BRANCEPETH B
1613-1645X CARR B
1975-   CARR OF HADLEY B(L)
CARRICK
E(S) 1180-1271? Duncan
E(S) 1200-1306M Bruce
E(S) 1314-1371X Bruce
E(S) 1361-1363M Cunynghame   *
E(S) 1390-....M Stewart
E(S) 1630-1652X Stewart
E(I) 1748-   Butler
E(S) 1958-   Windsor
CARRICKFERGUS: See ENNISHOWEN &
                    CARRICKFERGUS
CARRINGTON
B   1643-1706X Smith
B(I) 1796-   Carrington
B   1797-   Carrington
E   1895-1928X Wynn-Carrington
See also: RAMSAY & CARRINGTON

* See also Addenda

Carrington
1796-   CARRINGTON B(I)
1797-   CARRINGTON B
CARROLL
1552-....? ELY O'CARROLL
CARRON
B(L) 1967-1969X Carron
Carron
1967-1969X CARRON B(L)
CARSON
B(L) 1921-1935X Carson
Carson
1921-1935X CARSON B(L)
Carter: See Bonham Carter
CARTERET
B   1681-1695X Carteret
Vss 1714-1776X Carteret
B   1784-1849X Thynne
Carteret
1681-1695X CARTERET B
1714-1776X CARTERET Vss
1714-1766X GRANVILLE E
CARVER
B(L) 1977-   Carver
Carver
1977-   CARVER B(L)
CARY
L(S) 1620-   Cary
Cary
1620-   CARY L(S)
1620-   FALKLAND V(S)
1832-1884X HUNSDON B
CARYSFORT
B(I) 1752-1909X Proby
E(I) 1789-1909X Proby
B   1801-1909X Proby
CASEY
B(L) 1960-1976X Casey
Casey
1960-1976X CASEY B
CASSILIS
E(S) 1502-   Kennedy
CASTLE
B(L) 1974-   Castle
Castle
1974-   CASTLE B(L)
CASTLEBAR
B(I) 1628-1671X Saville
CASTLECOMER
V(I) 1706-1784X Wandesford
CASTLECOOTE
B(I) 1800-1827X Coote
CASTLE CUFFE
V(I) 1793-1793C Cuffe

28

```
CASTLE DURROW                          Caulfield (Cont'd)
  B(I) 1733-      Flower                  1620-1892X CHARLEMONT B(I)
CASTLEHAVEN                               1665-1892X CHARLEMONT V(I)
  E(I) 1616-1777X Touchet                 1763-1892X CHARLEMONT E(I)
  L(S) 1685-1745F Mackenzie               1837-1892X CHARLEMONT B
  B    1861-      Mackenzie             Causton
  Bss  1861-      Leveson-Gower           1910-1929X SOUTHWARK B
CASTLEMAINE                             CAUTLEY
  V(I) 1628-1661F Monson                  B    1936-1946X Cautley
  E(I) 1661-1705X Palmer                Cautley
  V(I) 1718-1784X Child                   1936-1946X CAUTLEY B
  B(I) 1812-1839X Handcock              CAUZ
  V(I) 1822-1839X Handcock                B    1154/89-1216X Cauz, De
CASTLE MARTYR                          Cauz, De
  B(I) 1756-      Boyle                   1154/89-1216X CAUZ B
CASTLEREAGH                            CAVAN
  V(I) 1795-      Stewart                 B(I) 1617-      Lambart
CASTLEROSSE                              E(I) 1647-      Lambart
  B(I) 1798-1952X Browne               CAVE
  V(I) 1801-1952X Browne                 V    1918-1928X Cave
CASTLE STEWART                         CAVE OF RICHMOND
  B(I) 1619-      Stuart                  Vss  1928-1938X Cave
  V(I) 1793-      Stuart               Cave
  E(I) 1800-      Stuart                  1918-1928X CAVE V
CASTLETON                                1928-1938X CAVE OF RICHMOND Vss
  V(I) 1627-1723X Saunderson             See also: Otway Cave
  V    1716-1723X Saunderson                       Verney-Cave
  E    1720-1723X Saunderson           CAVENDISH OF BOLSOVER
CASTLETOWN                               B    1628-1691X Cavendish
  B    1869-1937X FitzPatrick          CAVENDISH OF HARDWICKE
CATHCART                                 B    1605-      Cavendish
  L(S) 1447-      Cathcart             CAVENDISH OF KEIGHLEY
  V    1807-      Cathcart               B    1831-      Cavendish
  E    1814-      Cathcart             Cavendish
Cathcart                                 1831-      BURLINGTON E
  1447-      CATHCART L(S)               1628-1691X CAVENDISH OF BOLSOVER B
  1807-      CATHCART V                  1605-      CAVENDISH OF HARDWICKE B
  1814-      CATHCART E                  1831-      CAVENDISH OF KEIGHLEY B
  1807-      GREENOCK B                  1858-      CHESHAM E
CATHERLOUGH                              1618-      DEVONSHIRE E
  B(I) 1733-1762X Fane                   1694-      DEVONSHIRE D
  E(I) 1762-1772X Knight                 1694-      HARTINGTON M
  M(I) 1714-1731X Wharton                1620-1691X MANSFIELD V
CATTO                                    1628-1691X NEWCASTLE E
  B    1936-      Catto                  1643-1691X NEWCASTLE M
Catto                                    1664-1691X NEWCASTLE D
  1936-      CATTO B                     1620-1691A OGLE B
CAULFIELD                                1792-      WATERPARK B(I)
  B(I) 1620-1763C Caulfield           Cavendish-Bentinck
  V(I) 1665-1763C Caulfield              1880-      BOLSOVER B
Caulfield                                See also: Bentinck
  1620-1763C CAULFIELD B(I)           CAVERSHAM
  1665-1763C CAULFIELD V(I)             V    1718-1726X Cadogan
```

29

```
CAWDOR                                    Chandos
  B    1796-      Campbell                  1337-1353A CHANDOS B
  E    1827-      Campbell               CHANNING OF WELLINGBOROUGH
CAWLEY                                      B    1912-1926X Channing
  B    1918-      Cawley                 Channing
Cawley                                      1912-1926A CHANNING OF WELLING-
  1918-    CAWLEY B                                   BOROUGH B
CAYZER                                    CHAPLIN
  B(L) 1982-      Cayzer                   V    1916-1982X Chaplin
Cayzer                                    Chaplin
  1982-     CAYZER B(L)                     1916-1982X CHAPLIN V
  1939-     ROTHERWICK B                  Chapman
CECIL OF CHELWOOD                           1975-     NORTHFIELD B(L)      *
  V    1923-1958X Gascoyne-Cecil         CHARLEMONT
CECIL OF ESSENDON                           B(I) 1620-1892X Caulfield
  B    1603-      Cecil                    V(I) 1665-1892X Caulfield
CECIL OF PUTNEY                             E(I) 1763-1892X Caulfield
  B    1625-1638X Cecil                    B    1837-1892X Caulfield
Cecil                                     CHARLEVILLE
  1892-      AMHERST OF HACKNEY B          B(I) 1718-1754X Brownlow
  1571-      BURGHLEY B                    E(I) 1758-1764X Moore
  1603-      CECIL OF ESSENDON B           V(I) 1800-1875X Bury
  1625-1638X CECIL OF PUTNEY B            E(I) 1806-1875X Bury
  1604-      CRANBORNE V                 CHARNWOOD
  1605-      EXETER E                      B    1911-1955X Benson
  1801-      EXETER M                    CHARTERIS OF AMISFIELD
  1934-      ROCKLEY B                     B(L) 1977-      Charteris
  1605-      SALISBURY E                 Charteris
  1780-      SALISBURY M                   1977-     CHARTERIS OF AMISFIELD B(L)
  1626-1638X WIMBLEDON V                   1821-     WEMYSS B
  See also: Gascoyne-Cecil                 See also: Douglas
CESSFORD                                  CHATFIELD
  M(S) 1707-      Ker                       B    1937-      Chatfield
CHALFONT                                  Chatfield
  B(L) 1964-      Gwynne Jones              1937-     CHATFIELD B
CHALMERS                                  CHATHAM
  B    1919-1938X Chalmers                  B    1705-1743X Campbell
Chalmers                                    Bss  1761-1835X Pitt
  1919-1938X CHALMERS B                     E    1766-1835X Pitt
Chaloner                                  CHATTISHAM
  1917-     GISBOROUGH B                    B    1945-1945X Brass
CHAMPION                                  CHAVENT: See CHAMPVENT
  B(L) 1962-      Champion               CHAWORTH (or CADURCIS)
Champion                                    B    1066/87-1272/1307X Cadurcis, De
  1962-     CHAMPION B(L)               CHAWORTH
CHAMPVENT (or CHAVENT)                      B    1299-....? Chaworth
  B    1299-1302L Champvent, De           V(I) 1627-1699X Chaworth
Champvent, De                              B    1831-      Brabazon
  1299-1302L CHAMPVENT B               Chaworth
CHANDOS                                     1299-....? CHAWORTH B
  B    1337-1353A Chandos                  1627-1699X CHAWORTH V(I)
  B    1554-1789D Brydges              CHEDWORTH
  D    1719-1789X Brydges                  B    1741-1804X Howe
  M    1822-1889X Grenville            CHELMER
  V    1954-      Lyttelton              B(L) 1963-      Edwards

                       30              *See Addenda
```

```
CHELMSFORD                              CHEYLESMORE
  B    1858-      Thesiger                 B    1887-1974X Eaton
  V    1921-      Thesiger              CHEYNE
CHELSEA                                   L(S) 1681-1738X Cheyne
  V    1800-      Cadogan              Cheyne
CHELWOOD                                  1681-1738X CHEYNE L(S)
  B(L) 1974-      Beamish                 1681-1738X NEWHAVEN V(S)
CHENEY                                  CHICHESTER
  B    1487-1499X Cheney                  B(I) 1612-1624X Chichester
CHENEY OF TODDINGTON                      E    1644-1653X Leigh
  B    1572-1587X Cheney                  E    1653-1667X Wriothesley
Cheney                                    E    1674-1774X Fitz-Roy
  1487-1499X CHENEY B                      E    1801-      Pelham
  1572-1587X CHENEY OF TODDDINGTON B    CHICHESTER OF BELFAST
CHEPSTOW                                  B(I) 1625-      Chichester
  B    1506-      Somerset             CHICHESTER OF CARRICKFERGUS
CHERLETON OF POWYS                        V(I) 1625-      Chichester
  B    1313-1422A Cherleton           Chichester
Cherleton                                 1625-      BELFAST B(I)
  1313-1422A CHERLETON OF POWYS B         1791-      BELFAST E(I)
CHERWELL                                  1612-1624X CHICHESTER B(I)
  B    1941-1957X Lindemann               1625-      CHICHESTER OFBELFAST
  V    1956-1957X Lindemann                          B(I)
CHESHAM                                   1625-      CHICHESTER OF CARRICK-
  B    1858-      Cavenish                           FERGUS V(I)
Cheshire                                  1647-      DONEGALL E(I)
  1978-      RYDER OF WARSAW Bss(L)        1791-      DONEGALL M(I)
CHESTER                                   1841-1883X ENNISHOWEN & CARRICK-
  E    1066-1070P Georbodus                          FERGUS B
  E    1070-1119P Abrincis                1790-      FISHERWICK B
  E    1119-1231C Meschines, De       Chichester-Clark
  E    1231-1246M Le Scot                 1971-      MOYOLA B(L)
  E    1253-1253X Plantagenet         Child
  E    1264-1265F Montfort  De            1718-1784X CASTLEMAINE V(I)
  E    1958-      Windsor       *         1718-1784X NEWTOWN B(I)
CHESTERFIELD                              1731-1784X TYLNEY E(I)
  E    1628-1967X Stanhope            Child-Villiers
  Css  1660-1667X Wotton                  1697-      JERSEY E
CHESTERFORD                             CHILSTON
  B    1706-1722X Howard                  V    1911-      Akers-Douglas
CHETWODE                                CHOLMONDELEY
  B    1945-      Chetwode                V(I) 1628-1659X Cholmondeley
Chetwode                                  B    1645-1659X Cholmondeley
  1945-      CHETWODE B                    V(I) 1661-      Cholmondeley
CHETWYND                                  B    1689-      Cholmondeley
  V(I) 1717-      Chetwynd                E    1706-      Cholmondeley
Chetwynd                                  M    1815-      Cholmondeley
  1717-      CHETWYND B(I)            Cholmondeley
  1717-      CHETWYND V(I)                 1628-1659X CHOLMONDELEY V(I)
Chetwynd-Talbot                           1645-1659X CHOLMONDELEY B
  1784-      INGESTRE V                    1661-      CHOLMONDELEY V(I)
  1784-      TALBOT E                      1689-      CHOLMONDELEY B
CHEWTON                                   1706-      CHOLMONDELEY E
  V    1729-      Waldegrave               1815-      CHOLMONDELEY M
```

* See also Addenda

31

Cholmondeley (Cont'd)
1821-   DELAMERE B
1645-1659X LEINSTER E(I)
1706-   MALPAS V
1714-   NEWBOROUGH B(I)
1716-   NEWBURGH B
1815-   ROCKSAVAGE E
CHORLEY
B   1945-   Chorley
Chorley
1945-   CHORLEY B
Chubb
1927-   HAYTER B
CHURCHILL
L(S) 1685-1722X Churchill
B   1685-   Churchill
B   1815-   Spemcer
V   1902-   Spencer
Churchill
1702-   BLANDFORD M
1685-1722X CHURCHILL L(S)
1685-   CHURCHILL B
1689-   MARLBOROUGH E
1702-   MARLBOROUGH D
See also: Spencer-Churchill
Churchman
1932-1949X WOODBRIDGE B
CHURSTON
B   1858-   Yarde-Buller
CHUTER-EDE
B(L) 1965-1965X Chuter-Ede
Chuter-Ede
1965-1965X CHUTER-EDE B(L)
CILCENNIN
V   1956-1960X Thomas
CIOCHES
B   1066/87-1205X Cioches, De
Cioches, De
1066/87-1205X CIOCHES
CIRENCESTER
B   1689-   Bentinck
CITRINE
B   1946-   Citrine
Citrine
1946-   CITRINE B
CLANBRASSILL
E(I) 1647-1675X Hamilton
E(I) 1756-1798X Hamilton
B   1821-1897X Jocelyn
CLANCARE
E(I) 1556-1597R M'Carthy
CLANCARTY
E(I) 1658-1770X M'Carty
E(I) 1803-   Trench
V   1823-   Trench

CLAN-CONAL: See DUNSANDLE & CLAN-CONAL
CLANDEBOYE
B(I) 1800-   Hamilton-Blackwood
B   1860-   Hamilton-Blackwood
V   1871-   Hamilton-Blackwood
CLANEBOYE
B(I) 1719-1798X Hamilton
V(I) 1622-1675X Hamilton
CLANEHUGH
B(I) 1673-   Forbes
CLANFIELD
V   1929-   Peel
CLANMALIER
B(I) 1550-1714X O'Dempsey
V(I) 1631-1714X O'Dempsey
CLANMAURICE
V(I) 1722-   Fitzmaurice
CLANMORRIS
B(I) 1800-   Bingham
CLANRICARDE
E(I) 1543-1916X De Burgh-Canning
M(I) 1644-1657X De Burgh-Canning
M(I) 1785-1797X De Burgh-Canning
E(I) 1800-   De Burgh
M(I) 1825-1916X De Burgh-Canning
CLANWILLIAM
V(I) 1766-   Meade
E(I) 1776-   Meade
B   1828-   Meade
CLARE
B   1066-1313X Clare, De
B   1309-....X Clare, De
E   1624-1711X Holles
M   1689-1711X Holles
E   1714-1768X Pelham/Holles
V(I) 1767-1788X Nugent
E(I) 1795-1864X Fitzgibbon
E   1798-1864X Fitzgibbon
Clare, De
1066-1313X CLARE B
1309-....X CLARE B
1226-1313X GLOUCESTER E
1135/54-1313X HERTFORD E
1138-1245X PEMBROKE E
CLARENCE
D   1362-1368X Plantagenet
D   1411-1421X Plantagenet
D   1461-1477F Plantagenet
D   1789-1830M Guelph
E   1881-1919S Guelph
CLARENCE & AVONDALE
D   1890-1892X Guelph
CLARENDON
E   1661-1723X Hyde
E   1776-   Villiers

32

CLARINA
  B(I) 1800-1952X Massey
CLARK
  B(L) 1969-1983X Clark
Clark
  1969-1983X CLARK B(L)
  See also: Chichester-Clark
Clarke
  1913-1933X SYDENHAM OF COMBE B
CLAUSON
  B   1942-1946X Clauson
Clauson
  1942-1946X CLAUSON B
CLAVERING
  B   1295-1332X Clavering
Clavering
  1295-1332X CLAVERING B
  See also: Fitzrobert
Clayton
  1735-1752X SUNDON B(I)
CLEDWYN OF PENRHOS
  B(L) 1979-   Hughes
Clegg-Hill: See Hill

CLEMENTS
  B   1831-1952X Clements
Clements
  1831-1952X CLEMENTS B
  1783-1952X LEITRIM B(I)
  1793-1952X LEITRIM V(I)
  1795-1952X LEITRIM E(I)
CLENAWLY: See GLENAWLEY
        (In Addenda)
CLERMONT
  B(I) 1770-1829X Fortescue
  V(I) 1776-1829X Fortescue
  E(I) 1777-1829X Fortescue
  B(I) 1852-1898X Parkinson-Fortescue
  B   1866-1887X Fortescue
CLERMONT & FETTERCAIRN
  L(S) 1660-1695F Middleton
CLEVELAND
  E   1626-1667X Wentworth
  Dss 1670-1709X Villiers
  D   1709-1774X Fitzroy
  M   1827-1891X Vane
  D   1833-1891X Vane
CLIFDEN
  B(I) 1776-1974X Agar-Robartes
  V(I) 1781-1974X Agar-Robartes
CLIFFORD
  B   1165-1285X Clifford, De
  B   1628-1639P Clifford

CLIFFORD, DE
  B   1299-   Clifford
CLIFFORD OF CHUDLEIGH
  B   1672-   Clifford
CLIFFORD OF LANESBOROUGH
  B   1644-1753X Boyle
Clifford
  1299-   CLIFFORD, DE B
  1628-1639P CLIFFORD B
  1672-   CLIFFORD OF CHUDLEIGH B
  1525-1643X CUMBERLAND E
Clifford, De
  1165-1285C CLIFFORD B
CLIFTON
  B   1376-1394A Clifton
CLIFTON OF LEIGHTON BROMSWOLD
  B   1608-   Bligh
CLIFTON OF RATHMORE
  B(I) 1721-   Bligh
Clifton
  1376-1394A CLIFTON B
Clifton-Hastings-Campbell
  1880-1927X DONINGTON B
CLINTON
  B   1299-1957A Clinton, De
  B   1330-1354X Clinton, De
  E   1746-1751X Fortescue
Clinton, De
  1299-1957A CLINTON B
  1330-1354X CLINTON B
  1337-1354X HUNTINGDON E
  1572-   LINCOLN E
CLITHEROE
  B   1955-   Assheton
CLIVE
  B(I) 1762-   Clive
  B   1794-   Clive
  V   1804-   Clive
Clive
  1762-   CLIVE B(I)
  1794-   CLIVE B
  1804-   CLIVE V
  1804-   HERBERT OF CHIRBURY B
  1794-   POWIS B
  1804-   POWIS E
CLOGHGRENAN
  B(I) 1693-1759X Butler
CLONAWLY: See GLENAWLEY
        (In Addenda)
CLONBROCK
  B(I) 1790-1926X Dillon
CLONCURRY
  B(I) 1789-1929X Lawless
  B   1831-1929X Lawless

33

Cloncurry
1789-1929X CLONCURRY B(I)
1831-1929X CLONCURRY B
CLONMELL
V(I) 1789-1935X Scott
E(I) 1793-1935X Scott
CLONMORE
V(I) 1676-1677X Butler
B(I) 1776-1978X Forward-Howard
CLONTARFE
V(I) 1541-1560L Rawson
Clotworthy
1660-   LOUGHNEAGH B(I)
1660-   MASSEREENE V(I)
CLUN
B   1627-   Howard
CLWYD
B   1919   Roberts
CLYDE
L(S) 1858-1863X Campbell
CLYDESDALE
M(S) 1643-   Hamilton
CLYDESMUIR
B   1948-   Colville
CLYVEDON
B   1294-....X Clyvedon, De
Clyvedon, De
1294-....X CLYVEDON B
Coats
1916-1971X GLENTANAR B
COBBOLD
B   1960-   Cobbold
Cobbold
1960-   COBBOLD B
COBHAM
B   1313-1409P Cobham, De
B   1409-1417F Oldcastle
B   1445-1607F Brooke
B   1645-1651X Brooke
B   1747-1787P Boothby
B   1787-1789A Disney
B   1933-1951A Alexander
COBHAM OF KENT
B   1313-1604F Cobham, De
B   1714-   Temple
V   1718-   Temple
COBHAM OF NORFOLK
B   1324-1325L Cobham, De
COBHAM OF RUNDELL
B   1326-1334L Cobham, De
COBHAM OF STERBOROUGH
B   1342-1372X Cobham, De
Cobham, De
1313-1409P COBHAM

Cobham, De (Cont'd)
1313-1604F COBHAM OF KENT B
1324-1325L COBHAM OF NORFOLK B
1326-1334L COBHAM OF RUNDELL B
1342-1372X COBHAM OF STERBOROUGH
COCHRANE OF DUNDONALD
L(S) 1647-   Cochrane
COCHRANE OF CULTS
B   1919-   Cochrane
COCHRANE OF PAISLEY & OCHILTREE
L(S) 1669-   Cochrane
Cochrane
1919-   COCHRANE OF CULTS B
1647-   COCHRANE OF DUNDONALD L(S)
1669-   COCHRANE OF PAISLEY &
              OCHILTREE L(S)
1669-   DUNDONALD E(S)
Cochrane-Baillie
1880-1951X LAMINGTON B
COCKERMOUTH
B   1749-1845X Seymour
COCKFIELD
B(L) 1978-   Cockfield
Cockfield
1978-   COCKFORD B(L)
Cocks
1784-1883X SOMERS B
See also: Somers-Cocks
COGGAN
B(L) 1980-   Coggan
Coggan
1980-   COGGAN B(L)
COHEN
B(L) 1951-1973X Cohen
COHEN OF BIRKENHEAD
B   1956-1977X Cohen
COHEN OF BRIGHTON
B(L) 1965-1966X Cohen
Cohen
1951-1973X COHEN B(L)
1956-1977X COHEN OF BIRKENHEAD B
1965-1966X COHEN OF BRIGHTON B(L)
Cokayne
1642-1813X CULLEN V(I)
1920-   CULLEN OF ASHBOURNE B
COKE
V   1744-1759X Coke
V   1837-   Coke
Coke
1744-1759X COKE V
1837-   COKE V
1744-1759X LEICESTER E
1837-   LEICESTER E
COLBORNE
B   1839-1854X Colborne

34

Colborne
 1839-1854X COLBORNE B
Colborne-Vivian
 1839-1955X SEATON B
COLCHESTER
 V   1621-1728X Savage
 B   1817-1919X Abbot
COLE
 V(I) 1776-   Cole
 B(L) 1965-   Cole
Cole
 1776-   COLE V(I)
 1965-   COLE B(L)
 1776-   ENNISKILLEN V(I)
 1789-   ENNISKILLEN E(I)
 1815-   GRINSTEAD B
 1760-   MOUNTFLORENCE B(I)
 1715-1754X RANELAGH B(I)
COLEBROOKE
 B   1906-1939X Colebrooke
Colebrooke
 1906-1939X COLEBROOKE B
COLEPEPER
 B   1644-1725X Colepeper
Colepeper
 1644-1725X COLEPEPER B
COLERAINE
 B(I) 1625-....X Hare
 B(I) 1762-1824X Hanger
 B   1954-   Law
COLERIDGE
 B   1873-   Coleridge
Coleridge
 1873-   COLERIDGE B
COLESHILL
 V   1790-1856X Digby
COLGRAIN
 B   1946-   Campbell
Colley: See Wesley
Collier
 1885-   MONKSWELL B
COLLINGWOOD
 B   1805-1810X Collingwood
Collingwood
 1805-1810X COLLINGWOOD B
COLLINS
 B(L) 1907-1911X Collins
Collins
 1907-1911X COLLINS B(L)
 1958-1971X STONEHAM B(L)
COLLISON
 B(L) 1964-   Collison
Collison
 1964-   COLLISON B(L)

COLONSAY
 B   1867-1874X McNeill
Colston
 1916-1944X ROUNDWAY B
COLUMBERS
 B   1314-1342X Columbers
Columbers
 1314-1342X COLUMBERS B
COLVILL
 B   1264-1294A Colvill
COLVILL OF OCHILTRIE
 L(S) 1537-1782X Colvill
Colvill
 1264-1294A COLVILL B
 1537-1782X COLVILL OF OCHILTRIE L(S)
COLVILLE OF CULROSS
 L(S) 1604-   Colville
 B   1885-   Colville
 V   1902-   Colville
Colville
 1604-   COLVILLE OF CULROSS L(S)
 1885-   COLVILLE OF CULROSS B
 1902-   COLVILLE OF CULROSS V
 1948-   CLYDESMUIR B
COLWYN
 B   1917-   Smith
COLYEAR
 L(S) 1703-1835X Colyear
Colyear
 1703-1835X COLYEAR L(S)
 1703-1835X MILSINGTON V(S)
 1699-1835X PORTMORE L(S)
 1703-1835X PORTMORE E(S)
COLYTON
 B   1956-   Hopkinson
COMBERMERE
 B   1814-   Stapleton-Cotton
 V   1826-   Stapleton-Cotton
COMPTON
 B   1572-1855A Compton
 E   1812-   Compton
Compton
 1572-1855A COMPTON B
 1812-   COMPTON E
 1618-   NORTHAMPTON E
 1812-   NORTHAMPTON M
 1730-1743X PEVENSEY V
 1728-1743X WILMINGTON B
 1730-1743X WILMINGTON E
 1812-   WILMINGTON B
Comyn
 1068-1069X NORTHUMBERLAND E
CONESFORD
 B   1955-1974X Strauss

35

CONGLETON
B   1841-   Parnell
CONINGSBY
B(I) 1693-1729X Coningsby
B   1715-1761X Coningsby
E   1719-1761X Coningsby
Coningsby
1693-1729X CONINGSBY B(I)
1715-1761X CONINGSBY B
1719-1761X CONINGSBY E
1716-1761X HAMPTON COURT Bss
CONNAUGHT & STRATHEARN
D   1874-1943X Guelph
CONNEMARA
B   1887-1902X Bourke
Conolly-Carew
1834-   CAREW B(I)
1838-   CAREW B
CONSTABLE
L(S) 1620-1718D Constable
Constable
1620-1718D CONSTABLE L(S)
1620-1718D DUNBAR V(S)
Constable-Maxwell
1884-1908X HERRIES B
CONSTANTINE
B(L) 1969-1971X Constantine
CONSTANTINE OF STANMORE
B(L) 1981-   Constantine
Constantine
1969-1971X CONSTANTINE B(L)
1981-   CONSTANTINE OF STANMORE
              B(L)
Consul
1109-1176P GLOUCESTER E
CONWAY
B   1624-1683X Conway
V   1626-1683X Conway
E   1679-1683X Conway
CONWAY OF ALLINGTON
B   1931-1937X Conway
CONWAY & KILLULTAGH
B(I) 1712-   Seymour
CONWAY OF RAGLEY
B   1703-   Seymour
Conway
1624-1683X CONWAY B
1626-1683X CONWAY V
1679-1683X CONWAY E
1931-1937X CONWAY OF ALLINGTON B
1626-1683X KILLULTAGH V(I)
1750-   RAGLEY B
Conwy: See Rowley-Conwy

CONYERS
B   1509-1948A D'Arcy
CONYNGHAM
B(I) 1753-1781P Conyngham
V(I) 1756-1781P Conyngham
B(I) 1781-   Conyngham
V(I) 1789-   Conyngham
E(I) 1797-   Conyngham
M(I) 1816-   Conyngham
Conyngham
1753-1781P CONYNGHAM B(I)
1756-1781P CONYNGHAM V(I)
1781-   CONYNGHAM B(I)
1789-   CONYNGHAM V(I)
1797-   CONYNGHAM E(I)
1816-   CONYNGHAM M(I)
1821-   MINSTER B
1753-1781P MOUNT CHARLES B(I)
1797-   MOUNT CHARLES V(I)
1816-   MOUNT CHARLES E(I)
1816-   SLANE V
CONYNGSBY: See CONINGSBY
COOPER
B   1672-   Ashley-Cooper
COOPER OF CULROSS
B   1954-1955X Cooper
Cooper
1954-1955X COOPER OF CULROSS B
1952-   NORWICH
COOTE OF COLOONY
B(I) 1660-1800X Coote
Coote
1660-1800X COOTE OF COLOONY B(I)
1689-1766X BELLAMONT E(I)
1767-1800X BELLAMONT E(I)
1800-1827X CASTLECOOTE B(I)
1660-1802X MOUNTRATH E(I)
COPE
B   1945-1946X Cope
Cope
1945-1946X COPE B
Copley
1827-1863X LYNDHURST B
See also: Cromwell
Copsi
1068-1068X NORTHUMBERLAND E
CORBET
B   1295-1322X Corbet
Vss 1679-1688X Corbet
Corbet
1295-1322X CORBET B
1679-1688X CORBET Vss
Corbett
1911-   ROWALLAN B

36

CORK
  E(I) 1620-   Boyle
CORMEILES
  B   1066/87-1217X Cormeiles, De
Cormeiles, De
  1066/87-1217X CORMEILES B
CORNBURY
  V   1661-1753X Hyde
CORNWALL
  E   1068-1104F Moreton
  E   1140-1175X Dunstanville, De
  E   1226-1300X Plantagenet
  E   1308-1314X Gaveston
  E   1330-1336X Plantagenet
  D   1337-   Plantagenet *
Cornwall
  1438-1443X FANHOPE B
  1442-1443X MILBROKE B
CORNWALLIS
  B   1661-1852X Cornwallis
  E   1753-1852X Cornwallis
  M   1792-1823X Cornwallis
  B   1927-   Cornwallis
Cornwallis
  1661-1852X CORNWALLIS B
  1753-1852X CORNWALLIS E
  1792-1823X CORNWALLIS M
  1927-   CORNWALLIS B
CORRY
  V(I) 1789-   Corry
Corry
  1789-   CORRY V(I)
  See also: Lowry-Corry
Cosby
  1768-1774X SYDNEY B(I)
Cospatrick
  1069-1070X NORTHUMBERLAND E
COTTENHAM
  B   1836-   Pepys
  E   1850-   Pepys
COTTESLOE
  B   1874-   Fremantle
COTTINGTON
  B   1631-1653X Cottington
Cottington
  1631-1653X COTTINGTON B
  1631-1653X HANWORTH B
Cotton: See Stapleton-Cotton
COUPAR
  L(S) 1607-1669P Elphinstone
Courcy, De
  1366-1397X BEDFORD E
  1223-   KINGSALE B(I)
  1181-   RINGRONE B(I)
  1181-1204X ULSTER E(I)

COURTAULD-THOMSON
  B   1944-1954X Courtauld-Thomson
Courtauld-Thomson
  1944-1954X COURTAULD-THOMSON B
COURTENAY
  B   1299-1461F Courtenay
  V   1762-1835X Courtenay
Courtenay
  1299-1461F COURTENAY B
  1762-1835X COURTENAY V
  1335-1461F DEVON E
  1485-1539D DEVON E   *
  1526-1539F EXETER M
  1553-1556X EXETER M
COURTHOPE
  B   1945-1955X Courthope
Courthope
  1945-1955X COURTHOPE B
COURTNEY OF PENWITH
  B   1906-1918X Courtney
Courtney
  1906-1918X COURTNEY OF PENWITH B
COURTOWN
  B(I) 1758-   Stopford
  E(I) 1762-   Stopford
COUTANCHE
  B(L) 1961-1973X Coutanche
Coutanche
  1961-1973X COUTANCHE B(L)
Coutts: See Burdett-Coutts
          Money-Coutts
COVENTRY
  E   1623-1687X Villiers
  B   1628-1719X Coventry
  E   1697-   Coventry
Coventry
  1628-1719X COVENTRY B
  1697-   COVENTRY E
  1697-   DEERHURST V
COWAL: See CAMPBELL & COWAL
COWDRAY
  B   1910-   Pearson
  V   1917-   Pearson
COWELELYENE
  B(I) 1554-....L Kavanagh
COWLEY
  E   1857-   Wellesley
COWLEY OF WELLESLEY
  B   1828-   Wellesley
COWPER
  B   1706-1905X Cowper
  E   1718-1905X Cowper
Cowper
  1666-1905A BUTLER B
  1706-1905X COWPER B

Cowper (Cont'd)
1718-1905X FORDWICH V
Cowper-Temple
1880-1888X MOUNT-TEMPLE B
COX
Bss(L) 1982-   Cox
Cox
1982-   COX Bss(L)
See also: Roxbee Cox
COZENS-HARDY
B   1914-1975X Cozens-Hardy
Cozens-Hardy
1914-1975X COZENS-HARDY B
Cradock
1819-1873X HOWDEN B(I)
1831-1873X HOWDEN B
Craig
1927-   CRAIGAVON V
CRAIGAVON
V   1927-   Craig
CRAIGMYLE
B   1929-   Shaw
CRAIGTON
B(L) 1959-   Browne
CRAMOND
L(S) 1628-1735X Richardson
CRANBORNE
V   1604-   Cecil
CRANBROOK
V   1878-   Gathorne-Hardy
E   1892-   Gathorne-Hardy
CRANFIELD
B   1621-1674X Cranfield
B   1675-1843X Sackville
Cranfield
1621-1674X CRANFIELD B
1622-1674X MIDDLESEX E
CRANLEY
B   1776-   Onslow
V   1801-   Onslow
CRANSTOUN
B   1609-1869X Cranstoun
Cranstoun
1609-1869X CRANSTOUN B
CRANWORTH
B   1850-1868X Rolfe
B   1899-   Gurdon
CRATHORNE
B   1959-   Dugdale
CRAVEN
B   1626-   Craven
V   1665-1697X Craven
E   1665-1697X Craven
E   1801-   Craven

CRAVEN OF RYTON
B   1642-1650X Craven
Craven
1626-   CRAVEN B
1665-1697X CRAVEN V
1665-1697X CRAVEN E
1801-   CRAVEN E
1642-1650X CRAVEN OF RYTON B
1801-   UFFINGTON V
CRAWFORD
E(S) 1398-   Lindsay
Crawford
1951-1966X HUNGARTON B
See also: Lindsay-Crawford
CRAWSHAW
B   1892-   Brooks
CREMORNE
V(I) 1785-1813X Dawson
B   1797-1933X Dawson
CRETING
B   1332-....X De Creting
Creting, De
1332-....X CRETING B
CREW
B   1661-1721X Crew
Crew
1661-1721X CREW B
CREWE
B   1806-1894X Crewe
E   1895-1945X Crewe-Milnes
M   1911-1945X Crewe-Milnes
Crewe
1806-1894X CREWE B
Crewe-Milnes
1895-1945X CREWE E
1911-1945X CREWE M
1863-1945X HOUGHTON B
1911-1945X MADELEY E
CRICHTON
L(S) 1445-1484F Crichton
L(S) 1487-   Crichton
L(S) 1642-1690F Crichton
Crichton
1622-   AIR V(S)
1450-1455X CAITHNESS E(S)
1445-1484F CRICHTON L(S)
1487-   CRICHTON L(S)
1642-1690F CRICHTON L(S)
1633-   DUMFRIES E(S)
1768-   ERNE B(I)
1781-   ERNE V(I)
1789-   ERNE E(I)
1876-   FERMANAGH B
1642-1690F FRENDRAUGHT V(S)

CRIKETOFT
  B   1216/72-1307/27X Criketoft,De
Criketoft, De
  1216/72-1307/27X CRIKETOFT B
Cripps
  1914-   PARMOOR B
Crittall
  1948-1961X BRAINTREE B
CROFT
  B   1940-   Croft
Croft
  1940-   CROFT B
CROFTON
  B(I) 1797-   Crofton
Crofton
  1797-   CROFTON B(I)
CROFTS
  B   1658-1677X Crofts
Crofts
  1658-1677X CROFTS B
CROHAM
  B(L) 1977-   Allen
CROMARTIE
  E   1861-   Mackenzie
CROMARTY
  E(S) 1703-1745F Mackenzie
CROMER
  B   1892-   Baring
  V   1899-   Baring
  E   1901-   Baring
CROMWELL
  B   1308-1471A Cromwell
  B   1540-1687X Cromwell
  B   1375-   Cromwell
CROMWELL OF WIMBLEDON
  B   1536-1540 Cromwell
Cromwell
  1645-1687X ARDGLASS E(I)
  1308-1471A CROMWELL B
  1540-1687X CROMWELL B
  1375-   CROMWELL B
  1536-1540F CROMWELL OF WIMBLEDON B
  1539-1540F ESSEX E
  1624-1687X LECALE V(I)
CROOK
  B   1947-   Crook
Crook
  1947-   CROOK B
CROOKSHANK
  V   1956-1961X Crookshank
Crookshank
  1956-1961X CROOKSHANK V
CROSBIE
  V(I) 1771-1815X Crosbie

Crosbie
  1758-1832X BRANDON B(I)
  1771-1815X CROSBIE V(I)
  1776-1826X GLANDORE E(I)
CROSS
  V   1886-   Cross
CROSS OF CHELSEA
  B(L) 1971-   Cross
Cross
  1886-   CROSS B
  1971-   CROSS OF CHELSEA B(L)
Crossley
  1916-   SOMERLEYTON B
CROWHURST
  V   1850-   Pepys
CROWTHER
  B(L) 1968-1972X Crowther
Crowther
  1968-1972X CROWTHER B(L)
CROWTHER-HUNT
  B(L) 1973-   Crowther-Hunt
Crowther-Hunt
  1973-   CROWTHER-HUNT B(L)
Cubitt
  1892-   ASHCOMBE B
CUDLIPP
  B(L) 1974-   Cudlipp
Cudlipp
  1974-   CUDLIPP B(L)
Cuffe
  1793-1793C CASTLE CUFFE V(I)
  1733-1934X DESART B(I)
  1781-1934X DESART V(I)
  1793-1934X DESART E(I)
  1909-1934X DESART B
  1797-1821X TYRAWLEY B(I)
CULLEN
  V(I) 1642-1813X Cokayne
CULLEN OF ASHBOURNE
  B   1920-   Cokayne
CULLODEN
  B   1801-1904X Guelph
  B   1928-   Windsor
CULMORE
  B(I) 1725-1802X Bateman
CUMBERLAND
  E   1525-1643X Clifford
  D   1644-1682X Rupert
  D   1689-1708X Denmark, Prince of
  D   1726-1765X Guelph
  D   1766-1790X Guelph
CUMBERLAND & TEVIOTDALE
  D   1799-1919F Guelph

39

CUMBERNAULD
L(S) 1606-1747X Fleming
CUMBRAE: See MOUNTSTUART, CUMBRAE &
                INCHMARNOCK
Cummin
  1240-1306X BADENOCH L(S)
Cumyn
  1221-1320F BUCHAN E(S)
Cuninghame
  1796-   ROSSMORE B(I)
CUNLIFFE
  B   1914-   Cunliffe
Cunliffe
  1914-   CUNLIFFE B
Cunliffe-Lister
  1891-1924X MASHAM B
  1935-   MASHAM B
  1970-   MASHAM OF ILTON Bss(L)
  1935-   SWINTON V
  1955-   SWINTON E
CUNNINGHAM OF HYNDHOPE
  B   1945-1963X Cunningham
  V   1946-1963X Cunningham
Cunningham
  1945-1963X CUNNINGHAM OF HYNDHOPE B
  1946-1963X CUNNINGHAM OF HYNDHOPE V
Cunynghame
  1361-1363M CARRICK E(S)
  1488-1796D GLENCAIRN E(S)
  1450-1796D KILMAURS L(S)
CURRIE
  B   1899-1906X Currie
Currie
  1899-1906X CURRIE B
CURZON
  B   1794-   Curzon
  V   1802-   Curzon
CURZON OF KEDLESTONE
  B(I) 1898-1925X Curzon
  E   1911-1925X Curzon
  M   1921-1925X Curzon
Curzon
  1794-   CURZON B
  1802-   CURZON V
  1898-1925X CURZON OF KEDLESTONE B(I)
  1911-1925X CURZON OF KEDLESTONE E
  1921-1925X CURZON OF KEDLESTONE M
  1788-   HOWE B
  1821-   HOWE E
  1921-1925X KEDLESTON E
  1761-   SCARSDALE B
  1911-   SCARSDALE V
  1829-   ZOUCHE Bss

CUSHENDEN
  B   1927-1934X McNeill
Cust
  1815-1921X ALFORD V
  1776-1921X BROWNLOW B
  1815-1921X BROWNLOW E
CUTTS
  B(I) 1690-1706X Cutts
Cutts
  1690-1706X CUTTS B

(TITLES are in CAPITALS
 Surnames in smalls)

40

D'ABERNON
B   1914-1941X Vincent
V   1926-1941X Vincent
DACRE
B   1321-   Dacre
DACRE OF GILLESLAND
B   1482-1569A Dacre
B   1661-   Howard
Dacre
1321-   DACRE Bss
1482-1569A DACRE OF GILLESLAND B
See also: Multon
DAER & SHORTCLEUCH
L(S) 1646-1885D Douglas
DAGWORTH
B   1347-1359X Dagworth
Dagworth
1347-1359X DAGWORTH B
DALHOUSIE
E(S) 1633-   Ramsay
B   1815-1860X Ramsay
M   1838-1860X Ramsay
DALKEITH
L(S) 1458-   Douglas
L(S) 1580-1672X Stewart
E(S) 1673-1685F Scott
DALLING & BULWER
B   1871-1872X Bulwer
DALMENY & PRIMROSE
L(S) 1700-   Primrose
DALRYMPLE
V(S) 1703-   Dalrymple
Dalrymple
1703-   DALRYMPLE V(S)
1690-   GLENLUCE & STRANRAER
           L(S)
1703-   NEWLISTON L(S)
1841-   OXENFOORD B
1690-   STAIR V(S)
1703-   STAIR E(S)
DALTON
B(L) 1960-1962X Dalton
Dalton
1960-1962X DALTON B(L)
Daly
1845-1911X DUNSANDLE & CLAN-
           CONAL B(I)
DALZELL
L(S) 1628-1941D Dalzell
DALZELL & LIBERTON
L(S) 1639-1941D Dalzell
Dalzell
1639-1941D CARNWATH E(S)
1628-1941D DALZELL L(S)

Dalzell (Cont'd)
1639-1941D DALZELL & LIBERTON L(S)
1628-1941D LIBERTON L(S)
DALZIEL OF KIRKCALDY
B   1921-1935X Dalziel
DALZIEL OF WOOLER
B   1927-1928X Dalziel
Dalziel
1921-1935X DALZIEL OF KIRKCALDY B
1927-1928X DALZIEL OF WOOLER B
Damer
1792-1808X DORCHESTER E
1753-1808X MILTON B(I)
1762-1808X MILTON B
1792-1808X MILTON V
D'AMORIE
B   1317-1404F D'Amorie
D'Amorie
1317-1404F D'AMORIE B
DANBY
E   1625-1644X Danvers
E   1674-1964X Osborne
DANESFORT
B   1924-1935X Butcher
DANGAN
V   1857-   Wellesley
Daniel
1475-....X RATHWIER B(I)
DANVERS
B   1603-1643X Danvers
Danvers
1625-1644X DANBY E
1603-1643X DANVERS B
D'ARCY
B   1299-....A D'Arcy
B(I) 1721-1733X D'Arcy
DARCY OF CHICHE
B   1551-1639X Darcy
DARCY OF DARCY
B   1509-1538F Darcy
B   1548-1635X D'Arcy
DARCY OF KNAITH
B   1332-1418A D'Arcy
DARCY & CONYERS
B   1641-1778X Darcy
D'Arcy
1299-....A DARCY B
1332-1418A DARCY OF KNAITH B
1548-1635X DARCY OF DARCY B
1721-1733X D'ARCY B(I)
Darcy
1509-1948A CONYERS B
1509-1538F DARCY OF DARCY B
1551-1639X DARCY OF CHICHE B

41

Darcy (Cont'd)
1641-1778X DARCY & CONYERS B
1682-1778X HOLDERNESSE E
DARESBURY
B   1927-   Greenall
DARLING
B   1924   Darling
DARLING OF HILLSBOROUGH
B(L) 1974-   Darling
Darling
1924-   DARLING B
1974-   DARLING OF HILLS-
             BOROUGH B(L)
DARLINGTON
Bss 1686-1692X Sidley
Css 1722-1730X Kielmansegg
E   1754-1891X Powlett
DARNLEY
L(S) 1460-1576X Stewart
E(S) 1581-1672X Stewart
E(S) 1675-   Lennox
V(I) 1723-   Bligh
E(I) 1725-   Bligh
DARTMOUTH
B   1675-1680X Fitzcharles
B   1682-   Legge
E   1711-   Legge
DARTREY
B(I) 1770-1813X Dawson
B   1847-1933X Dawson
E   1866-1933X Dawson
DARWEN
B   1946-   Davies
DARYNGTON
B   1923-   Pease
Dashwood
1763-1781A DESPENCER B
DAUBENEY
B   1295-1636A Daubeney
B   1486-1548A Daubeney
Daubeney
1295-1636A DAUBENEY
1486-1548A DAUBENEY
D'Aubeney
1538-1548X BRIDGEWATER E
D'AUNEY
B   1327-....X Dauney
Dauney
1327-....X D'AUNEY
DAUNTSEY
B   1644-1667X Stewart
B   1667-1671X Stewart
DAVENTRY
V   1943-   FitzRoy

DAVEY
B(L) 1894-1907X Davey
Davey
1894-1907X DAVEY B(L)
DAVID
Bss(L) 1978-   David
David
1978-   DAVID Bss(L)
DAVIDSON
V   1937-   Davidson
DAVIDSON OF LAMBETH
B   1928-1930X Davidson
Davidson
1937-   DAVIDSON V
1928-1930X DAVIDSON OF LAMBETH B
1963-   NORTHCHURCH Bss(L)
DAVIES
B   1932-   Davies

DAVIES OF LEEK
B(L) 1970-   Davies
DAVIES OF PENRHYS
B(L) 1974-   Davies
Davies
1946-   DARWEN B
1932-   DAVIES B
1970-   DAVIES OF LEEK B(L)
1974-   DAVIES OF PENRHYS B(L)
See also: Prys-Davies
          Edmund-Davies
          Llewelyn-Davies
          Vaughan-Davies
Davison
1945-   BROUGHSHANE B
Davys
1706-1719X MOUNT CASHEL V(I)
DAWICK
V   1919-   Haig
DAWNAY
B   1796-1832X Dawnay
B   1897-   Dawnay
Dawnay
1796-1832X DAWNAY B
1897-   DAWNAY B
1680-   DOWNE V(I)
1796-1832X DOWNE B
DAWSON
B(I) 1770-   Dawson
DAWSON OF PENN
B   1920-1945X Dawson
V   1936-1945X Dawson

42

Dawson
1776-   CARLOW V(I)
1785-1813X CREMORNE V(I)
1797-1933X CREMORNE B(I)
1771-1813X DARTREY B(I)
1847-1933X DARTREY B
1866-1933X DARTREY E
1770-   DAWSON B(I)
1920-1945X DAWSON OF PENN B
1936-1945X DAWSON OF PENN V
1785-   PORTARLINGTON E(I)
DE & DE LA prefixes:
    See under final part of TITLE or Name
DEAN OF BESWICK
    B(L) 1983-   Dean
Dean
    1983-   DEAN OF BESWICK B(L)
Deane
    1781-   MUSKERRY B(I)
DECHMONT
    L(S) 1696-1951D Fitz-Maurice
    L(S) 1696-   Hamilton
DECIES
    V(I) 1673-1704X Le Poer
    B(I) 1812-   De La Poer Beresford
DEERHURST
    V   1697-   Coventry
DEINCOURT
    B   1299-1487F Deincourt
DEINCOURT OF SUTTON
    B   1624-1736X Leke
Deincourt
    1299-1487F DEINCOURT B
DELACOURT-SMITH
    B(L) 1967-1972X Delacourt-Smith
DELACOURT-SMITH OF ALTERYN
    Bss(L) 1974-   Delacourt-Smith
Delacourt-Smith
    1967-1972X DELACOURT-SMITH B(L)
    1974-   DELACOURT-SMITH OF
               ALTERYN
DELAMERE
    B   1821-   Cholmondeley
DELAVAL
    B(I) 1783-1808X Delaval
    B   1786-1808X Delaval
Delaval
    1783-1808X DELAVAL B(I)
    1786-1808X DELAVAL B
Delawarde
    1299-1334X DE LA WARDE B
DELFONT
    B(L) 1976-   Delfont

Delfont
    1976-   DELFONT B(L)
DELORAINE
    E(S) 1706-1807X Scott
DELVIN
    B(I) 1486-   Nugent
DENBIGH
    B   1563-1588X Dudley
    E   1622-   Feilding
DENHAM
    B   1937-   Bowyer
DENINGTON
    Bss(L) 1978-   Denington
Denington
    1978-   DENINGTON Bss(L)
Denison
    1850-   LONDESBOROUGH B
    1887-1937X LONDESBOROUGH E
    1872-1873X OSSINGTON V
    1887-1937X RAINCLIFFE V
Denison-Pender
    1937-   PENDER B
DENMAN
    B   1834-   Denman
Denman
    1834-   DENMAN B
Denmark, Prince of
    1689-1708X CUMBERLAND D
    1689-1708X WOKINGHAM B
DENNEY
    B   1604-1660X Denney
Denney
    1604-1660X DENNEY B
DENNING
    B(L) 1957-   Denning
Denning
    1957-   DENNING B(L)
Dennis
    1780-   TRACTON B(I)
DENNISTON
    L(S) 1375-1394X Denniston
Denny
    1626-1630X NORWICH E
Dent
    1295-1968A FURNIVALL B
    1932-   FURNIVAL B
DENTON
    B   1914-   Kitchener
DERAMORE
    B   1885-   Yarburgh-Bateson,
                    De

43

DERBY
 E 1137-1265F Ferrers
 E 1337-1399M Plantagenet
 E 1485- Stanley
D'ERVILL
 B 1264-....X Dewill
DERWENT
 B 1881- Vanden-Bempde-Johnson
DERWENTWATER
 E 1688-1716F Radcliffe
DESART
 B(I) 1733-1934X Cuffe
 V(I) 1781-1934X Cuffe
 E(I) 1793-1934X Cuffe
 B 1909-1934X Cuffe
DESBOROUGH
 B 1905-1945X Grenfell
DESMOND
 E(I) 1329-1398A Fitzmaurice
 E(I) 1422-1582F Fitzmaurice
 B(I) 1600-1601F Fitzgerald
 E(I) 1622- Feilding
DESPENCER
 B 1066/87-1251X Despencer
 B 1264-1399F Despencer
 B 1461-1461A Despencer
 B 1604-1762A Fane
 B 1763-1781A Dashwood
 B 1788-1831M Stapleton
Despencer
 1066/87-1251X DESPENCER B
 1264-1399F DESPENCER B
 1461-1461A DESPENCER B
 1397-1400F GLOUCESTER E
 1322-1326X WINCHESTER E
DEVEREUX
 B 1299-1397M Devereux
Devereux
 1299-1397M DEVEREUX B
 1572-1646X ESSEX E
 1461-1600F FERRERS OF CHARTLEY B
 1603-1646A FERRERS OF CHARTLEY B
 1550- HEREFORD V
 1135/54-1189/99X SALISBURY E
DEVLIN
 B(L) 1961- Devlin
Devlin
 1961- DEVLIN B(L)
DEVON
 E 1100/35-1293X Redvers, De
 E 1335-1461F Courtenay
 E 1485-1539D Courtenay
 E 1553-1556A Courtenay

DEVON (Cont'd)
 E 1603-1606X Blount
 E 1803- Courtenay
DEVONPORT
 B 1910- Kearley
 V 1917- Kearley
DEVONSHIRE
 E 1618- Cavendish
 D 1694- Cavendish
DEWAR
 B 1919-1930X Dewar
Dewar
 1919-1930X DEWAR B
 1917- FORTEVIOT B
Dewill
 1264-....X D'ERVILL B
DIAMOND
 B(L) 1970- Diamond
Diamond
 1970- DIAMOND B(L)
DICKINSON
 B 1930- Dickinson
Dickinson
 1930- DICKINSON B
Dickson-Poynder
 1910-1936X ISLINGTON B
DIGBY
 B 1618-1698X Digby
 B 1765- Digby
 E 1790-1856X Digby
 B(I) 1620- Digby
Digby
 1622-1698X BRISTOL E
 1790-1856X COLESHILL V
 1618-1698X DIGBY B
 1765- DIGBY B
 1790-1856X DIGBY E
 1620- DIGBY B(I)
Digby alias Fitzgerald
 1620-1658X OFFALEY Bss(I)
DILHORNE
 B 1954- Manningham-Buller
 V 1964- Manningham-Buller
DILLON
 B(I) 1619-1850D Dillon
 V(I) 1622- Dillon
Dillon
 1790-1926X CLONBROOK B(I)
 1619-1850D DILLON B(I)
 1622- DILLON V(I)
 1619- KILKENNY B(I)
 1622-1850D ROSCOMMON E(I)

44

DINAN
B   1066/87-1258X Dinan
B   1295-1509X Dinan
Dinan
1066/87-1258X DINAN B
1295-1509X DINAN B
DINGWALL
L(S) 1584-1589X Keith
L(S) 1609-1715F Preston
DINORBEN
B   1831-1852X Hughes
DIPLOCK
B(L) 1968-   Diplock
Diplock
1968-   DIPLOCK B(L)
DIRLETON
L(S) 1603-   Erskine
DIRLETOUN
E(S) 1646-....X Maxwell
Disney
1787-1789A COBHAM B
Disraeli
1868-1872X BEACONSFIELD Vss
1876-1881X BEACONSFIELD E
Dixon
1939-   GLENTORAN B
DOCKWRA
B(I) 1621-1631X Dockwra
Dockwra
1621-1631X DOCKWRA B(I)
Dodington
1761-1762X MELCOMBE B
Dodson
1884-   MONK BRETTON B
DONALDSON OF KINGSBRIDGE
B(L) 1967-   Donaldson
Donaldson
1967-   DONALDSON OF KINGS-
              BRIDGE B(L)
DONAMORE
B(I) 1646-1772X Hawley
DONCASTER
B   1618-1660X Hay
V   1663-1685F Scott
E   1663-1685F Scott
E   1743-   Scott
DONEGALL
E(I) 1647-   Chichester
M(I) 1791-   Chichester
DONERAILE
V(I) 1703-1767X St Leger
B(I) 1776-   St Leger
V(I) 1785-   St Leger

DONINGTON
B   1880-1927X Clifton-Hastings-
              Campbell
DONNET OF BALGAY
B(L) 1978-   Donnet
Donnet
1978-   DONNET OF BALGAY B(L)
DONOUGHMORE
B(I) 1783-   Hely-Hutchinson
V(I) 1797-   Hely-Hutchinson
E(I) 1801-   Hely-Hutchinson
DONOVAN
B(L) 1963-1971X Donovan
Donovan
1963-1971X DONOVAN B(L)
DORCHESTER
B   1628-1631X Carlton
M   1646-1680X Pierrepont
Css 1686-1692X Sidley
M   1706-1773X Pierrepont
B   1786-1897X Carleton
E   1792-1808X Damer
B   1899-1963X Carleton
DORMER
B   1615-   Dormer
Dormer
1615-   DORMER B
1628-1709X ASCOTT V
1628-1709X CARNARVON E
DORSET
E   1066/87-....X Osmund
M   1397-1426X Beaufort
E   1411-1426X Beaufort
E   1441-1463F Beaufort
M   1442-1463F Beaufort
M   1475-1554F Grey
E   1603-1843X Sackville
D   1720-1843X Sackville
DOUGLAS
E(S) 1357-1456F Douglas
M(S) 1633-   Douglas
L(S) 1703-1761X Douglas
D(S) 1703-1761X Douglas
B   1875-   Douglas-Home
DOUGLAS OF AMESBURY
B   1786-1810X Douglas
DOUGLAS OF BAADS
B   1911-   Akers-Douglas
DOUGLAS OF BARLOCH
B   1950-1980X Douglas
DOUGLAS OF CLEVELAND
B(L) 1967-1978X Douglass
DOUGLAS OF DOUGLAS CASTLE
L(S) 1790-1857X Stewart

DOUGLAS OF KIRTLESIDE
B   1948-1969X Douglas
DOUGLAS OF LOCHLEVEN
B   1791-1827X Douglas
DOUGLAS OF HAWICK & TIBBERS
L(S) 1628-   Douglas
DOUGLAS OF KINMONT, MIDDLEBIE &
DORNOCH
L(S) 1706-   Scott
DOUGLAS OF NEIDPATH, LYNE & MUNARD
L(S) 1697-   Douglas
Douglas
 1351-1458M ABERDOUR L(S)
 1638-   ABERDOUR L(S)
 1703-1761X ABERNETHY M(S)
 1633-   ABERNETHY & JEDBURGH
              FOREST L(S)
 1389-   ANGUS E(S)
 1703-1761X ANGUS M(S)
 1341-1371M ATHOLL E(S)
 1437-1456F AVONDALE E(S)
 1633-1639X BELHAVEN V(S)
 1708-1778M BEVERLEY M
 1651-1761X BOTHWELL L(S)
 1609-1638R CARLYLE L(S)
 1646-1885D DAER & SHORTCLEUCH L(S)
 1458-   DALKEITH L(S)
 1357-1456F DOUGLAS E(S)
 1633-   DOUGLAS M(S)
 1703-1761X DOUGLAS L(S)
 1703-1761X DOUGLAS D(S)
 1786-1810X DOUGLAS OF AMESBURY B
 1950-1980X DOUGLAS OF BARLOCH B
 1948-1969X DOUGLAS OF KIRTLESIDE B
 1791-1827X DOUGLAS OF LOCHLEVEN B
 1628-   DOUGLAS OF HAWICK &
              TIBBERS L(S)
 1697-   DOUGLAS OF NEIDPATH, LYNE
              & MUNARD L(S)
 1708-1778X DOVER D
 1400-   DRUMLANRIG L(S)
 1628-   DRUMLANRIG V(S)
 1675-1725X DUMBARTON E(S)
 1651-1715P FORFAR E(S)
 1800-1823X GLENBERVIE B(I)
 1660-1694X HAMILTON D(S)
 1651-1761P HARTSIDE L(S)
 1703-1761X JEDBURGH FOREST V(S)
 1893-1894X KELHEAD B
 1697-   MARCH E(S)
 1641-1791X MORDINGTON L(S)
 1458-   MORTON E(S)
 1697-   MUNARD L(S)

Douglas (Cont'd)
 1445-1455F ORMONDE E(S)
 1651-1715P ORMONDE E(S)
 1697-   PEEBLES V(S)
 1633-   QUEENSBERRY E(S)
 1682-   QUEENSBERRY M(S)
 1708-1778X RIPPON B
 1646-1885D SELKIRK E(S)
 1706-1778P SOLWAY E(S)
 1833-1837X SOLWAY B
 1706-1778P TIBBERS V(S)
 1681-   TORTHORWALD V(S)
 See also: Akers-Douglas
Douglas-Hamilton
 1445-1711M HAMILTON L(S)
 1599-1711M HAMILTON M(S)
 1643-1711M HAMILTON D(S)
Douglas-Home
 1875-   DOUGLAS B
 1605-   DUNGLASS L(S)
 1605-   HOME E(S)
 1974-   HOME OF THE HIRSEL B(L)
Douglas-Pennant
 1866-   PENRHYN B
Douglas-Scott-Montagu
 1885-   MONTAGU OF BEAULIEU B
Douglass
 1967-1978X DOUGLAS OF CLEVELAND B(L)
DOUNE
 L(S) 1581-   Stuart
DOURO
 B   1809-   Wellesley
 M   1814-   Wellesley
DOVER
 E   1628-1677X Carey
 B   1685-1703M Jermyn
 D   1708-1778X Douglas
 B   1788-1792X Yorke
 B   1831-1899X Agar-Ellis
Dover, De
 1100/35-1216/72X DOVOR B
DOVERCOURT
 B   1954-1961X Holmes
DOVERDALE
 B   1917-1949X Partington
DOVOR
 B   1100/35-1216/72X Dover, De
DOWDING
 B   1943-   Dowding
Dowding
 1943-   DOWDING B
DOWNE
 E(I) 1628-1668X Pope

46

DOWNE (Cont'd)
V(I) 1680-   Dawnay
B   1796-1832X Dawnay
DOWNES
B   1822-1864X Burgh
DOWNHAM
B   1918-1920X Fisher
DOWNPATRICK
B   1934-   Windsor
DOWNSHIRE
M(I) 1789-   Hill
DOWNTON
B   1747-1763X Duncombe
D'OYLEY
B   1066/87-1232X D'Oyley
D'Oyley
1066/87-1232X D'OYLEY B
DRAYCOTE
B   1297-1297X Draycote, De
Draycote, De
1297-1297X DRAYCOTE B
Dreux, De
1230-1399F RICHMOND E
Driberg
1975-1976X BRADWELL B(L)
DROGHEDA
E(I) 1661-   Moore
M(I) 1791-1892X Moore
DROMORE
B(I) 1628-1716X Scudamore
DRUMALBYN
B   1963-   Macpherson
DRUMLANRIG
L(S) 1400-   Douglas
V(S) 1628-   Douglas
DRUMLANRIG & SANQUHAR
E(S) 1684-   Scott
DRUMMOND
L(S) 1686-   Drummond
B   1797-1800X Drummond
DRUMMOND OF CROMLIX
L(S) 1686-   Drummond
Drummond
1686-   DRUMMOND L(S)
1797-1800X DRUMMOND B
1686-   DRUMMOND OF CROMLIX
1686-1902D FORTH V(S)
1609-   MADERTY L(S)
1686-1902D MELFORT E(S)   *
1605-   PERTH E(S)
1797-1800X PERTH B
1686-   STRATHALLAN V(S)
See also: Heathcote-Drummond-
Willoughby
      * See also Addenda

DRUMRY: See KILBURNIE, KINGSBURN &
DRUMRY
DUBLIN
M   1385-1388F Vere
E   1850-1901M Guelph
DUCIE
B   1720-1770X Moreton
B   1763-   Moreton
E   1837-   Moreton
DUDHOPE
V(S) 1641-   Scrimgeour
L(S) 1686-1688M Graham
DUDLEY
B   1308-1322X Somerie
B   1342-1643P Sutton, De
B   1644-1757A Ward
B   1916-   Smith
Dss 1644-1670 Dudley
V   1860-   Ward
E   1860-   Ward
DUDLEY & WARD
V   1763-1833X Ward
DUDLEY OF DUDLEY CASTLE
E   1827-1833X Ward
Dudley
1563-1588X DENBIGH B
1644-1670X DUDLEY Dss
1563-1588X LEICESTER E
1541-1553F L'ISLE B
1542-1553F L'ISLE V
1561-1589S L'ISLE B
1551-1553F NORTHUMBERLAND D
1561-1589X WARWICK E

Duff
1735-1912D BRACO B(I)
1759-1912D FIFE E(I)
1790-1809X FIFE B
1827-1857X FIFE B
1885-1912X FIFE E
1889-1912X FIFE D
1759-1912D MACDUFF V(I)
1889-1912X MACDUFF M
1857-1912X SKENE B
DUFFERIN
E   1871-   Hamilton-Blackwood
DUFFERIN & AVA
M   1888-   Hamilton-Temple-
                      Blackwood
DUFFERIN & CLANDEBOYE
B(I) 1800-   Blackwood
DUFFUS
B   1650-1715F Dunbar
B   1826-1876X Dunbar

47

DUGAN OF VICTORIA
B   1949-1951X Dugan
Dugan
1949-1951X DUGAN OF VICTORIA B
Dugdale
1959-   CRATHORNE B
Duke
1925-   MERIVALE B
Dukes
1947-1948X DUKESTON B
DUKESTON
B   1947-1948X Dukes
DULVERTON
B   1929-   Wills
DUMBARTON
E(S) 1675-1725X Douglas
DUMFRIES
E(S) 1633-   Crichton
DUMFRIESSHIRE
M(S) 1684-   Scott
DUNALLEY
B(I) 1800-   Prittie
DUNBAR
E(S) 1178-1434F Dunbar
E(S) 1605-1611X Home
V(S) 1620-1718D Constable
Dunbar
1650-1715F DUFFUS B
1826-1876X DUFFUS B
1178-1434F DUNBAR E(S)
1060-1419D MARCH E(S)
1360-1455F MURRAY E(S)
DUNBOYNE
B(I) 1324-   Butler
B(I) 1541-   Butler
B(I) 1719-   Grimston
DUNCAN OF CAMPERDOWN
V   1797-1933X Haldane-Duncan
DUNCAN OF LUNDIE
B   1797-1933X Haldane-Duncan
Duncan
1180-1271? CARRICK E(S)
DUNCAN-SANDYS
B(L) 1974-   Duncan-Sandys
Duncan-Sandys
1974-   DUNCAN-SANDYS B(L)
DUNCANNON
V(I) 1722-   Ponsonby
B   1834-   Ponsonby
Dunch
1658-1660X BURNELL B
Duncombe
1747-1763X DOWNTON B

Duncombe (Cont'd)
1747-1763X FEVERSHAM B
1826-   FEVERSHAM B
1868-1963X FEVERSHAM E
1868-1963X HELMSLEY V
DUNDAFF
V(S) 1707-   Graham
DUNDALK
Bss(I) 1716-1743X Schulenburg
DUNDAS
B   1794-   Dundas
Dundas
1832-1832X AMESBURY B
1794-   DUNDAS B
1802-   DUNEIRA B
1802-   MELVILLE V
1892-   RONALDSHAY E
1838-   ZETLAND E
1892-   ZETLAND M
DUNDEE
E(S) 1660-   Scrimgeour
V(S) 1688-1746F Graham
DUNDONALD
E(S) 1669-   Cochrane
DUNEDIN
B   1905-1942X Murray
V   1926-1942X Murray
DUNEIRA
B   1802-   Dundas
DUNFERMLINE
E(S) 1605-1694X Seton
B   1839-1868X Abercromby
DUNGAN
V(I) 1661-1715X Dungan
Dungan
1661-1715X DUNGAN V(I)
1685-1715X LIMERICK E(I)
DUNGANNON
B(I) 1542-1612X O'Neill
V(I) 1661-1706X Trevor
Css(I) 1716-1743X Schulenburg
Mss(I) 1716-1743X Schulenburg
V(I) 1765-1862X Trevor
DUNGARVAN
V(I) 1616-   Boyle
DUNGLASS
L(S) 1605-   Douglas-Home
DUNKELD
L(S) 1645-1689F Galloway
DUNKELLIN
B(I) 1543-1916X Burgh-Canning, De
DUNKERRON
V(I) 1719-1751X Petty
B(I) 1751-   Petty-Fitzmaurice

48

```
DUNLEATH                            Dutton
  B    1892-    Mulholland            1784-     SHERBORNE B
DUNLO                               DUVEEN
  V(I) 1801-    Trench                B    1933-1939X Duveen
DUNLUCE                             Duveen
  V(I) 1618-1791X McDonnell          1933-1939X DUVEEN B
  V(I) 1785-    McDonnell          DYNEVOR
DUNMORE                              B    1780-     Rhys
  E(S) 1686-    Murray             DYSART
  B    1831-    Murray              E(S) 1643-     Greaves
DUNNING
  B    1869-    Rollo
Dunning
  1782-1823X ASHBURTON B
DUNOON
  L(S) 1706-1761X Campbell
DUNRAVEN & MOUNT-EARL
  E(I) 1822-    Quin
DUNROSSIL
  V    1959-    Morrison
DUNSANDLE & CLAN-CONAL
  B(I) 1845-1911X Daly
DUNSANY
  B(I) 1439-    Plunkett
DUNSFORD
  V    1920-    Brodrick
DUNSMORE
  B    1628-1653X Leigh
DUNSTANVILLE, DE
  B    1796-1835X Basset
Dunstanville, De
  1140-1175X CORNWALL E
DUNWICH
  V    1821-    Rous
DU PARCQ
  B(L) 1946-1949X Du Parcq
Du Parcq
  1946-1949X DU PARCQ B(L)
DUPPLIN
  V(S) 1627-    Hay
DURAS
  B    1673-1709X Duras
Duras
  1673-1709X DURAS B
  1676-1709X FEVERSHAM E
DURHAM
  E    1075-1080X Lorraine, De
  B    1828-    Lambton
  E    1833-    Lambton
DURSLEY
  V    1679-1942X Berkeley
DUTTON                              (TITLES are in CAPITALS
  B    1711-    Hamilton             Surnames in smalls)
                      49
```

Eady
1919-   SWINFEN B
EARDLEY
B(I) 1789-1825X Eardley
Eardley
1789-1825X EARDLEY B(I)
EARLSFORT
B(I) 1784-1935X Scott
EASTBARNS
L(S) 1600-1625X Ramsay
EASTNOR
V   1821-1823X Somers-Cocks
Eaton
1887-1974X CHEYLESMORE B
EBBISHAM
B   1928-   Blades
EBRINGTON
V   1789-   Fortescue
EBURY
B   1857-   Grosvenor
ECCLES
V   1964-   Eccles
Eccles
1964-   ECCLES V
ECHINGHAM
B   1311-1326X Echingham
Echingham
1311-1326X ECHINGHAM B
EDDISBURY
B   1848-   Stanley
Ede: See Chuter-Ede
EDEN OF WINTON
B(L) 1983-   Eden
Eden
1789-   AUCKLAND B(I)
1793-   AUCKLAND B
1839-1849X AUCKLAND E
1961-   AVON E
1983-   EDEN OF WINTON B(L)
1799-   HENLEY B(I)
1885-   NORTHINGTON B
EDENDERRY
B(I) 1720-1756X Blundell
EDGCUMBE
B   1742-   Edgcumbe
Edgcumbe
1742-   EDGCUMBE B
1789-   MOUNT EDGCUMBE E
1781-   MOUNT EDGCUMBE &
         VALLETORT V
1781-1789M VALLETORT V

EDINBURGH
D   1726-1760M Guelph
D   1764-1834X Guelph
D   1866-1900X Guelph
D   1947-   Mountbatten
See also: GLOUCESTER & EDINBURGH
EDIRDALE
E(S) 1488-1504X Stewart
Edmondson
1945-   SANDFORD B
EDMUND-DAVIES
B(L) 1974-   Edmund-Davies
Edmund-Davies
1974-   EDMUND-DAVIES B(L)
EDNAM
V   1827-1833X Ward
V   1860-   Ward
EDRINGTON
B   1336-1336X Edrington
Edrington
1336-1336X EDRINGTON B
Edwardes
1776-   KENSINGTON B(I)
1886-   KENSINGTON B
Edwards
1963-   CHELMER B(L)
EFFINGHAM
E   1731-1816X Howard
E   1837-   Howard
EGERTON OF TATTON
B   1859-1958X Egerton
E   1897-1909X Egerton
Egerton
1616-1829X BRACKLEY V
1720-1803X BRACKLEY M
1617-1829X BRIDGEWATER E
1720-1803X BRIDGEWATER D
1859-1958X EGERTON OF TATTON B
1897-1909X EGERTON OF TATTON E
1603-1829X ELLESMERE B
1801-   GREY DE WILTON V
1897-1909X SALFORD V
1801-   WILTON E
See also: Grey-Egerton
         Leveson-Gower
EGLINTON
E(S) 1508-   Montgomerie
EGMONT
E(I) 1733-   Perceval
EGREMONT
B   1449-1460X Percy

50

EGREMONT (Cont'd)
E   1749-1750P Seymour
E   1750-1845X Wyndham
B   1963-   Wyndham
ELBOTTLE
L(S) 1646-....X Maxwell
ELCHO & METHEL
L(S) 1633-   Wemyss
ELDON
B   1799-   Scott
E   1821-   Scott
ELGIN
E(S) 1633-   Bruce
Elias
1937-1946X SOUTHWOOD B
1946-1946X SOUTHWOOD V
ELIBANK
L(S) 1643-   Erskine-Murray
V   1911-1962X Murray
ELIOT
B   1784-   Eliot
Eliot
1784-   ELIOT B
1815-   ST GERMANS E
ELLENBOROUGH
B   1802-   Law
E   1844-1871X Law
ELLES
Bss(L) 1972-   Elles
Elles
1972-   ELLES Bss(L)
ELLESMERE
B   1603-1829X Egerton
E   1846-   Leveson-Gower
ELLIOT OF HARWOOD
Bss(L) 1958-   Elliot
Elliot
1958-   ELLIOT OF HARWOOD Bss(L)
1787-1813X HEATHFIELD B
1813-   MELGUND V
1797-   MINTO B
1813-   MINTO V
1813-   MINTO E
Ellis
1794-   MENDIP B
1826-   SEAFORD B
See also: Agar-Ellis
ELMLEY
V   1815-1979X Lygon
ELPHINSTONE
L(S) 1509-   Elphinstone
B   1885-   Elphinstone

Elphinstone
1603-1746F BALMERINO L(S)
1607-1669P COUPAR L(S)
1509-   ELPHINSTONE L(S)
1885-   ELPHINSTONE B
1797-1823X KEITH B(I)
1803-1867X KEITH B
ELTHAM
E   1726-1760M Guelph
E   1917-1981X Cambridge
ELTISLEY
B   1934-1942X Newton
ELTON
B   1934-   Elton
Elton
1934-   ELTON B
ELVEDEN
V   1919-   Guinness
ELWORTHY
B(L) 1972-   Elworthy
Elworthy
1972-   ELWORTHY B(L)
ELWYN JONES
B(L) 1974-   Jones
ELY
V(I) 1622-1725X Loftus
M   1726-1760M Guelph
E(I) 1766-1783X Loftus
E(I) 1794-   Tottenham
M(I) 1801-   Tottenham
ELY O'CARROLL
B(I) 1552-....? Carroll
ELYSTAN-MORGAN
B(L) 1981-   Morgan
EMLY
B   1874-1932X Monsell
EMLYN
V   1827-   Campbell
EMMETT OF AMBERLEY
Bss(L) 1964-   Emmett
Emmett
1964-   EMMETT OF AMBERLEY Bss(L)
EMMOTT
B   1911-1926X Emmott
Emmott
1911-1926X EMMOTT B
EMSLIE
B(L) 1980-   Emslie
Emslie
1980-   EMSLIE B(L)
ENCOMBE
V   1821-   Scott

51

ENERGLYN
  B(L) 1968-   Evans
ENFIELD
  B   1695-1830X Nassau
  V   1847-   Byng
ENGAINE
  B   1299-1367X Engaine
Engaine
  1299-1367X ENGAINE B
ENNALS
  B(L) 1983-   Ennals
Ennals
  1983-   ENNALS B(L)
ENNISDALE
  B   1619-1651X Hamilton
  B   1939-1963X Lyons
ENNISHOWEN & CARRICKFERGUS
  B   1841-1883X Chichester
ENNISKILLEN
  B(I) 1627-1644F Maguire
  V(I) 1776-   Cole
  E(I) 1789-   Cole
ENNISMORE
  B(I) 1800-   Hare
ENNISMORE & LISTOWEL
  V(I) 1816-   Hare
ENZIE
  E(S) 1599-   Gordon
EPSOM
  B   1911-   Primrose
ERLEIGH
  V   1917-   Isaacs
ERNE
  B(I) 1768-   Crichton
  V(I) 1781-   Crichton
  E(I) 1789-   Crichton
ERNLE
  B   1919-1937X Prothero
ERNLEY
  B   1661-1787X Ernley
Ernley
  1661-1787X ERNLEY B
ERRINGTON
  V   1901-   Baring
ERRIS
  B(I) 1800-   King
ERROLL
  E(S) 1452-   Hay
ERROLL OF HALE
  B   1964-   Erroll
Erroll
  1964-   ERROLL OF HALE B

ERSKINE
  B   1806-   Erskine
ERSKINE OF DIRLETON
  L(S) 1459-   Erskine
ERSKINE OF RERRICK
  B   1964-   Erskine
Erskine
  1610-   CARDROSS L(S)
  1603-   DIRLETON L(S)
  1806-   ERSKINE B
  1459-   ERSKINE OF DIRLETON L(S)
  1964-   ERSKINE OF RERRICK B
  1606-   FENTOUN V(S)
  1619-   KELLIE E(S)
  1565-   MAR E(S)
Erskine-Murray
  1643-   ELIBANK L(S)
ESHER
  B   1885-   Brett
  V   1897-   Brett
ESKDALE
  L(S) 1620-1716F Maxwell
ESLINGTON
  B   1874-1904X Liddell
ESMONDE
  B(I) 1622-1646X Esmonde
Esmonde
  1622-1646X ESMONDE B(I)
ESPEC
  B   1158-....X L'Espec
ESSENDON
  B   1932-1978X Lewis
ESSEX
  E   1135/54-1189X Mandeville, De
  E   1199-1227C Fitz-Piers
  E   1239-1372X Bohun, De
  E   1461-1539X Bourchier
  E   1539-1540F Cromwell
  E   1543-1571X Parr
  E   1572-1646X Devereux
  E   1661-   Capel
ESTCOURT
  B   1903-1915X Sotheran-Estcourt
ETTRICK
  B   1872-   Napier
EURE
  B   1544-1698X Eure
Eure
  1544-1698X EURE B
Eustace
  1541-1585F BALTINGLASS V(I)
  1541-1585F KILCULLEN B(I)
  1462-1585F PORTLESTER B(I)

52

```
EUSTON                                 EXMOUTH
  E    1672-       FitzRoy               B    1814-      Pellew
EVANS                                    V    1816-      Pellew
  B    1957-1963X Evans                EYRE
EVANS OF CLAUGHTON                       B(I) 1768-1781X Eyre
  B(L) 1978-       Evans              Eyre
EVANS OF HUNGERSHALL                     1768-1781X EYRE B(I)
  B(L) 1967-1982X Evans              Eyres Monsell
Evans                                    1935-      MONSELL V
  1968-       ENERGLYN B(L)          EYTHEN
  1957-1963X EVANS B                   L(S) 1642-1647X King
  1978-       EVANS OF CLAUGHTON B(L) EZRA
  1967-1982X EVANS OF HUNGERSHALL      B(L) 1983-      Ezra
              B(L)                    Ezra
  1945-       MOUNTEVANS B              1983-      EZRA B(L)
Evans-Freke
  1715-       CARBERY B(I)
Eve
  1963-       SILSOE B
Evereux
  1216-1226P GLOUCESTER E
EVERINGHAM
  B    1309-1371A Everingham
Everingham
  1309-1371A EVERINGHAM B
EVERSHED
  B    1956-1966X Evershed
Evershed
  1956-1966X EVERSHED B
EVERSLEY                         *
  B    1906-1928X Shaw-Lefevre
EWART-BIGGS
  Bss(L) 1981-       Ewart-Biggs
Ewart-Biggs
  1981-       EWART-BIGGS Bss(L)
Ewing: See Orr-Ewing
EWE
  B    1066/87-1154/89X Ewe, De
  B    1199/1216-1216/72X Ysondon
Ewe, De
  1066/87-1154/89X EWE B
EWYAS
  B    1154/89-....X Ewyas, De
Ewyas, De
  1154/89-....X EWYAS B
EXETER
  D    1397-1400F Holland
  D    1416-1426X Beaufort
  D    1443-1461F Holland
  M    1526-1539F Courtenay
  M    1553-1556X Courtenay
  E    1605-       Cecil           (TITLES are in CAPITALS
  M    1801-       Cecil               Surnames in smalls)
      * See also Addenda      53
```

FABER
B   1905-1920X Faber
Faber
    1905-1920X FABER B
    1918-1931X WITTENHAM B
FAIRFAX
    V(I) 1628-1741X Fairfax
FAIRFAX OF CAMERON
    L(S) 1627-   Fairfax
Fairfax
    1628-1741X FAIRFAX V(I)
    1627-   FAIRFAX OF CAMERON L(S)
FAIRFIELD
    B   1939-1945X Greer
FAIRFORD
    V   1772-   Hill
FAIRHAVEN OF ANGLESEY ABBEY
    B   1961-   Broughton
FAIRHAVEN OF LODE
    B   1929-1966X Broughton
FAIRLIE
    B   1897-   Boyle
FAITHFULL
    Bss(L) 1975-   Faithfull
Faithfull
    1975-   FAITHFULL Bss(L)
FALCONER OF GLENFARQUHAR
    B   1724-1727X Falconer
FALCONER OF HALKERTON
    L(S) 1646-1966D Keith
Falconer
    1724-1727X FALCONER OF GLENFAR-
                QUHAR B
    1647-1677M HALKERTOUN B
FALKENDER
    Bss(L) 1974-   Falkender
Falkender
    1974-   FALKENDER Bss(L)
FALKLAND
    V(S) 1620-   Cary
Falle
    1934-1948X PORTSEA B
FALMOUTH
    E   1664-1665X Berkeley
    V   1674-1716X Fitz-Roy
    V   1720-   Boscawen
    E   1808-1852X Boscawen
FALVERSLEY
    B   1383-1392X Falversley
Falversley
    1383-1392X FALVERSLEY B
FANE
    V(I) 1718-1766X Fane

Fane
    1624-   BURGHERSH B
    1733-1762X CATHERLOUGH B(I)
    1604-1762A DESPENCER B
    1718-1766X FANE V(I)
    1718-1766X LOUGHGUYRE B(I)
    1624-   WESTMORLAND E
FANHOPE
    B   1438-1443X Cornwall
FANSHAWE   *
    V(I) 1661-1716X Fanshawe
Fanshawe
    1661-1716X FANSHAWE V(I)
FAREHAM
    Css 1673-1734X Querouaille
FARINGDON
    B   1916-   Henderson
FARNBOROUGH
    B   1826-1838X Long
    B   1886-1886X May
FARNHAM
    B(I) 1756-   Maxwell
    V(I) 1760-1779X Maxwell
    E(I) 1763-1779X Maxwell
    V(I) 1781-1823X Maxwell
    E(I) 1781-1823X Maxwell
FARQUHAR
    B   1898-1923X Farquhar
    V   1917-1923X Farquhar
    E   1922-1923X Farquhar
Farquhar
    1898-1923X FARQUHAR B
    1917-1923X FARQUHAR V
    1922-1923X FARQUHAR E
FARRER
    B   1893-1964X Farrer
Farrer
    1893-1964X FARRER B
FAUCONBERG
    B   1295-1376C Fauconberg
    B   1429-1462A Nevill
    B   1903-1926P Lane-Fox
    B   1926-1948A Anderson-Pelham
    V   1643-1815X Belasyse
    E   1689-1700X Belasyse
FAUCONBERG OF YARM
    B   1627-1815X Belasyse
Fauconberg
    1295-1376C FAUCONBERG B
FAULKNER OF DOWNPATRICK
    B(L) 1977-1977X Faulkner
Faulkner
    1977-1977X FAULKNER OF DOWNPATRICK
                B(L)

54   * See also Addenda

FEATHER
  B(L) 1974-1976X Feather
Feather
  1974-1976X FEATHER B(L)
FEILDING
  B   1620-   Feilding
  V   1620-   Feilding
Feilding
  1622-   CALLAN V(I)
  1622-   DENBIGH E
  1622-   DESMOND E(I)
  1620-   FEILDING B
  1620-   FEILDING V
  1663-   ST LIZ B
Fellowes
  1921-   AILWYN B
  1887-   RAMSEY, DE B
FELTON
  B   1313-1358X Felton
Felton
  1313-1358X FELTON B
FENTOUN
  V(S) 1606-   Erskine
Fergaunt, or Alan
  1066/87-1230P RICHMOND E
Ferguson: See Munro-Ferguson
Fergusson
  1972-   BALLANTRAE B(L)
FERMANAGH
  V(I) 1703-1791X Verney
  Bss(I) 1792-1810X Verney
  B   1876-   Crichton
Fermor
  1721-1867X POMFRET E
Fermor-Hesketh
  1935-   HESKETH B
FERMOY
  V(I) 1490-1703? Roche
  B(I) 1856-   Roche
FERRARD
  B(I) 1715-1731X Tichborne
  Vss(I) 1797-1831X Foster
FERRERS
  E   1711-   Shirley
FERRERS OF CHARTLEY
  B   1299-1449C Ferrers
  B   1461-1600F Devereux
  B   1603-1646A Devereux
  B   1677-1741 Shirley
  B   1751-1855A Townshend

FERRERS OF GROBY
  B   1297-1445P Ferrers
  B   1445-1483F Grey
  B   1485-1554F Grey
FERRERS OF OKEHAM
  B   1154/89-1189/99X Ferrers
FERRERS OF WEMME
  B   1375-1410A Ferrers
Ferrers
  1137-1265F DERBY E
  1299-1449C FERRERS OF CHARTLEY B
  1297-1445P FERRERS OF GROBY
  1154/89-1189/99X FERRERS OF
          OKEHAM B
  1375-1410A FERRERS OF WEMME B
FERRIER
  B(L) 1958-   Noel-Paton
Ferris- See Grant-Ferris
FETHARD
  B(I) 1695-   Vaughan
FETTERCAIRN
  L(S) 1660-1695F Middleton
  See also: CLERMONT & FETTERCAIRN
FEVERSHAM
  E   1676-1709X Duras
  E   1676-1709X Sondes
  Css 1719-1743X Schulenburg
  B   1747-1763X Duncombe
  B   1826-   Duncombe
  E   1868-1963X Duncombe
FFRENCH
  B(I) 1798-   ffrench
ffrench
  1798-   FFRENCH B(I)
FIELD
  B   1890-1907X Field
Field
  1890-1907X FIELD B
Fienes or Fiennes
  1458-1541F DACRE B
  1558-1611P DACRE B
  1447-   SAYE & SELE B
  1624-1781X SAYE & SELE V
FIFE
  E(S) 1057-1425X MacDuff
  M(S) 1567-1575F Hepburn
  E(I) 1759-1812D Duff
  B   1790-1809X Duff
  B   1827-1857X Duff
  E   1885-1912X Duff
  D   1885-1912X Duff
  D   1900-   Carnegie

55

```
FINCASTLE                            FITZALAN
   V(S) 1686-        Murray             B    1066/87-1216/72M Fitzalan
FINCH                                   B    1295-1305A Fitzalan
   B    1640-1660X Finch                B    1627-       Howard
   B    1673-       Finch            FITZALAN OF BEDALE
Finch                                   B    1154/89-1216/72A Fitzalan
   1714-       AYLESFORD E           FITZALAN OF DERWENT
   1640-1660X FINCH B                   V    1921-1962X Fitzalan-Howard
   1673-       FINCH B              Fitzalan or FitzAlan or Fitz-Alan  *
   1660-1729X FITZHERBERT B            1289-1326F ARUNDEL E
   1702-       GUERNSEY B             1331-1347F ARUNDEL E
   1623-       MAIDSTONE V            1400-1580  ARUNDEL E
   1681-       NOTTINGHAM E           1433-       ARUNDEL E
   1628-       WINCHILSEA E           1066/87-1216/72M FITZALAN B
FINDLATER                              1295-1305A FITZALAN B
   E(S) 1638-1811X Ogilvy             1154/89-1216/72A FITZALAN OF BEDALE B
FINGALL                                1347-1397F SURREY E
   E(I) 1628-1984X Plunkett           1400-1475X SURREY E
   B    1831-1984X Plunkett         Fitzalan-Howard
FINLAY                                 1921-1962X FITZALAN OF DERWENT V
   B    1916-1945X Finlay             1490-       HERRIES OF TERREGLES L(S)
   V    1919-1945X Finlay             1869-       HOWARD OF GLOSSOP B
Finlay                               FITZANCULF
   1916-1945X FINLAY B                  B    1066/87-....X Fitzanculf
   1919-1945X FINLAY V              Fitzanculf
FINTRIE: See ABERUTHVEN, MUGDOCK       1066/87-....X FITZANCULF B
   & FINTRIE                         FITZBADERON
FISHER                                  B    1066/87-1257X MONMOUTH B
   B    1909-       Fisher           FITZBERNARD
FISHER OF CAMDEN                        B    1313-1350X Fitzbernard
   B(L) 1974-       Fisher           Fitzbernard
FISHER OF LAMBETH                      1313-1350X FITZBERNARD B
   B(L) 1961-1972X Fisher           Fitzcharles
FISHER OF REDNAL                       1675-1680X DARTMOUTH B
   Bss(L) 1974-       Fisher         1675-1680X PLYMOUTH E
Fisher                                 1675-1680X TOTNESS V
   1918-1920X DOWNHAM B             FITZ-CLARENCE
   1909-       FISHER B                V    1831-       Fitz-Clarence
   1974-       FISHER OF CAMDEN B(L) Fitz-Clarence or FitzClarence
   1961-1972X FISHER OF LAMBETH B(L) 1831-       FITZ-CLARENCE V
   1974-       FISHER OF REDNAL       1831-       MUNSTER E
               Bss(L)                 1831-       TEWKESBURY B
FISHERWICK                           FITZGERALD
   B    1790-       Chichester          B(I) 1826-1843X Fitzgerald
FISKE                                   B    1835-1860X Fitzgerald
   B(L) 1957-1975 Fiske             FITZGERALD OF KILMARNOCK
Fiske                                   B(L) 1882-1889X Fitzgerald
   1957-1975X FISKE B(L)            FITZGERALD & VESEY
FITT OF BELL'S HILL                     B    1826-1860X Fitzgerald
   B(L) 1983-       Fitt
Fitt                                          * See also Addenda
   1983-       FITT OF BELL'S HILL B(L)
```

Fitzgerald
  1600-1601F DESMOND B(I)
  1826-1843X FITZGERALD B(I)
  1835-1860X FITZGERALD B
  1882-1889X FITZGERALD OF KILMAR-
            NOCK B(L)
  1826-1860X FITZGERALD & VESEY B
  1316-   KILDARE E(I)
  1761-   KILDARE M(I)
  1870-   KILDARE B
  1800-1810X LECALE B(I)
  1747-   LEINSTER V
  1766-   LEINSTER D(I)
  1203-   OFFALY B(I)
  1761-   OFFALY E(I)
Fitzgerald, Digby alias: See Digby
FITZGEROLD
  B   1066/87-1154/89? Fitzgerold
Fitzgerold
  1066/87-1154/89? FITZGEROLD B
FITZGIBBON
  B(I) 1789-1864X Fitzgibbon
  B   1799-1864X Fitzgibbon
Fitzgibbon
  1795-1864X CLARE E(I)
  1798-1864X CLARE E
  1789-1864X FITZGIBBON B(I)
  1799-1864X FITZGIBBON B
FITZHAMON
  B   1066/87-1107X Fitzhamon
Fitzhamon
  1066/87-1107X FITZHAMON B
FITZHARDING
  V(I) 1661-1712X Berkeley
FITZHARDINGE
  E   1841-1857X Berkeley
  B   1861-1916X Berkeley
FITZHARRIS
  V   1800-   Harris
FITZHENRY
  B   1295-1325X Fitzhenry
Fitzhenry
  1295-1325X FITZHENRY
FITZHERBERT
  B   1199/1216-1272/1307X
                Fitzherbert
  B   1660-1729X Finch
Fitzherbert
  1194/1216-1272/1307X FITZHERBERT B
  1791-1839X ST HELENS B (I)
  1801-1839X ST HELENS B
  1640-   STAFFORD B

FITZHUGH
  B   1066/87-1304L Fitzhugh
  B   1321-1512A Fitzhugh
Fitzhugh
  1066/87-1304L FITZHUGH B
  1321-1512A FITZHUGH B
Fitzjames
  1687-1695F BERWICK D
  1687-1695F BOSWORTH B
  1687-1695F TINMOUTH E
FITZJOHN
  B   1216/72-1258L Fitzjohn
  B   1264-1276X Fitzjohn
  B   1295-1297X Fitzjohn
Fitzjohn
  1216/72-1258L FITZJOHN B
  1264-1276X FITZJOHN B
  1295-1297X FITZJOHN B
Fitzmaure
  1329-1398A DESMOND E(I)
  1422-1582F DESMOND E(I)
FITZMAURICE
  V(I) 1751-   Petty-Fitzmaurice
  B   1906-1935X Fitzmaurice
Fitzmaurice
  1722-   CLANMAURICE V(I)
  1696-1951D DECHMONT L(S)
  1906-1935X FITZMAURICE B
  1722-   KERRY E(I)
  1264-1697X KERRY & LIXNAW B(I)
  1696-1951D KIRKWALL V(S)
  1696-1951D ORKNEY E(S)
  See also: Hamilton
  See also: Petty-Fitmaurice
Fitzosborne
  1066/87-1074X HERFORD E
Fitzpatrick
  1869-1937X CASTLETOWN B
  1715-1818X GOWRAN B(I)

  1751-1818X UPPER OSSORY E(I)
  1794-1818X UPPER OSSORY B
FITZPAYNE
  B   1154/89-1216/72L Fitzpayne
  B   1299-1354A Fitzpayne
Fitzpayne
  1154/89-1216/72L FITZPAYNE B
  1299-1354A FITZPAYNE B
Fitzpiers
  1199-1227C ESSEX E
FITZRALPH
  B   1066/87-1216/72X Fitzralph

57

Fitzralph
  1066/87-1216/72X FITZRALPH B
FITZRANULPH
  B   1154/80-1216/72X Fitzranulph
Fitzranulph
  1154/80-1216/72X FITZRANULPH B
FITZREGINALD
  B   1135/54-1216/72L Fitzreginald
  B   1299-1307X Fitzreginald
Fitzreginald
  1135/54-1216/72L FITZREGINALD B
  1299-1307X FITZREGINALD B
FITZROBERT
  B   1299-1332A Fitzrobert alias
                  Clavering
Fitzrobert alias Clavering
  1299-1332A FITZROBERT
FITZROGER
  B   1299-1299X Fitzroger
Fitzroger
  1299-1299X FITZROGER B
Fitzroy/FitzRoy/Fitz-Roy
  1664-1936A ARLINGTON E
  1672-1936A ARLINGTON E
  1674-1774X CHICHESTER E
  1709-1774X CLEVELAND D
  1943-   DAVENTRY V
  1672-   EUSTON E
  1674-1716X FALMOUTH V
  1675-   GRAFTON D
  1672-   IPSWICH E
  1674-1716X NORTHUMBERLAND E
  1683-1716X NORTHUMBERLAND D
  1525-1536X NOTTINGHAM E
  1674-1716X POMFRET B
  1525-1536X RICHMOND D
  1525-1536X SOMERSET D
  1674-1774X SOUTHAMPTON D
  1780-   SOUTHAMPTON B
  1672-   SUDBURY B
  1672-1936A THETFORD V
  See also: Scot
  See also: Villiers
FITZSWAINE
  B   1154/89-....X Fitzswaine
Fitzswaine
  1154/89-....X FITZSWAINE B
FITZWALTER
  B   1100/35-1234L Fitzwalter
  B   1295-1432X Fitzwalter
  B   1485-1495F Ratcliffe
  V   1525-1641X Ratcliffe

FITZWALTER (Cont'd)
  B   1669-1756A Mildmay
  E   1730-1756X Mildmay
  B   1868-1875X Bridges
  B   1924-1932X Plumptre
FITZWALTER OF DAVENTRY
  B   1272/1307-....X Fitzwalter
Fitzwalter
  1100/35-1234L FITZWALTER B
  1295-1432X FITZWALTER B
  1272/1307-....X FITZWALTER OF
                  DAVENTRY B
FITZWARINE
  B   1189/99-1216/72L Fitzwarine
  B   1295-1429P Fitzwarine
  B   1292-1636A Bourchier
  B   1342-....X Fitzwarine
Fitzwarine
  1189/99-1216/72L FITZWARINE B
  1295-1429P FITZWARINE B
  1342-....X FITZWARINE B
FITZWILLIAM
  B   1327-....L Fitzwilliam
  B(I) 1620-1979X Fitzwilliam
  E(I) 1716-1979X Fitzwilliam
  B   1742-1979X Fitzwilliam
  E   1746-1979X Fitzwilliam
  B(I) 1629-1833X Fitzwilliam
  V(I) 1629-1833X Fitzwilliam
FITZWILLIAM OF GRIMTHORPE
  B   1295-1316X Fitzwilliam
Fitzwilliam
  1327-....L FITZWILLIAM B
  1620-1979X FITZWILLIAM B(I)
  1716-1979X FITZWILLIAM E(I)
  1742-1979X FITZWILLIAM B
  1746-1979X FITZWILLIAM E
  1629-1833X FITZWILLIAM B(I)
  1629-1833X FITZWILLIAM V(I)
  1716-   MILTON V(I)
  1742-   MILTON B
  1746-   MILTON V
  1537-1543X SOUTHAMPTON E
  1663-1667X TYRCONNEL E(I)
  1295-1316X FITZWILLIAM OF
                  GRIMTHORPE B
FLECK
  B   1961-1968X Fleck
Fleck
  1961-1968X FLECK B

58

FLEMING
  E(S) 1341-1747L Fleming
  L(S) 1451-1747L Fleming
  L(S) 1606-1747L Fleming
Fleming
  1606-1747X CUMBERNAULD L(S)
  1341-1747L FLEMING E(S)
  1451-1747L FLEMING L(S)
  1606-1747L FLEMING L(S)
  1713-1726F LONGFORD V(I)
  1185-1726L SLANE B(I)
  1341-1371X WIGTON E(S)
  1606-1747L WIGTON E(S)
FLETCHER
  B(L) 1970-   Fletcher
Fletcher
  1970-   FLETCHER B(L)
  1942-1961X WINSTER B
Fletcher-Vane
  1964-   INGLEWOOD B
FLOREY
  B(L) 1965-1968X Florey
Florey
  1965-1968X FLOREY B(L)
Flower
  1751-   ASHBROOK V(I)
  1892-1907X BATTERSEA B
  1733-   CASTLE DURROW B(I)
FLOWERS
  B(L) 1979-   Flowers
Flowers
  1979-   FLOWERS B(L)
Foix, De
  1446-1485? KENDAL E
FOLEY
  B   1712-1716X Foley
  B   1776-   Foley
Foley
  1712-1716X FOLEY B
  1776-   FOLEY B

FOLIOT
  B   1295-1297A Foliot
Foliot
  1295-1297A FOLIOT B
Foljambe
  1893-   HAWKESBURY B
  1905-   HAWKESBURY V
  1905-   LIVERPOOL E
FOLKESTONE
  V   1747-   Bouverie, De

FOLLIOTT
  B(I) 1619-1716X Folliott
Folliott
  1619-1716X FOLLIOTT B(I)
FOOT
  B(L) 1967-   Foot
Foot
  1964-   CARADON B(L)
  1967-   FOOT B(L)
FORBES
  L(S) 1445-   Forbes
  B(I) 1673-   Forbes
  B   1806-   Forbes
FORBES OF PITSLIGO
  L(S) 1633-1745F Forbes
Forbes
  1673-   CLANEHUGH B(I)
  1445-   FORBES L(S)
  1633-1745F FORBES OF PITSLIGO L(S)
  1673-   FORBES B(I)
  1806-   FORBES B
  1675-   GRANARD V(I)
  1684-   GRANARD E(I)
  1806-   GRANARD B
Forbes-Leith
  1905-1925X LEITH OF FYVIE B
FORDWICH
  V   1718-1905X Cowper
FORESTER
  B   1821-   Weld-Forester
FORFAR
  E(S) 1651-1715P Douglas
FORMARTINE
  V(S) 1682-   Gordon
FORRES
  B   1922-   Williamson
FORREST
  B   1918-1918X Forrest
Forrest
  1918-1918X FORREST B
FORRESTER OF CORSTORPHINE
  L(S) 1633-   Forrester
Forrester
  1633-   FORRESTER OF CORSTORPHINE L
FORSTER
  B   1919-1936X Forster
FORSTER OF HARRABY
  B   1959-1972X Forster
Forster
  1919-1936X FORSTER B
  1959-1972X FORSTER OF HARRABY B

FORTE
B(L) 1982-   Forte
Forte
1982-   FORTE B(L)
FORTESCUE
B   1746-   Fortescue
E   1789-   Fortescue
B(I) 1746-1781X Fortescue-Aland
Fortescue
1770-1806X CLERMONT B(I)
1776-1829X CLERMONT V(I)
1777-1829X CLERMONT E(I)
1866-1887X CLERMONT B
1746-1751X CLINTON E
1789-   ERRINGTON V
1746-   FORTESCUE B
1789-   FORTESCUE E
See also: Parkinson-Fortescue
Fortescue-Aland
1746-1781X FORTESCUE B(I)
FORTEVIOT
B   1917-   Dewar
FORTH
V(S) 1686-1902D Drummond
E(S) 1642-1651X Ruthven
Fortibus
1190-1216/72X ALANBROOKE Count
1212-1273X ALBEMARLE E
FORTROSE
B(I) 1766-1815X Mackenzie
Forward-Howard
1776-1978X CLONMORE B(I)
1785-1978X WICKLOW V(I)
1793-1978X WICKLOW E(I)
FOSSARD
B   1100/35-1135/54X Fossard
Fossard
1100/35-1135/54X FOSSARD B
Foster
1797-   FERRARD V(I)
1910-1952X ILKESTON B
1790-1831X ORIEL Bss(I)
1821-   ORIEL B
See also: Hylton-Foster
Fowler
1908-1943X WOLVERHAMPTON V
FOX
Bss(L) 1981-   Fox
Fox
1981-   FOX Bss(L)
1762-1859X HOLLAND OF HOLLAND B
See also: Lane-Fox

FOXFORD
B   1815-   Pery
Fox-Strangways
1741-   ILCHESTER B
1756-   ILCHESTER E
1747-   ILCHESTER & STAVORDALE B
1747-   REDLYNCH B
1741-   STRANGWAYS B
FRANCIS-WILLIAMS
B(L) 1962-1970X Williams
FRANKFORT
B(I) 1800-1817D Morres
FRANKFORT DE MONTMORENCY
V(I) 1816-1917D Montmorency, De

FRANKLEY
B   1794-   Lyttelton
FRANKS
B(L) 1962-   Franks
Franks
1962-   FRANKS B(L)
FRASER
L(S) 1633-1720D Fraser
FRASER OF ALLANDER
B   1964-   Fraser
FRASER OF KILMORACK
B(L) 1974-   Fraser
FRASER OF LONSDALE
B(L) 1958-1974X Fraser
FRASER OF NORTH CAPE
B   1946-1981X Fraser
FRASER OF TULLYBELTON
B(L) 1975-   Fraser
Fraser
1633-1720D FRASER L(S)
1964-   FRASER OF ALLANDER B
1974-   FRASER OF KILMORACK B(L)
1958-1974X FRASER OF LONSDALE B(L)
1946-1981X FRASER OF NORTH CAPE B
1975-   FRASER OF TULLYBELTON B(L)
1458-   LOVAT L(S)
1837-   LOVAT B
1445-   SALTOUN L(S)
1955-   STRATHALMOND B

Freeman-Mitford
1802-1886X REDESDALE B
1877-1886X REDESDALE E

60

Freeman-Thomas
    1931-   RATENDONE V
    1910-1979X WILLINGDON B
    1924-1979X WILLINGDON V
    1936-1979X WILLINGDON M
Freke: See Evans-Freke
Fremantle
    1874-   COTTESLOE B
FRENCH OF YPRES
    V   1916-
French
    1839-1856X FREYNE OF ARTAGH, DE B
    1851-   FREYNE, DE
    1916-   FRENCH OF YPRES V
    1922-   YPRES E
FRENDRAUGHT
    V(S) 1642-1690F Crichton
FRESCHVILLE
    B   1297-....L Freschville
    B   1664-1682X Freschville
Freschville
    1297-....L FRESCHVILLE B
    1664-1682X FRESCHVILLE B
FREVILLE
    B   1327-....L Freville
Freville
    1327-....L FREVILLE B
FREYBERG
    B   1951-   Freyberg
Freyberg
    1951-   FREYBERG B
FREYNE, DE
    B   1851-   French
FREYNE OF ARTAGH, DE
    B   1839-1856X French
Fuller-Acland-Hood
    1911-1971X ST AUDRIES B
FULTON
    B(L) 1966-   Fulton
Fulton
    1966-   FULTON B(L)
FURNEAUX
    V   1922-   Smith
FURNESS
    B   1910-   Furness
    V   1918-   Furness
Furness
    1910-   FURNESS B
    1918-   FURNESS V
Furniss
    1930-1939X SANDERSON B

FURNIVAL
    B   1216/72-1279L Furnival, De
    B   1295-1383C Furnival, De
    B   1406-1442P Nevill
    B   1442-1616A Talbot
    B   1677-1777A Howard
    B   1913-1920A Petre
    B   1932-1968A Dent
Furnival, De
    1216/72-1279L FURNIVAL B
    1295-1383C FURNIVAL B
FURNIVALL
    B   1839-1849X Talbot
Fyfe
    1954-1967X KILMUIR B
    1962-1967X KILMUIR E
FYVIE
    L(S) 1598-1715F Seton

(TITLES are in CAPITALS
Surnames in smalls)

61

GAGE
  B(I) 1720-   Gage
  V(I) 1720-   Gage
  B   1780-   Gage
  B   1790-1791X Gage
Gage
  1720-   GAGE B(I)
  1720-   GAGE V(I)
  1780-   GAGE B
  1790-1791X GAGE B
GAINFORD
  B   1917-   Pease
GAINSBOROUGH
  E   1682-1798X Noel
  E   1841-   Noel
GAITSKELL
  Bss(L) 1963-   Gaitskell
Gaitskell
  1963-   GAITSKELL Bss(L)
Galbraith
  1955-   STRATHCLYDE B
GALLACHER
  B(L) 1982-   Gallacher
Gallacher
  1982-   GALLACHER B(L)
GALLEN RIDGEWAY
  B(I) 1616-1714X Ridgeway
GALLOWAY
  L(S) 1140-1234X Galloway, De
  E(S) 1623-   Stewart
Galloway
  1645-1689F DUNKELD L(S)
Galloway, De
  1140-1234X GALLOWAY L(S)
GALMOYE
  V(I) 1646-1697F Butler
GALPERN
  B(L) 1979-   Galpern
Galpern
  1979-   GALPERN B(L)
GALWAY
  V(I) 1687-1691X Burke
  V(I) 1692-1720X Massue
  E(I) 1697-1720X Massue
  V(I) 1727-   Monckton
GAMBIER
  B   1807-1833X Gambier
Gambier
  1807-1833X GAMBIER B
GANT
  B   1066/87-1189/99X Gant
  B   1264-1297X Gant

Gant
  1066/87-1189/99X GANT B
  1216-1217X LINCOLN E
  1264-1297X GANT B
Ganzoni
  1938-   BELSTEAD B
GARDINER
  B(L) 1963-   Gardiner
Gardiner
  1816-1829X BLESSINGTON E(I)
  1963-   GARDINER B(L)
  1785-1829X MOUNTJOY B(I)
  1795-1829X MOUNTJOY V(I)
GARDNER OF PARKES
  Bss(L) 1981-   Gardner
Gardner
  1895-1921X BURGHCLERE B
  1981-   GARDNER OF PARKES Bss(L)
GARDYNE: See BRUCE-GARDYNE*
GARIOCH
  L(S) 1295-   Mar, Of
GARLIES
  L(S) 1607-   Stewart
GARMOYLE
  V   1878-   Cairns
GARNER
  B(L) 1969-1983X Garner
Garner
  1969-1983X GARNER B(L)
GARNOCK
  V(S) 1703-1808D Lindsay
GARNSWORTHY
  B(L) 1967-1974X Garnsworthy
Garnsworthy
  1967-1974X GARNSWORTHY B(L)
GARVAGH
  B(I) 1818-   Canning
GARVIACH: See MARR & GARVIACH
Gascoyne-Cecil
  1923-1958X CECIL OF CHELWOOD V
  1941-1956X QUICKSWOOD B
  See also: Cecil
GASK: See MURRAY, BALVENIE & GASK
Gathorne-Hardy
  1878-   CRANBROOK V
  1892-   CRANBROOK E
  1892-   MEDWAY B
GAUGI
  B   1154/89-1286X Gaugi, De
Gaugi, De
  1154/89-1286X GAUGI B
Gaveston
  1308-1314X CORNWALL E

GEDDES
B 1942-   Geddes
GEDDES OF EPSOM
B(L) 1958-1983X Geddes
Geddes
  1942-   GEDDES B
  1958-1983X GEDDES OF EPSOM B(L)
GENEVILL
B 1299-1307A Genevill
Genevill
  1299-1307A GENEVILL B
GEOFFREY-LLOYD
B(L) 1974-   Lloyd
Georbodus
  1066-1070P CHESTER E
George, Prince of Denmark
  1689-1708X KENDAL E
George: See Lloyd George
GEORGE-BROWN
B(L) 1970-   George-Brown
George-Brown
  1970-   GEORGE-BROWN B(L)
GERARD
B 1603-1707X Gerard
B 1876-   Gerard
GERARD OF BRANDON
B 1645-1702X Gerard
Gerard
  1679-1702M BRANDON V
  1603-1707X GERARD B
  1876-   GERARD B
  1645-1702X GERARD OF BRANDON
  1679-1702X MACCLESFIELD E
GHISNES
B 1154/89-1272/1307L Ghisnes
B 1295-1335X Ghisnes
Ghisnes
  1154/89-1272/1307L GHISNES B
  1295-1335X GHISNES B
Gibbs   *
  1896-   ALDENHAM B
  1928-   WRAXALL B
GIBSON
B(L) 1975-   Gibson
Gibson
  1885-   ASHBOURNE B
  1975-   GIBSON B(L)
Gibson-Carmichael
  1912-1926X CARMICHAEL B
GIBSON-WATT
B(L) 1979-   Gibson-Watt
Gibson-Watt
  1979-   GIBSON-WATT B(L)

GIFFARD
B 1066/87-1199/1216L Giffard
B 1295-1327A Giffard
B 1199/1216-1272/1307X Giffard
Giffard
  1066-1166X BUCKINGHAM E
  1066/87-1199/1216L GIFFARD B
  1295-1327A GIFFARD B
  1199/1216-1272/1307X GIFFARD B
  1885-   HALSBURY B
  1898-   HALSBURY E
  1898-   TIVERTON V
GIFFORD
B 1824-   Gifford
E(S) 1694-   Hay
Gifford
  1824-   GIFFORD B
Gilbey: See Vaux
Gilchrist
  1120-1343 ANGUS E(S)
GILLFORD
B(I) 1766-   Meade
Ginkel
  1692-1844X ATHLONE E
GISBOROUGH
B 1917-   Chaloner
GLADSTONE
V 1910-1930X Gladstone
GLADSTONE OF HAWARDEN
B 1932-1935X Gladstone
Gladstone
  1910-1930X GLADSTONE V
  1932-1935X GLADSTONE OF HAWARDEN B
GLADWYN
B 1960-   Jebb
GLAMIS
L(S) 1445-   Lyon
GLAMIS, TANNADYCE, SIDLAW &
  STRATHDICHTIE
L(S) 1677-   Lyon
GLANDINE
V(I) 1827-   Toler
GLANDORE
E(I) 1776-1826X Crosbie
GLANELY
B 1918-1942X Tatem
GLANTAWE
B 1906-1915X Jenkins
GLANUSK
B 1899-   Bailey
GLANVILL
B 1066/87-1189X Glanvill, De
*See also Addenda

63

Glanvill, De
1066/87-1189X GLANVILL B
GLASFOORD
  L(S) 1685-1703L Abercromby
GLASGOW
  E(S) 1703-   Boyle
GLASSARY
  B   1954-   Scrymgeour
GLASTONBURY
  Bss 1719-1743X Schulenburg
  B   1797-1826X Grenville
GLEAN-O'MALLAN
  B(I) 1622-....? O'Mullane
GLENALMOND
  V(S) 1696-1724L Murray
  See also: BALWHIDDER, GLENALMOND
    & GLENLYON
GLENAPP
  V   1929-   Mackay
GLENARTHUR
  B   1918-   Arthur
GLENAVY
  B   1921-1984X Campbell *
GLENBERVIE
  B(I) 1800-1823X Douglas
GLENCAIRN
  E(S) 1488-1796D Cunynghame
GLENCONNER
  B   1911-   Tennant
GLENDALE
  V   1695-1701X Grey
GLENDEVON
  B   1964-   Hope
GLENDYNE
  B   1922-   Nivison
GLENELG
  B   1835-1866X Grant
GLENESK
  B   1895-1908X Borthwick
GLENGALL
  E   1816-1858X Butler
GLENILLA: See LOCHOW & GLENILLA
GLENKINGLAS
  B(L) 1974-1984X Noble
GLENLUCE & STRANRAER
  L(S) 1690-   Dalrymple
GLENLYON
  B   1821-1957X Stewart-Murray
  See also: BALWHIDDER, GLENALMOND
    & GLENLYON

    * See Addenda

GLENORCHY, BENEDARALOCH, ORMELIE &
  WEICK
  L(S) 1677-   Campbell
GLENRAVEL
  B   1936-1937X Benn
GLENTANAR
  B   1916-1971X Coats
GLENTORAN
  B   1939-   Dixon
GLENTWORTH
  B(I) 1790-   Pery
GLERAWLY
  V(I) 1766-   Annesley
GLOUCESTER
  E   1109-1176P Consul
  E   1176-1199P Plantagenet
  E   1213-1216P Mandeville, De
  E   1216-1226P Evereux
  E   1226-1313X Clare, De
  E   1337-1347X Audley
  D   1385-1399X Plantagenet
  E   1397-1400F Despencer
  D   1414-1446X Plantagenet
  D   1461-1483M Plantagenet
  D   1659-1660X Stuart
  D   1689-1700X Stuart
  D   1928-   Windsor
GLOUCESTER & EDINBURGH
  D   1764-1834X Guelph
GLOUCESTER & HERTFORD
  E   1299-1306L Monthermer
GLYN
  B   1953-1960X Glyn
Glyn
  1953-1960X GLYN B
  1869-   WOLVERTON B
GODBER
  B   1956-1976X Godber
GODBER OF WILLINGTON
  B(L) 1979-1980X Godber
Godber
  1956-1976X GODBER B
  1979-1980X GODBER OF WILLINGTON B(L)
GODDARD
  B(L) 1944-1971X Goddard
Goddard
  1944-1971X GODDARD B(L)
GODERICH
  V   1706-1740X Grey
  V   1827-1923X Robinson

64

Godley
 1909-   KILBRACKEN B
GODOLPHIN
 B   1684-1766X Godolphin
 E   1706-1766X Godolphin
 B   1832-1859M Osborne
GODOLPHIN OF HELSTON
 B   1735-1785X Godolphin
Godolphin
 1684-1766X GODOLPHIN B
 1706-1766X GODOLPHIN E
 1735-1785X GODOLPHIN OF HELSTON B
GOODMAN
 B(L) 1965-   Goodman
Goodman
 1965-   GOODMAN B(L)
GORDON
 L(S) 1376-1836X Gordon
 D(S) 1684-1836X Gordon
 B   1784-1836X Gordon
 V   1814-   Gordon
GORDON OF DRUMEARN
 B(L) 1876-1879X Gordon
Gordon
 1682-   ABERDEEN E(S)
 1814-   ABERDEEN V
 1632-1643F ABOYNE V(S)
 1599-   ENZIE E(S)
 1682-   FORMARTINE V(S)
 1376-1836X GORDON L(S)
 1684-1836X GORDON D(S)
 1784-1836X GORDON B
 1814-   GORDON V
 1876-1879 GORDON OF DRUMEARN B(L)
 1916-   HADDO E
 1682-   HADDO, METHLIC, TARVES
            & KELLIE L(S)
 1450-   HUNTLY E(S)
 1599-   HUNTLY M(S)
 1684-1836X INVERNESS V(S)
 1633-1847D KENMURE V
 1633-1847D LOCHINVAR L(S)
 1815-   MELDRUM B
 1627-1630X MELGUM V(S)
 1784-1836X NORWICH E
 1682-   TARVES L(S)
 See also: Hamilton-Gordon
Gordon-Lennox
 1876-   KINRARA E
 See also: Lennox
GORDON-WALKER
 B(L) 1974-   Gordon Walker

Gordon Walker
 1974-   GORDON-WALKER B(L)
GORE
 B(I) 1764-1802X Gore
Gore
 1766-1784X ANNALY B(I)
 1789-1793X ANNALY B(I)
 1762-   ARRAN E(I)
 1768-1802X BELLEISLE V(I)
 1764-1802X GORE B(I)
 1772-1802X ROSS E(I)
 1758-   SAUNDERS B(I)
 1758-   SUDLEY V(I)
 1884-   SUDLEY B
 See also: Ormsby-Gore

GORE-BOOTH
 B(L) 1969-1984X Gore-Booth
Gore-Booth
 1969-1984X GORE-BOOTH B(L)
GORELL
 B   1909-   Barnes
GORGES
 B   1309-1400A Gorges
 B(I) 1620-1712X Gorges
Gorges
 1309-1400A GORGES B
 1620-1712X GORGES B(I)
GORING
 B   1628-1672X Goring
Goring
 1628-1672X GORING B
 1645-1672X NORWICH E
GORMANSTON
 B(I) 1370-   Preston
 V(I) 1478-   Preston
 B   1868-   Preston
GORMLEY
 B(L) 1982-   Gormley
Gormley
 1982-   GORMLEY B(L)
GORONWY-ROBERTS
 B(L) 1974-1981X Roberts
GORT
 V(I) 1816-   Vereker
 V   1946-1946X Vereker
GOSCHEN
 V   1900-   Goschen
Goschen
 1900-   GOSCHEN V
GOSFORD
 B(I) 1776-   Acheson
 V(I) 1785-   Acheson
 E(I) 1806-   Acheson

65

```
Gospatric                              1722-      GRAHAM E
  1069-1072F NORTHUMBERLAND E          1688-1746F GRAHAM L(S)
Gotha: See Saxe-Coburg                 1983-      GRAHAM OF EDMONTON B(L)
GOUGH                                  1681-1739X GRAHAM OF ESK L(S)
  B    1846-       Gough               1707-      GRAHAM & BUCHANAN M(S)
  V    1849-       Gough               1707-      KINCARDINE E(S)
Gough                                  1814-1843X LYNEDOCH B
  1846-      GOUGH B                   1427-1694D MONTEITH & AIRTH E(S)
  1849-      GOUGH V                   1505-      MONTROSE E(S)
Gough-Calthorpe                        1644-      MONTROSE M(S)
  1796-      CALTHORPE B               1707-      MONTROSE D(S)
Gould                                  1681-1739X PRESTON V(S)
  1799-1800P GREY DE RUTHYN B          1427-1427P STRATHERN E(S)
Goulding                             Graham-Toler: See Toler
  1922-1936X WARGRAVE B              GRAHAM & BUCHANAN
GOWER                                  M(S) 1707-      Graham
  B    1703-       Leveson-Gower     GRANARD
  E    1746-       Leveson-Gower       V(I) 1673-       Forbes
Gower: See Leveson-Gower               E(I) 1684-       Forbes
GOWRAN                                 B    1806-       Forbes
  E(I) 1676-1677X Butler            GRANBY
  B(I) 1715-1818X Fitzpatrick          M    1703-       Manners
GOWRIE                               GRANDISON
  E(S) 1581-1600F Ruthven              B    1299-1305X Grandison
  B    1935-       Ruthven             B    1299-1375D Grandison
  E    1945-       Ruthven             V(I) 1620-1630  Villiers
GRADE                                  E(I) 1721-1800X Villiers
  B(L) 1976-       Grade               Vss(I) 1746-1809X Villiers
Grade                                  Css(I) 1766-1809X Villiers
  1976-      GRADE B(L)             Grandison
GRAFTON                                1299-1305X GRANDISON B
  D    1675-       FitzRoy             1299-1375D GRANDISON B
GRAHAM                               GRANEY
  L(S) 1445-       Graham              V(I) 1535-1541F Grey
  M(S) 1707-       Graham           Grant
  B    1722-       Graham              1835-1866X GLENELG B
  E    1722-       Graham              See also: Ogilvie-Grant
  L(S) 1688-1746F Graham            Grant-Ferris
                               *       1974-      HARVINGTON B(L)
GRAHAM OF ESK                        GRANTCHESTER
  L(S) 1681-1739X Graham              B    1953-       Suenson-Taylor
Graham                               GRANTHAM
  1707-      ABERUTHVEN, MUGDOCK &     E    1698-1754X Nassau
             FINTRIE L(S)             B    1761-1923X Robinson
  1633-1694D AIRTH & MONTEITH E(S)  GRANTLEY
  1917-1938X ATHOLSTAN B              B    1782-       Norton
  1686-1688M DUDHOPE L(S)          GRANVILLE
  1707-      DUNDAFF V(S)             B    1661-1711X Granville
  1688-1746F DUNDEE V(S)             V    1661-1711X Granville
  1445-      GRAHAM L(S)              E    1661-1711X Granville
  1707-      GRAHAM M(S)              B    1702-1707X Granville
  1722-      GRAHAM B
                                       * See also Addenda
                          66
```

GRANVILLE (Cont'd)
E   1715-1776X Carteret
V   1815-   Leveson-Gower
E   1833-   Leveson-Gower
GRANVILLE OF EYE
B(L) 1967-   Granville
GRANVILLE OF KILHAMPTON
B   1689-1711X Granville
GRANVILLE OF POTHERIDGE
B   1702-1707X Granville
Granville
   1661-1711X BATH E
   1661-1711X GRANVILLE B
   1661-1711X GRANVILLE V
   1661-1711X GRANVILLE E
   1702-1707X GRANVILLE B
   1967-   GRANVILLE OF EYE B(L)
   1689-1711X GRANVILLE OF
              KILHAMPTON B
   1702-1707X GRANVILLE OF
              POTHERIDGE B
   1711-1734X LANSDOWNE B
GRANVILLE-WEST
B(L) 1958-1984X West
GRAVES
B(I) 1794-   Graves
Graves
   1794-   GRAVES B(I)
GRAY   *
L(S) 1445-   Campbell-Gray
Gray: See also Anstruther-Gray
Greaves
   1643-   DYSART E(S)
GREDINGTON
B   1788-   Kenyon
Greenall
   1927-   Daresbury B
GREENE
B   1941-1952X Greene
GREENE OF HARROW WEALD
B(L) 1974-   Greene
Greene
   1941-1952X GREENE B
   1974-   GREENE OF HARROW
              WEALD B(L)
GREENHILL
B   1950-   Greenhill
GREENHILL OF HARROW
B(L) 1974-   Greenhill
Greenhill
   1950-   GREENHILL B
   1974-   GREENHILL OF
              HARROW B(L)
      * See also Addenda   67

GREENOCK
B   1807-   Cathcart
GREENWAY
B   1927-   Greenway
Greenway
   1927-   GREENWAY B
GREENWICH
E   1705-1743X Campbell
D   1719-1743X Campbell
Bss 1767-1794X Townshend
B   1947-   Mountbatten
GREENWOOD
B   1929-   Greenwood
V   1937-   Greenwood
GREENWOOD OF ROSSENDALE
B(L) 1970-1982X Greenwood
Greenwood
   1929-   GREENWOOD B
   1937-   GREENWOOD V
   1970-1982X GREENWOOD OF ROSSEN-
              DALE B(L)
Greer
   1939-1945X FAIRFIELD B
GREGSON
B(L) 1975-   Gregson
Gregson
   1975-   GREGSON B(L)
GRENDON
B   1299-1331A Grendon
Grendon
   1299-1331A GRENDON B
GRENFELL
B   1902-   Grenfell
Grenfell
   1905-1945X DESBOROUGH B
   1902-   GRENFELL B
   1935-1984X ST JUST B
GRENTMAISNILL
B   1066/87-1154/89X Grentmaisnill, De
Grentmaisnill, De
   1066/87-1154/89X GRENTMAISNILL B
GRENVILLE
B   1790-1834X Grenville
Grenville
   1784-1889X BUCKINGHAM M
   1822-1889X BUCKINGHAM D
   1822-1889X CHANDOS M
   1797-1826X GLASTONBURY B
   1790-1834X GRENVILLE B
   See also: Freeman-Grenville
GRESLEY
B   1100/35-1154/89X Gresley
B   1307-1347X Gresley

Gresley
   1100/35-1154/89X GRESLEY B
   1307-1347X GRESLEY B
GRETTON
   B   1944-   Gretton
Gretton
   1944-   GRETTON B
GREVILLE
   B   1869-   Greville
Greville
   1621-   BROOKE B
   1746-   BROOKE E
   1869-   GREVILLE B
   1759-   WARWICK E
GREY
   B   1784-1814X Grey

GREY OF CHILLINGHAM
   B   1624-1706X Grey
GREY OF CODNOR
   B   1299-1496A Grey
GREY OF FALLODON
   V   1916-1933X Grey
GREY OF GROBY
   B   1330-1554F Grey
   B   1603-1976X Grey
GREY OF HOWICK
   E   1806-   Grey
GREY OF NAUNTON
   B(L) 1968-   Grey
GREY OF POWYS
   B   1482-1552A Grey
GREY OF ROLLESTON
   B   1673-1734X North
GREY OF ROTHERFIELD
   B   1199/1216-1295L Grey
   B   1297-1487F Grey
GREY OF WERKE
   B   1624-1706X Grey
GREY OF WILTON
   B   1216/72-1265L Grey
   B   1295-1604F
GREY DE RADCLIFFE
   B   1875-1885X Grey-Egerton
GREY DE RUTHYN
   B   1342-1639P Grey
   B   1639-1643P Longueville
   B   1643-1799P Yelverton
   B   1799-1800P Gould
   B   1800-1868A Yelverton
   B   1940-1963A Butley-Bowdon
GREY DE WILTON
   V   1801-   Egerton

GREY, DE
   M   1740-1797X Grey
GREY OF WREST, DE
   E   1816-1923X Robinson
Grey
   1475-1554F DORSET M
   1445-1483F FERRERS OF GROBY B
   1485-1554F FERRERS OF GROBY B
   1695-1701X GLENDALE V
   1706-1740X GODERICH V
   1535-1541F GRANEY V(I)
   1784-1814X GREY
   1624-1706X GREY OF CHILLINGHAM B
   1299-1496A GREY OF CODNOR B
   1916-1933X GREY OF FALLODON V
   1330-1554F GREY OF GROBY B
   1603-1976X GREY OF GROBY B
   1806-   GREY OF HOWICK E
   1968-   GREY OF NAUNTON B(L)
   1482-1552A GREY OF POWYS B
   1199/1216-1295L GREY OF ROTHERFIELD B
   1297-1487F GREY OF ROTHERFIELD B
   1624-1706X GREY OF WERKE
   1216/72-1265L GREY OF WILTON
   1295-1604F GREY OF WILTON
   1342-1639P GREY DE RUTHYN B
   1801-   GREY DE WILTON V
   1740-1770X GREY, DE M
   1706-1741X HAROLD E
   1806-1806M HOWICK V
   1471-1475R HUNTINGDON E
   1465-1741X KENT E
   1706-1741X KENT M
   1710-1741X KENT D
   1475-1512X L'ISLE B
   1483-1512X L'ISLE V
   1769-1883X MERE, DE LA
   1628-1976X STAMFORD E
   1551-1554F SUFFOLK D
   1418-1459A TANKERVILLE E
   1695-1701X TANKERVILLE E
   1796-1883X WARRINGTON E
   See also: Ferrers
Grey, De
   1780-   WALSINGHAM B
Grey-Egerton
   1875-1885X GREY DE RADCLIFFE B
GREYSTOCK
   B   1199/1216-1288L Greystock
   B   1295-1569A Greystock
Greystock
   1199/1216-1288L GREYSTOCK B
   1295-1569A GREYSTOCK B

```
GRIDLEY                                  Guelph (Cont'd)
  B     1955-      Gridley                  1881-1919S ATHLONE B
Gridley                                    1890-1892X ATHLONE E
  1955-      GRIDLEY B                      1726-1765X BERKHAMSTED M
GRIFFIN                                    1706-1727M CAMBRIDGE D
  B     1688-1742X Griffin                  1801-1904X CAMBRIDGE D
Griffin                                    1789-1830M CLARENCE D
  1788-           BRAYBROOKE B              1881-1919S CLARENCE E
  1688-1742X GRIFFIN B                      1890-1892X CLARENCE & AVONDALE D *
Grigg                                      1801-1904X CULLODEN B
  1945-      ALTRINCHAM B                   1726-1765X CUMBERLAND D
GRIMOND                                    1766-1790X CUMBERLAND D
  B(L) 1983-      Grimond                   1799-1919F CUMBERLAND & TEVIOTDALE D
Grimond                                    1850-1901M DUBLIN E
  1983-      GRIMOND B(L)                   1726-1760M EDINBURGH D
GRIMSTON                                   1764-1834X EDINBURGH D
  B(I) 1719-      Grimston                  1866-1900X EDINBURGH D
  V(I) 1719-      Grimston                  1726-1760M ELTHAM E
GRIMSTON OF WESTBURY                        1726-1760M ELY M
  B     1964-      Grimston                 1764-1834X GLOUCESTER & EDINBURGH D
Grimston                                    1874-          GUELPH E
  1719-           DUNBOYNE B(I)             1801-1843X INVERNESS E(I) *      *
  1719-           GRIMSTON B(I)             1799-1820X KENT D
  1719-           GRIMSTON V(I)             1866-1900X KENT E               *
  1964-           GRIMSTON OF WESTBURY B    1726-1760M LAUNCESTON V
  1719-           VERULAM V(I)              1706-1727M MILFORD HAVEN E
  1790-           VERULAM B                 1789-1830M MUNSTER E(I)
  1815-           VERULAM E                 1706-1727M NORTHALLERTON V
GRIMTHORPE                                 1789-1830M ST ANDREWS D
  B     1886-      Beckett                  1801-1843X SUSSEX D
GRINSTEAD                                  1799-1799M TEVIOTDALE D
  B     1815-      Cole                     1801-1904X TIPPERARY E
GROSMONT                                   1726-1765X TREMATON V
  V     1644-      Somerset                 1716-1728X ULSTER E(I)
GROSVENOR                                  1760-1767X ULSTER E(I)
  B     1761-      Grosvenor                1784-1827X ULSTER E(I)
  E     1784-      Grosvenor                1866-1900X ULSTER E
Grosvenor                                  1716-1728X YORK D
  1784-           BELGRAVE V                1760-1767X YORK D
  1857-           EBURY B                   1784-1827X YORK D             *
  1761-           GROSVENOR B             GUERNSEY
  1784-           GROSVENOR E               B     1702-      Finch
  1886-1949X STALYBRIDGE B               GUEST
  1831-           WESTMINSTER M             B(L) 1961-      Guest
  1874-           WESTMINSTER D           Guest
GUELPH                                      1910-      ASHBY ST LEDGERS B
  E     1874-      Guelph                   1880-      WIMBORNE B
Guelph                            *        1918-      WIMBORNE V
  1881-1919S ALBANY D                   *   1961-      GUEST B(L)
  1801-1843X ARKLOW B(I)                  See also: HADEN-GUEST
  1799-1919F ARMAGH E(I)
                                               * See also Addenda
```

69

```
GUILDFORD
  Css  1660-1673X Boyle
  E    1674-1682X Maitland
GUILFORD
  B    1683-      North
  E    1752-      North
GUILLAMORE
  V(I) 1831-1955X O'Grady
Guinness
  1880-1915X ARDILAUN B
  1919-      ELVEDEN V
  1891-      IVEAGH B
  1905-      IVEAGH V
  1919-      IVEAGH E
  1932-      MOYNE B
Gully
  1905-      SELBY V
Gurdon
  1899-      CRANWORTH B
GURNAY
  B    1066/87-1290X Gurnay, De
Gurnay, De
  1066/87-1290X GURNAY B
GWYDIR
  B    1796-1915X Burrell
GWYNEDD
  V    1945-      Lloyd George
Gwynne Jones
  1964-      CHALFONT B(L)
```

NOTE

Each TITLE is shown in CAPITALS,
then in Year order of creations,
preceded by Rank and followed by
Surname

Each Surname is shown in Smalls,
then in Alphabetical Order of
TITLES, preceded by Year and
followed by Rank

SEE PAGE vi OF INTRODUCTION FOR
ABBREVIATIONS

HACCHE
B   1299-1306D Hacche
Hacche
1299-1306D HACCHE B
HACKING
B   1945-   Hacking
Hacking
1945-   HACKING B
HADDINGTON
V(S) 1606-1625X Ramsay
E(S) 1619-   Baillie-Hamilton
HADDO
E   1916-   Gordon
HADDO, METHLIC, TARVES & KELLIE
L(S) 1682-   Gordon
HADEN-GUEST
B   1950-   Haden-Guest
Haden-Guest
1950-   HADEN-GUEST B
HAIG
E   1919-   Haig
Haig
1919-   DAWICK V
1919-   HAIG E
HAILES
B   1957-1974X Buchan-Hepburn
HAILEY
B   1936-1969X Hailey
Hailey
1936-1969X HAILEY B
HAILSHAM
B   1928-   Hogg
V   1929-   Hogg
HAILSHAM OF ST MARYLEBONE
B(L) 1970-   Hogg
HAIRE OF WHITEABBEY
B(L) 1965-1966X Haire
Haire
1965-1966X HAIRE OF WHITEABBEY B(L)
HALDANE
V   1911-1928X Haldane
Haldane
1911-1928X HALDANE V
Haldane-Duncan
1831-1933X CAMPERDOWN E
1797-1933X DUNCAN OF LUNDIE B
1797-1933X DUNCAN OF CAMPERDOWN V
HALDON
B   1880-1939X Palk
HALE
B(L) 1972-   Hale
Hale
1972-   HALE B(L)

HALES
L(S) 1467-1575X Hepburn
HALIBURTON
B   1898-1907X Haliburton
Haliburton
1898-1907X HALIBURTON B
HALIFAX
V   1668-1700X Savile
E   1679-1700X Savile
M   1682-1700X Savile
B   1700-1772X Montagu
E   1714-1715X Montagu
E   1715-1772X Montagu
V   1866-   Wood
E   1944-   Wood
HALKERTOUN
B   1647-1677M Falconer
HALL
V   1946-   Hall
Hall
1946-   HALL V
1859-1867X LLANOVER B
1977-   LOCKWOOD Bss(L)
See also: King-Hall
HALSBURY
B   1885-   Giffard
E   1898-   Giffard
HALYBURTON
L(S) 1441-1600F Halyburton
Halyburton
1441-1600F HALYBURTON L(S)
HAMBLEDEN
V   1891-   Smith
HAMILTON
L(S) 1445-   Hamilton
M(S) 1599-   Hamilton
D(S) 1643-   Hamilton
L(S) 1581-1672X Stewart
L(S) 1606-   Hamilton
V   1786-   Hamilton
M   1868-   Hamilton
D(S) 1660-1694X Douglas
B   1776-   Campbell
B   1831-   Hamilton
HAMILTON OF DALZELL
B   1886-   Hamilton
HAMILTON OF GLENAWLEY
B(I) 1660-1680X Hamilton
HAMILTON OF STACKALLAN
B(I) 1715-   Hamilton

71

Hamilton
1608-1649D ABERBROTHWICK L(S)
1603-   ABERCORN L(S)
1606-   ABERCORN E(S)
1790-   ABERCORN M
1503-   ? ARRAN E(S)
1643-   ARRAN, LANARK & CAMBRIDGE
            E(S)
1643-   AVEN & INNERDALE L(S)
1639-1736D BARGENY L(S)
1647-   BELHAVEN & STENTON L(S)
1715-   BOYNE B(I)
1717-   BOYNE V(I)
1711-   BRANDON D
1619-   BYRES & BINNING L(S)
1619-1651X CAMBRIDGE E
1647-1675X CLANBRASSILL E(I)
1756-1798X CLANBRASSILL E(I)
1622-1675X CLANEBOY V(I)
1719-1798X CLANEBOY E(I)
1643-   CLYDESDALE M(S)
1696-   DECHMONT L(S)
1711-   DUTTON B
1619-1651X ENNISDALE B
1606-1686M HAMILTON L(S)
1786-   HAMILTON V
1868-   HAMILTON M(I)
1643-   HAMILTON D(S)
1831-   HAMILTON B
1886-   HAMILTON OF DALZELL B
1660-1680X HAMILTON OF GLENAWLEY B(I)
1715-   HAMILTON OF STACKALLAN
            B(I)
1665-1810X HILLHOUSE L(S)
1897-   HOLM PATRICK B
1696-   KIRKWALL V(S)
1639-   LANARK E(S)
1719-1798X LIMERICK V(I)
1643-   MACHANSIRE & POLMONT L(S)
1619-1627 MELROSE E(S)
1827-1858X MELROSE B
1606-   MOUNTCASTLE L(S)
1701-   MOUNTCASTLE B(I)
1696-1951D ORKNEY E(S)
1587-   PAISLEY L(S)
1606-   PAISLEY, HAMILTON, MOUNT-
            CASTELL & KILPATRICK L(S)
1697-1810X RICCARTOUN V(S)
1697-1810X RUGLEN E(S)
1617-1   STRABANE B(I)
1701-   STRABANE V(I)

Hamilton (Cont'd)
1913-1934X SUMNER B(L)
1927-1934X SUMNER V
See also: Baillie-Hamilton
See also: Douglas-Hamilton
Hamilton-Blackwood
1800-   CLANDEBOYE B(I)
1860-   CLANDEBOYE B
1871-   CLANDEBOYE V
1871-   DUFFERIN E
Hamilton-Gordon
1893-1957X STANMORE B
Hamilton-Russell
1866-   BRANCEPETH B
Hamilton-Temple-Blackwood
1888-   AVA E
1888-   DUFFERIN & AVA M
HAMMOND OF KIRKELLA
B   1874-1890X Hammond
Hammond
1874-1890X HAMMOND OF KIRKELLA B
HAMNETT
B(L) 1970-   Hamnett
Hamnett
1970-   HAMNETT B(L)
HAMPDEN
B   1776-1824X Trevor
V   1884-   Brand
HAMPTON
B   1874-   Pakington
HAMPTON COURT
Bss L716-1761X Coningsby
Hanbury: See Bateman-Hanbury
Hanbury-Tracy
1838-   SUDELEY B
Handcock
1812-   CASTLEMAINE B(I)
1822-1839X CASTLEMAINE V(I)
HANDLO
B   1342-1346X Handlo
Handlo
1330-1420A BURNELL B
1342-1346X HANDLO B
Hanger
1762-1824X COLERAINE B(I)
HANKEY
B   1939-   Hankey
Hankey
1939-   HANKEY B
HANMER
B   1872-1881X Hanmer

Hanmer
1872-1881X HANMER B
HANNEN
B(L) 1891-1894X Hannen
HANSELYN
B   1066/87-1135/54X Hanselyn
Hanselyn
1066/87-1135/54X HANSELYN B
HANSON
B(L) 1983-   Hanson
Hanson
1983-   HANSON B(L)
HANWORTH
B   1631-1653X Cottington
B   1926-   Pollock
V   1936-   Pollock
HARBERTON
B(I) 1783-   Pomeroy
V(I) 1791-   Pomeroy
Harbord
1786-   SUFFIELD B
HARBOROUGH
B   1714-1859X Sherard
E   1719-1859X Sherard
HARCLA
B   1321-1323F Harcla
Harcla
1322-1323F CARLISLE E
1321-1323F HARCLA B
HARCOURT
B   1711-1830X Harcourt
V   1721-1830X Harcourt
E   1749-1830X Harcourt
V   1917-1979X Harcourt
Harcourt
1711-1830X HARCOURT B
1721-1830X HARCOURT V
1749-1830X HARCOURT E
1917-1979X HARCOURT V
1749-1830X NUNEHAM V
1917-   NUNEHAM B
HARDERESHULL
B   1342-1342A Hardereshull
Hardereshull
1342-1342A HARDERESHULL B
HARDING OF PETHERTON
B   1958-   Harding
Harding
1958-   HARDING OF PETHERTON
HARDINGE
V   1846-   Hardinge
HARDINGE OF PENSHURST
B   1910-   Hardinge

Hardinge
1846-   HARDINGE V
1910-   HARDINGE OF PENSHURST B
HARDWICKE
B   1733-   Yorke
E   1754-   Yorke
Hardy: See Cozens-Hardy
       See Gathorne-Hardy
HARE
B   1869-   Hare
Hare
1963-   BLAKENHAM V
1625-....X COLERAINE B(I)
1800-   ENNISMORE B(I)
1816-   ENNISMORE & LISTOWEL V(I)
1869-   HARE B
1816-   LISTOWEL V(I)
1822-   LISTOWEL E(I)
HAREWOOD
B   1790-1795X Lascelles
B   1796-   Lascelles
E   1812-   Lascelles
HARINGTON
B   1324-1554F Harington
HARINGTON OF EXTON
B   1603-1614X Harington
Harington
1324-1554F HARINGTON B
1603-1614X HARINGTON OF EXTON B
HARLECH
B   1876-   Ormsby-Gore
HARLEY
B   1711-1853X Harley
Harley
1711-1853X HARLEY B
1711-1853X MORTIMER E
1711-1853X OXFORD E
HARMAR-NICHOLLS
B(L) 1974-   Harmar-Nicholls
Harmar-Nicholls
1974-   HARMAR-NICHOLLS B(L)
HARMSWORTH
B   1939-   Harmsworth
Harmsworth
1939-   HARMSWORTH B
1905-   NORTHCLIFFE B
1917-1922X NORTHCLIFFE V
1914-   ROTHERMERE B
1919-   ROTHERMERE V
HAROLD
E   1706-1741X Grey

73

HARRINGTON
B   1730-   Stanhope
E   1742-   Stanhope
HARRIS
B   1815-   Harris
HARRIS OF GREENWICH
B(L) 1974-   Harris
HARRIS OF HIGH CROSS
B(L) 1979-   Harris
Harris
1800-   FITZHARRIS V
1815-   HARRIS B
1974-   HARRIS OF GREENWICH
                   B(L)
1979-   HARRIS OF HIGH CROSS
                   B(L)
1788-   MALMESBURY B
1800-   MALMESBURY E
HARROWBY
B   1776-   Ryder
E   1809-   Ryder
HARTFELL
E(S) 1643-1808X Johnstone
HARTINGTON
M   1694-   Cavendish
HARTISMERE
B   1866-   Henniker-Major
HARTLAND
B(I) 1800-1845X Mahon
HARTSIDE
L(S) 1651-1761X Douglas
HARTWELL
B(L) 1968-   Berry
HARVEY OF PRESTBURY
B(L) 1971-   Harvey
HARVEY OF TASBURGH
B   1954-   Harvey
Harvey
1971-   HARVEY OF PRESTBURY
                   B(L)
1954-   HARVEY OF TASBURGH
                   B(L)
Harvie-Anderson
1979-1979X SKRIMSHIRE OF QUARTER
           Bss(L)
HARVINGTON
B(L) 1974-   Grant-Ferris
HARWICH
M   1689-1719X Schomberg
V   1730-1756X Mildmay
B   1756-   Hill

HASTANG
B   1311-1342A Hastang
Hastang
1311-1342A HASTANG B
HASTINGS
B   1264-   Hastings
M   1816-1868X Rawdon-Hastings
HASTINGS OF GRESSINGHALL
B   1342-1359X Hastings
HASTINGS OF HASTINGS
B   1461-1960A Hastings
HASTINGS OF LOUGHBOROUGH
B   1558-1558X Hastings
B   1643-1666X Hastings
HASTINGS OF MENTEITH
B   1299-1313X Hastings
Hastings
1272-1391X ABERGAVENNY B
1264-.   HASTINGS B
1342-1359X HASTINGS OF GRESSING-
           HALL B
1461-1960A HASTINGS OF HASTINGS B
1558-1558X HASTINGS OF LOUGH-
           BOROUGH B
1643-1666X HASTINGS OF LOUGH-
           BOROUGH B
1299-1313X HASTINGS OF MENTEITH B
1529-   HUNTINGDON E
1339-1391X PEMBROKE E
1468-1503X WELLES B
See also: Clifton-Hastings-
          Campbell
HATCH OF LUSBY
B(L) 1978-   Hatch
Hatch
1978-   HATCH OF LUSBY B(L)
HATHERLEY
B   1868-1881X Wood
HATHERTON
B   1835-   Littleton
HATTON
B   1642-1762X Hatton
V   1682-1762X Hatton
Hatton
1642-1762X HATTON B
1682-1762X HATTON V
HAUSTED
B   1332-1332X Hausted
Hausted
1332-1332X HAUSTED B

74

HAVERSHAM
B   1696-1745X Thompson
B   1906-1917X Hayter
HAWARDEN
V(I) 1791-   Maude
HAWKE
B   1776-   Hawke
Hawke
1776-   HAWKE B
HAWKESBURY
B   1786-1851X Jenkinson
B   1893-   Foljambe
V   1905-   Foljambe
Hawkins
1899-1907X BRAMPTON B
HAWLEY
B(I) 1646-1790X Hawley
Hawley
1646-1790X DONAMORE B(I)
1646-1790X HAWLEY B(I)
HAY
L(S) 1449-1453M Hay
HAY OF KINFAUNS
L(S) 1627-   Hay
B   1711-   Hay
HAY OF SALVLEY
B   1615-1660X Hay
HAY OF YESTER
L(S) 1488-   Hay
Hay
1609-1660X BEWLIE L(S)
1622-1660X CARLISLE E
1618-1660X DONCASTER B
1627-   DUPPLIN V(S)
1452-   ERROLL E(S)
1694-   GIFFORD E(S)
1449-1453M HAY L(S)
1627-   HAY OF KINFAUNS L(S)
1711-   HAY OF KINFAUNS B
1615-1660X HAY OF SALVLEY B
1488-   HAY OF YESTER L(S)
1633-   KINNOULL E(S)
1633-   KINNOULL V(S)
1452-   SLAINS L(S)
1646-   TWEEDDALE E(S)
1694-   TWEEDDALE M(S)
1881-   TWEEDDALE B
1694-   WALDEN V(S)
HAYTER
B   1927-   Chubb

* See also Addenda

Hayter
1906-1917X HAVERSHAM B
HAZLERIGG
B   1945-   Hazlerigg
Hazlerigg
1945-   HAZLERIGG B
HEAD
V   1960-   Head
Head
1960-   HEAD V
HEADFORT
B(I) 1760-   Taylour
V(I) 1762-   Taylour
M(I) 1800-   Taylour
HEADLEY
B(I) 1797-   Allanson-Winn
Heathcoat-Amory: See Amory
Heathcote
1856-   AVELAND B
Heathcote-Drummond-Willoughby
1892-   ANCASTER E
HEATHFIELD
B   1787-1813X Elliot
HEDINGTON
B   1676-   Beauclerk
HEDON
B   1742-1764X Pulteney
HELMSLEY
V   1868-1963X Duncombe
HELSBY
B(L) 1968-1978X Helsby
Helsby
1968-1978X HELSBY B(L)
Hely-Hutchinson
1783-   DONOUGHMORE B(I)
1797-   DONOUGHMORE V(I)
1801-   DONOUGHMORE E(I)
1821-   HUTCHINSON V
HEMINGFORD
B   1943-   Herbert
HEMPHILL
B   1906-   Martyn-Hemphill
HENDERSON   *
B   1945-1984X Henderson
HENDERSON OF ARDWICK
B   1950-1950X Henderson
Henderson
1916-   FARINGDON B
1945-1984X HENDERSON B
1950-1950X HENDERSON OF ARDWICK B
1966-1968X ROWLEY B(L)

75

HENEAGE
  B   1896-1967X Heneage
Heneage
  1896-1967X HENEAGE B
HENLEY
  B   1760-1786X Henley
  B(I) 1799-   Eden
Henley
  1760-1786X HENLEY B
Henly
  1764-1786X NORTHINGTON E
Hennessy
  1937-   WINDLESHAM B
HENNIKER
  B(I) 1800-   Henniker-Major
Henniker-Major
  1866-   HARTISMERE B
  1800-   HENNIKER B(I)
Henry, Prince of Scotland
  1139-1152X NORTHUMBERLAND E
Hepburn
  1488-1567F BOTHWELL E(S)
  1567-1575F FIFE M(S)
  1467-1575X HALES L(S)
  1567-1567F ORKNEY D(S)
  See also: Buchan-Hepburn
Hepburne-Scott
  1450-   POLWARTH L(S)
HERBERT
  B(I) 1624-1801X Herbert
HERBERT OF CARDIFF
  B   1551-   Herbert
HERBERT OF HERBERT, & OF RAGLAND,
  CHEPSTOW & GOWER
  B   1461-1506X Herbert
  B   1506-   Somerset
HERBERT OF CHIRBURY
  B   1629-1691X Herbert
  B   1694-1738X Herbert
HERBERT OF CHIRBURY & LUDLOW
  B   1743-1801X Herbert
  B   1804-   Clive
HERBERT OF LEA
  B   1861-   Herbert
HERBERT OF SHURLAND
  B   1605-   Herbert
Herbert
  1793-   CARNARVON E
  1943-   HEMINGFORD B
  1624-1801X HERBERT B(I)
  1551-   HERBERT OF CARDIFF B

Herbert (Cont'd)
  1629-1691X HERBERT OF CHIRBURY B
  1694-1738X HERBERT OF CHIRBURY B
  1743-1801X HERBERT OF CHIRBURY &
     LUDLOW B
  1461-1506X HERBERT OF HERBERT, & OF
     RAGLAND, CHEPSTOW &
     GOWER
  1861-   HERBERT OF LEA B
  1605-   HERBERT OF SHURLAND B
  1479-1487X HUNTINGDON E
  1748-1801X LUDLOW V
  1605-   MONTGOMERY E
  1468-1472S PEMBROKE E
  1551-   PEMBROKE E
  1780-   PORCHESTER B
  1629-1748X POWIS B
  1674-1748X POWIS E
  1687-1748X POWIS M
  1748-1801X POWIS B
  1748-1801X POWIS E
  1963-1973X TANGLEY B(L)
  1689-1716X TORRINGTON E
  1917-1933X TREOWEN B
HEREFORD
  E   1066/87-1074X Fitzosborne
  E   1199-1372X Bohun, De
  E   1140-1154X Milo de Gloucester
  D   1397-1399M Plantagenet
  V   1550-   Devereux
HERMITAGE
  V(S) 1706-1807X Scott
Hermon-Hodge
  1919-   WYFOLD B
HERON
  B   1199/1216-1296X Heron
  B   1371-....X Heron
  B   1393-1404X Heron
Heron
  1199/1216-1296X HERON B
  1371-....X HERON B
  1393-1404X HERON B
HERRIES
  B   1884-1908X Constable-Maxwell
HERRIES OF TERREGLES
  L(S) 1490-   Fitzalan-Howard
HERSCHELL
  B   1886-   Herschell
Herschell
  1886-   HERSCHELL B

HERTFORD
E   1135/54-1313X Clare
E   1537-1552F Seymour
E   1559-1750X Seymour
M   1640-1750X Seymour
E   1750-   Seymour
M   1793-   Seymour
  See also: GLOUCESTER & HERTFORD
HERVEY
  B(I) 1620-1642X Hervey
  B   1628-1642X Hervey
HERVEY OF ICKWORTH
  B   1703-   Hervey
Hervey
  1714-   BRISTOL E
  1826-   BRISTOL M
  1620-1642X HERVEY B(I)
  1628-1642X HERVEY B
  1703-   HERVEY OF ICKWORTH B
  1820-   JERMYN E
HESKETH
  B   1935-   Fermor-Hesketh
HEWART
  B   1922-1964X Hewart
  V   1922-1964X Hewart
Hewart
  1922-1964X HEWART B
  1922-1964X HEWART V
HEWETT
  V(I) 1689-1689X Hewett
Hewett
  1689-1689X HEWETT V(I)
  1689-1689X JAMESTOWN B
Hewitt
  1768-   LIFFORD B(I)
  1781-   LIFFORD V(I)
HEWLETT
  B(L) 1972-   Hewlett
Hewlett
  1972-   HEWLETT B(L)
HEYCOCK
  B(L) 1967-   Heycock
Heycock
  1967-   HEYCOCK B(L)

HEYTESBURY
  B   1828-   Holmes à Court
HEYWORTH
  B   1955-1974X Heyworth
Heyworth
  1955-1974X HEYWORTH B

Hibbert: See Holland-Hibbert
HICKS
  B   1628-1798X Hicks
Hicks
  1628-1629X CAMPDEN V
  1628-1798X HICKS B
  See also: Joynson-Hicks
Hicks-Beach
  1915-   QUENINGTON V
  1906-   ST ALDWYN V
  1906-   ST ALDWYN E
HIGHAM
  V   1734-1782X Wentworth
HILL
  B(I) 1717-   Hill
  B   1814-1842X Hill
  B   1816-   Hill
  V   1842-   Hill
HILL OF LUTON
  B(L) 1963-   Hill
HILL OF WIVENHOE
  B(L) 1967-1969X Hill
Hill
  1784-1953X BERWICK B
  1789-   DOWNSHIRE M(I)
  1772-   FAIRFORD V
  1756-   HARWICH B
  1717-   HILL B(I)
  1814-1842X HILL B
  1816-   HILL B
  1842-   HILL V
  1963-   HILL OF LUTON B(L)
  1967-1969X HILL OF WIVENHOE B(L)
  1717-   HILLSBOROUGH V(I)
  1751-   HILLSBOROUGH E(I)
  1772-   HILLSBOROUGH E
  1751-   KILWARLIN V(I)
  1802-   SANDYS B
HILLHOUSE
  L(S) 1665-1810X Hamilton
HILLINGDON
  B   1886-1982X Mills
HILL-NORTON
  B(L) 1979-   Hill-Norton
Hill-Norton
  1979-   HILL-NORTON B(L)
HILLSBOROUGH
  V(I) 1717-   Hill
  E(I) 1751-   Hill
  E   1772-   Hill
Hill-Trevor
  1880-   TREVOR B

HILTON
　B　1295-1297A Hilton
　B　1332-1716F Hilton
HILTON OF UPTON
　B(L) 1965-1977X Hilton
Hilton
　1295-1297A HILTON B
　1332-1716F HILTON B
　1965-1967X HILTON OF UPTON B(L)
HINCHINGBROKE
　V　1660-　　Montagu
Hindley
　1931-1963X HYNDLEY B
　1948-1963X HYNDLEY V
HINDLIP
　B　1886-　　Allsopp
HINTON
　V　1706-1973X Poulett
HINTON OF BANKSIDE
　B(L) 1965-1983X Hinton
Hinton
　1965-1983X HINTON OF BANKSIDE B(L)
HIRSHFIELD
　B(L) 1967-　　Hirshfield
Hirshfield
　1967-　　HIRSHFIELD B(L)
HIRST
　B　1934-1943X Hirst
Hirst
　1934-1943X HIRST B
HIVES
　B　1950-　　Hives
Hives
　1950-　　HIVES B
Hoare
　1944-1959X TEMPLEWOOD V
HOBART
　B　1728-　　Hobart
Hobart
　1746-　　BUCKINGHAMSHIRE E
　1728-　　HOBART B
HOBHOUSE
　B　1885-1904X Hobhouse
Hobhouse
　1851-1869X BROUGHTON B
　1885-1904X HOBHOUSE B
HOBSON
　B(L) 1963-1966X Hobson
Hobson
　1963-1966X HOBSON B(L)
Hodge: See Hermon-Hodge

HODSON
　B(L) 1960-　　Hodson
Hodson
　1960-　　HODSON B(L)
HOESE
　B　1154/89-1272/1307X Hoese, De
　B　1295-1349X Hoese, De
　B　1348-1361X Hoese
Hoese, De
　1154/89-1272/1307X HOESE B
Hoese
　1348-1361X HOESE B
Hogg　　　　　　　　　　*
　1928-　　HAILSHAM B
　1929-　　HAILSHAM V
　1970-　　HAILSHAM OF ST MARYLE-
　　　　　　　BONE B(L)
HOLDEN
　B　1908-1951X Holden
Holden
　1908-1951X HOLDEN B
HOLDERNESS
　E　1621-1625X Ramsay
　E　1644-1682X Rupert
　E　1682-1778X Darcy
　B(L) 1979-　　Wood
HOLFORD
　B(L) 1965-1975X Holford
Holford
　1965-1975X HOLFORD B(L)
HOLLAND
　B　1314-1373C Holland
　B　1373-1487F Lovel
　B　1353-1407A Holland
HOLLAND OF ENMORE
　B　1762-　　Perceval
HOLLAND OF HOLLAND
　B　1624-1759X Rich
　B　1762-1859X Fox
　See also: BREADALBANE & HOLLAND
　See also: LOVEL & HOLLAND
Holland
　1397-1400F EXETER D
　1443-1461F EXETER D
　1314-1373C HOLLAND B
　1353-1407A HOLLAND B
　1387-1461F HUNTINGDON E
　1360-1407X KENT E
　1910-1950X ROTHERHAM B
　1397-1400X SURREY D
　1320-1407A WOODSTOCK B

　　　* See also Addenda

78

Holland-Hibbert
  1888-   KNUTSFORD B
  1895-   KNUTSFORD V
HOLLENDEN
  B   1912-   Hope-Morley
HOLLES
  B   1661-1694X Holles
Holles
  1624-1711X CLARE E
  1689-1711X CLARE M
  1714-1768X CLARE E
  1661-1694X HOLLES B
  1616-1711X HOUGHTON B
  1694-1711X NEWCASTLE D
  1715-1768X NEWCASTLE D
  1756-   NEWCASTLE-UNDER-LYME D
  1706-1768X PELHAM B
HOLMES
  B(I) 1760-1764X Holmes
  B(I) 1797-1804X Holmes
Holmes
  1954-1961X DOVERCOURT B
  1760-1764X HOLMES B(I)
  1797-1804X HOLMES B(I)
Holmes a Court
  1828-   HEYTESBURY B
HOLMESDALE
  V   1826-   Amherst
HOLM PATRICK
  B   1897-   Hamilton
Holroyd
  1816-1909X PEVENSEY V
  1783-   SHEFFIELD B(I)
  1781-1909X SHEFFIELD B(I)
  1802-1909X SHEFFIELD B
  1816-1909X SHEFFIELD E
HOLYROODHOUSE
  L(S) 1607-1635D Bothwell
HOME
  L(S) 1473-   Home
  E(S) 1605-   Douglas-Home
HOME OF THE HIRSEL
  B(L) 1974-   Douglas-Home
Home
  1605-1611X DUNBAR E(S)
  1473-   HOME L(S)
  See also: Douglas-Home
HOO
  B   1447-1454X Hoo
  B   1691-1691M Villiers
Hoo
  1447-1454X HOO B

HOOD
  B(I) 1782-   Hood
  B   1795-   Hood
  V   1796-   Hood
HOOD OF AVALON
  B   1892-1901X Hood
Hood
  1794-   BRIDPORT B(I)
  1796-1814X BRIDPORT B
  1801-1814X BRIDPORT V
  1868-   BRIDPORT V
  1782-   HOOD B(I)
  1795-   HOOD B
  1796-   HOOD V
  1892-1901X HOOD OF AVALON B
  See also: Fuller-Acland-Hood
HOOSON
  B(L) 1979-   Hooson
Hooson
  1979-   HOOSON B(L)
HOPE
  L(S) 1703-   Hope
Hope
  1703-   AITHRIE V(S)
  1964-   GLENDEVON B
  1703-   HOPE L(S)
  1703-   HOPETOUN L(S)
  1703-   HOPETOUN E(S)
  1809-   HOPETOUN B
  1902-   LINLITHGOW M
  1814-   NIDDRY B
  1932-   RANKEILLOUR B
Hope-Morley
  1912-   HOLLENDEN B
HOPETOUN
  L(S) 1703-   Hope
  E(S) 1703-   Hope
  B   1809-   Hope
Hopkinson
  1956-   COLYTON B
HOPTON
  B   1643-1652X Hopton
Hopton
  1643-1652X HOPTON B
Hopwood
  1917-   SOUTHBOROUGH B
HORDER
  B   1933-   Horder
Horder
  1933-   HORDER B
HORE-BELISHA
  B   1954-1957X Hore-Belisha

79

Hore-Belisha
  1954-1957X HORE-BELISHA B
HORNE
  B   1919-1929X Horne
HORNE OF SLAMANNAN
  V   1937-1940X Horne
Horne
  1919-1929X HORNE B
  1937-1940X HORNE OF SLAMANNAN V
HORNSBY-SMITH
  Bss(L) 1974-   Hornsby-Smith
Hornsby-Smith
  1974-   HORNSBY-SMITH Bss(L)
HORSBRUGH
  Bss(L) 1959-1969X Horsbrugh
Horsbrugh
  1959-1969X HORSBRUGH Bss(L)
HOTHAM
  B(I) 1797-   Hotham
Hotham
  1797-   HOTHAM B(I)
HOTHFIELD
  B   1881-   Tufton
HOUGHTON
  B   1616-1711X Holles
  B   1742-1797X Walpole
  B   1863-1945X Crewe-Milnes
HOUGHTON OF SOWERBY
  B(L) 1974-   Houghton
Houghton
  1974-   HOUGHTON OF SOWERBY B(L)
HOWARD
  B   1470-1777A Howard
HOWARD OF BINDON
  V   1559-1610X Howard
HOWARD OF CASTLE RISING
  B   1669-1777X Howard
HOWARD OF CHARLTON
  B   1622-   Howard
HOWARD OF EFFINGHAM
  B   1554-   Howard
HOWARD OF ESCRICK
  B   1628-1715X Howard
HOWARD OF GLOSSOP
  B   1869-   Fitzalan-Howard
HOWARD OF HENDERSKELFE
  B(L) 1983-1984X Howard
HOWARD OF MARNHULL
  B   1604-1614X Howard
HOWARD OF MORPETH
  V   1661-   Howard
HOWARD OF PENRITH
  B   1930-   Howard

HOWARD DE WALDEN
  B   1597-   Howard
  B   1826-   Howard
Howard
  1625-   ANDOVER V
  1626-   BERKSHIRE E
  1559-1691X BINDON V
  1706-1722X BINDON E
  1661-   CARLISLE E
  1706-1722X CHESTERFORD B
  1627-   CLUN B
  1661-   DACRE OF GILLESLAND B
  1731-1816X EFFINGHAM E
  1837-   EFFINGHAM E
  1627-   FITZALAN B
  1677-1777A FURNIVAL B
  1470-1777A HOWARD B
  1559-1610X HOWARD OF BINDON V
  1669-1777X HOWARD OF CASTLE
           RISING B
  1622-   HOWARD OF CHARLTON B
  1554-   HOWARD OF EFFINGHAM B
  1628-1715X HOWARD OF ESCRICK B
  1983-1984X HOWARD OF HENDERSKELFE
           B(L)
  1604-1614X HOWARD OF MARNHULL B
  1661-   HOWARD OF MORPETH V
  1930-   HOWARD OF PENRITH B
  1597-   HOWARD DE WALDEN B
  1826-   HOWARD DE WALDEN B
  1874-1880X LANERTON B
  1556-   MALTRAVERS B
  1483-   NORFOLK D
  1644-   NORFOLK E
  1604-1614X NORTHAMPTON E
  1672-1777X NORWICH E
  1597-1681X NOTTINGHAM E
  1627-   OSWALDESTRE B
  1640-1678F STAFFORD V
  1688-1693X STAFFORD Css
  1688-1762X STAFFORD B
  1603-   SUFFOLK E
  1483-   SURREY E
  See also: Fitzalan-Howard
  See also: Forward-Howard
HOWDEN
  B(I) 1819-1873X Cradock
  B   1831-1873X Cradock
HOWE
  V(I) 1701-1814X Howe
  V   1782-1799X Howe
  E   1788-1799X Howe

HOWE
B   1788-   Curzon
E   1821-   Curzon
Howe
1741-1804X CHEDWORTH B
1701-1814X GLENAWLEY B(I)
1701-1814X HOWE V(I)
1782-1799X HOWE V
1788-1799X HOWE E
HOWICK
V   1806-1806M Grey
HOWICK OF GLENDALE
B   1960-   Baring
HOWIE OF TROON
B(L) 1978-   Howie
Howie
1978-   HOWIE OF TROON B(L)
HOWLAND
B   1695-   Russell
HOWTH
B(I) 1461-1909X St Lawrence
E(I) 1767-1909X St Lawrence
B   1881-1909X St Lawrence
HOY
B(L) 1970-1976X Hoy
Hoy
1970-1976X HOY B(L)
Hozier
1898-1929X NEWLANDS B
Hubbard
1887-   ADDINGTON B
HUDSON
V   1952-1963X Hudson
Hudson
1952-1963X HUDSON V
Huggins
1955-   MALVERN V
HUGHES
B(L) 1961-   Hughes
Hughes
1979-   CLEDWYN OF PENRHOS B(L)
1831-1852X DINORBEN B
1961-   HUGHES B(L)
Hughes-Young
1964-   ST HELENS B
HUME
B   1604-1611X Hume
B   1776-1781X Hume
Hume
1604-1611X HUME B
1776-1781X HUME B
1697-1794D MARCHMONT E(S)

HUNGARTON
B   1951-1966X Crawford
HUNGERFORD
B   1426-1463X Hungerford
B   1482-   Hungerford
HUNGERFORD OF HEYTESBURY
B   1536-1541X Hungerford
Hungerford
1426-1463X HUNGERFORD B
1482-   HUNGERFORD B
1536-1541X HUNGERFORD OF HEYTES-
             BURY B
1445-   MOLINES B
HUNSDON
B   1559-1765X Carey
B   1832-1884X Cary
HUNSDON OF HUNSDON
B   1923-   Gibbs
HUNT
B(L) 1966-   Hunt
HUNT OF FAWLEY
B(L) 1973-   Hunt
HUNT OF TANWORTH
B(L) 1980-   Hunt
Hunt
1966-   HUNT B(L)
1973-   HUNT OF FAWLEY B(L)
1980-   HUNT OF TANWORTH B(L)
See also: Crowther-Hunt
HUNTER OF NEWINGTON
B(L) 1978-   Hunter
Hunter
1978-   HUNTER OF NEWINGTON B(L)
HUNTERCOMBE
B   1295-1312X Huntercombe
Huntercombe
1295-1312X HUNTERCOMBE B
HUNTINGDON
E   1068-1237M St Liz
E   1337-1354X Clinton, De
E   1387-1461F Holland
E   1471-1475R Grey
E   1479-1487X Herbert
E   1529-   Hastings
HUNTINGFIELD
B   1199/1216-1272/1307L Huntingfield
B   1351-1377X Huntingfield
B   1362-1362X Huntingfield
B(I) 1796-   Vanneck
Huntingfield
1199/1216-1272/1307L HUNTINGFIELD B
1351-1377X HUNTINGFIELD B
1362-1362X HUNTINGFIELD B

HUNTINGTOWER
 L(S) 1643-   Murray
 L(S) 1670-   Murray
HUNTLEY
 E(S) 1450-   Gordon
 M(S) 1599-   Gordon
HURCOMB
 B   1950-1975X Hurcomb
Hurcomb
 1950-1975X HURCOMB B
HURD
 B(L) 1964-1966X Hurd
Hurd
 1964-1966X HURD B(L)
HUSSEY
 B   1529-1536F Hussey
Hussey
 1529-1536F HUSSEY B
Hussey Montagu
 1762-1802X BEAULIEU B
 1784-1802X BEAULIEU E
HUTCHINSON
 B   1801-1832X Hutchinson
 V   1821-   Hely-Hutchinson
HUTCHINSON OF LULLINGTON
 B(L) 1978-
Hutchinson
 1801-1832X HUTCHINSON B
 1978-   HUTCHINSON OF LULL-
                INGTON B(L)
 1962-1974X ILFORD B(L)
 1800-   SUIRDALE V(I)
 See also Hely-Hutchinson
HUTCHISON OF MONTROSE
 B   1932-1950X Hutchison
Hutchison
 1932-1950X HUTCHISON OF MONTROSE B
HYDE
 B   1660-1753X Hyde
 B   1756-   Villiers
HYDE OF KENILWORTH
 V   1681-1753X Hyde
HYDE OF WOTTON BASSET
 B   1681-1753X Hyde
Hyde
 1771-1723X CLARENDON E
 1661-1753X CORNBURY V
 1660-1753X HYDE B
 1681-1753X HYDE OF KENILWORTH V
 1681-1753X HYDE OF WO
 1682-1753X ROCHESTER
 1681-1753X WOTTON BASSET B

HYLTON
 B   1866-   Jolliffe
HYLTON-FOSTER
 Bss(L) 1965-   Hylton-Foster
Hylton-Foster
 1965-   HYLTON-FOSTER Bss(L)
HYNDFORD
 E(S) 1701-1817X Carmichael
HYNDLEY
 B   1931-1963X Hindley
 V   1948-1963X Hindley
HYTHE
 V   1911-1919X Brassey

(TITLES are in CAPITALS
Surnames in smalls)

82

```
IBRACKAN                              INGRAM
  B(I) 1543-1774X Wyndham-O'Brien       L(S) 1661-1778X Ingram
IDDESLEIGH                            Ingram
  E    1885-       Northcote            1661-1778X INGRAM L(S)
IKERRIN                                1661-1778X IRVINE V(S)
  V(I) 1629-       Butler             INGROW
ILAY                                   B(L) 1982-       Taylor
  E(S) 1706-1761X Campbell
  V(S) 1706-1761X Campbell
ILCHESTER                            INMAN
  B    1741-       Fox-Strangways       B    1946-1979X Inman
  B    1747-       Fox-Strangways     Inman
  E    1756-       Fox-Strangways       1946-1979X INMAN B
ILCHESTER & STAVORDALE               INNERDALE: See AVEN & INNERDALE
  B    1747-       Fox-Strangways     INNES
ILFORD                                 E    1837-       Innes
  B    1962-1974X Hutchinson         Innes
ILIFFE                                 1837-       INNES E
  B    1933-       Iliffe            Inskip
Iliffe                                 1939-       CALDECOTE V
  1933-       ILIFFE B               INVERARAY, MULL, MORVERN & TIRY
ILKESTON                               L(S) 1701-       Campbell
  B    1910-1952X Foster            INVERBERVIE
ILLINGWORTH                            L(S) 1641-       Arbuthnott
  B    1921-1942X Illingworth       INVERCHAPEL
Illingworth                            B    1946-1951X Kerr Clark Kerr
  1921-1942X ILLINGWORTH B          INVERCLYDE
INCHCAPE                               B    1897-1957X Burns
  B    1911-       Mackay           INVERFORTH
  V    1924-       Mackay             B    1919-       Weir
  E    1929-       Mackay           INVERKEITHING
INCHIQUIN                              L(S) 1660-       Scrymgeour
  B(I) 1543-       O'Brien            L(S) 1703-       Primrose
  E    1654-1855X O'Brien          INVERNAIRN
INCHMARNOCK: See MOUNT STUART,         B    1921-1936X Beardmore
CUMRAE & INCHMARNOCK               INVERNESS                         *
INCHYRA                                V(S) 1684-1836X Gordon
  B    1962-       Millar            E(I) 1801-1843X Guelph
INGESTRE                               Dss  1840-1873X Underwood
  V    1784-       Chetwynd-Talbot    E    1920-1936M Windsor
INGHAM                               INVERURIE
  B    1328-1344A Ingham             L(S) 1677-       Keith
Ingham                               Ipre
  1328-1344A INGHAM B                 1141-1163X KENT E
INGLEBY                              IPSWICH
  V    1956-       Peake              V    1672-       FitzRoy
INGLEWOOD                            Irby
  B    1964-       Fletcher-Vane      1761-       BOSTON B
INGLISBERRY & NEMPHLAR              IRELAND
  V(S) 1701-1817X Carmichael         D(I) 1386-1388F Vere
INGLISMALDIE                         IRNHAM
  L(S) 1639-       Carnegie           B(I) 1768-1829X Luttrell

                          83         *See also Addenda
```

```
IRONSIDE                              JACKSON
   B    1941-      Ironside              B    1945-1954X Jackson
Ironside                              JACKSON OF BURNLEY
   1941-      IRONSIDE B                 B(L) 1967-1970X Jackson
IRVINE                                JACKSON OF LODSWORTH
   E(S) 1642-1660X Campbell             Bss(L) 1976-1981X Jackson
   V(S) 1661-1778X Ingram            Jackson
IRVING OF DARTFORD                      1902-      ALLERTON B
   B(L) 1979-      Irving              1945-1954X JACKSON B
Irving                                 1967-1970X JACKSON OF BURNLEY B(L)
   1979-      IRVING OF DARTFORD B(L)   1976-1981X JACKSON OF LODSWORTH
IRWIN                                            Bss(L)
   B    1925-      Wood              JACOBSON
Isaacs                                  B(L) 1975-      Jacobson
   1917-      ERLEIGH V              Jacobson
   1914-      READING B                1975-      JACOBSON B(L)
   1916-      READING V              JACQUES
   1917-      READING E                B(L) 1968-      Jacques
   1926-      READING M              Jacques
   1958-1971X SWANBOROUGH Bss(L)       1968-      JACQUES B(L)
ISLES, THE                            JAMES OF HEREFORD
   L(S) 1476-1493S Macdonald            B    1895-1911X James
   L(S) 1488/1513-     Stewart        JAMES OF RUSHOLME
ISLINGTON                               B(L) 1959-      James
   B    1910-1936X Dickson-Poynder   James
ISMAY                                    1895-1911X JAMES OF HEREFORD B
   B    1947-1965X Ismay               1959-      JAMES OF RUSHOLME
Ismay                                            B(L)
   1947-1965X ISMAY B                   1884-      NORTHBOURNE B
IVEAGH                                  1977-      SAINT BRIDES B(L)
   V(I) 1623-1693X Magennis          JAMESTOWN
   B    1891-      Guinness            B    1689-1689X Hewett
   V    1905-      Guinness          JANNER
   E    1919-      Guinness            B(L) 1970-1982X Janner
                                     Janner
                                        1970-1982X JANNER B(L)
                                     Jebb
                                        1960-      GLADWYN B
                                     JEDBURGH
                                        L(S) 1622-      Kerr
                                     JEDBURGH FOREST
                                        V(S) 1703-1761X Douglas
                                        See also: ABERNETHY & JEDBURGH
                                                  FOREST
                                     JEFFERYS
                                        B    1685-1703X Jefferys
            (TITLES are in CAPITALS   Jefferys
             Surnames in smalls)        1685-1703X JEFFERYS B
                                     JEFFREYS
                                        B    1952-      Jeffreys
                                     Jeffreys
                                        1952-      JEFFREYS B
                        84
```

JEGER
  Bss(L) 1979-   Jeger
Jeger
  1979-   JEGER Bss(L)
JELLICOE
  V   1917-   Jellicoe
  E   1925-   Jellicoe
Jellicoe
  1925-   BROCAS V
  1917-   JELLICOE V
  1925-   JELLICOE E
JENKINS
  B(L) 1959-1969X Jenkins
  B(L) 1981-   Jenkins
Jenkins
  1906-1915X GLANTAWE B
  1959-1969X JENKINS B(L)
  1981-   JENKINS B(L)
Jenkinson   *
  1796-1851X LIVERPOOL E
JERMYN
  B   1643-1703X Jermyn
  B   1685-1708X Jermyn
  E   1826-   Jermyn
Jermyn
  1685-1703M DOVER B
  1643-1703X JERMYN B
  1685-1708X JERMYN B
  1660-1683X ST ALBANS E
JERSEY
  E   1697-   Child-Villiers
JERVIS
  B   1797-1820X Jervis
Jervis
  1797-1820X JERVIS B
  1797-1823X ST VINCENT E
  1801-   ST VINCENT V
JESSEL
  B   1924-   Jessel
Jessel
  1924-   JESSEL B
Jeune
  1905-1905X ST HELIER B
JOCELYN
  V(I) 1755-   Jocelyn
Jocelyn
  1821-1897X CLANBRASSIL B
  1755-   JOCELYN V(I)
  1743-   NEWPORT B(I)
  1771-   RODEN E(I)
JOHN-MACKIE
  B(L) 1981-   Mackie

Johnson: See Webb-Johnson
Johnston: See Lawson-Johnston
JOHNSTONE
  L(S) 1633-1792X Johnstone
Johnstone
  1661-1792X ANNAND V(S)
  1701-1792A ANNANDALE M(S)
  1643-1808X HARTFELL E(S)
  1661-1808X HARTFELL E(S)
  1633-1792X JOHNSTONE L(S)
JOICEY
  B   1906-   Joicey
Joicey
  1906-   JOICEY B
Jolliffe
  1866-   HYLTON B
Jones
  1974-   ELWYN-JONES B(L)
  1966-1984X MAELOR B(L)
  1628-1885X NAVAN B(I)
  1628-1885X RANELAGH V(I)
  1674-1711X RANELAGH E(I)
  See also: Armstrong-Jones
  See also: Gwynne Jones
  See also: Leif-Jones
  See also: Wynne-Jones
Jones-Lloyd
  1850-   OVERSTONE B
JOWITT
  B   1945-1957X Jowitt
  V   1947-1957X Jowitt
  E   1951-1957X Jowitt
Jowitt
  1945-1957X JOWITT B
  1947-1957X JOWITT V
  1951-1957X JOWITT E
Joynson-Hicks
  1929-   BRENTFORD V
Juliers, De
  1340-1361X CAMBRIDGE E

* See also Addenda

(TITLES are in CAPITALS
  Surnames in smalls)

85

KABERRY OF ADEL
  B(L) 1983-   Kaberry
Kaberry
  1983-   KABERRY OF ADEL B(L)
KADOORIE
  B(L) 1981-   Kadoorie
Kadoorie
  1981-   KADOORIE B(L)
KAGAN
  B(L) 1976-   Kagan
Kagan
  1976-   KAGAN B(L)
KAHN
  B(L) 1965-   Kahn
Kahn
  1965-   KAHN B(L)
KALDOR
  B(L) 1974-   Kaldor
Kaldor
  1974-   KALDOR B(L)
Kavanagh
  1554-1555L BALLYANE B(I)
  1554-....L COWELELYENE B(I)
Kay-Shuttleworth
  1902-   SHUTTLEWORTH B
KEANE
  B   1839-1901X Keane
Keane
  1839-1901X KEANE B
Kearley
  1910-   DEVONPORT B
  1917-   DEVONPORT V
KEARTON
  B(L) 1970-   Kearton
Kearton
  1970-   KEARTON B(L)
KEDLESTON
  E   1921-1925X Curzon
KEITH
  L(S) 1587-1593X Keith
  B(I) 1797-1823X Elphinstone
  B   1803-1867X Elphinstone
  B   1801-1823X Keith
  V   1814-1823X Keith
KEITH OF AVONHOLM
  B(L) 1953-1964X Keith
KEITH OF INVERURIE & KEITH HALL
  L(S) 1677-   Keith
KEITH OF KINKEL
  B(L) 1976-   Keith

Keith
  1587-1593X ALTRIE L(S)
  1584-1589X DINGWALL L(S)
  1646-1966D FALCONER L(S)
  1677-   INVERURIE L(S)
  1587-1593X KEITH L(S)
  1801-1823X KEITH B
  1814-1823X KEITH V
  1953-1964X KEITH OF AVONHOLM B(L)
  1677-   KEITH OF INVERURIE &
              KEITH HALL L(S)
  1976-   KEITH OF KINKEL B(L)
  1677-   KINTORE E(S)
  1838-1966X KINTORE B
  1458-1715F MARISCHAL E(S)
KELBURN
  V(S) 1703-   Boyle
KELHEAD
  B   1893-1894X Douglas
KELLIE
  E(S) 1619-   Erskine
  See also: HADDO, METHLIC, TARVES
              & KELLIE
KELSO
  E(S) 1707-   Ker
KELVIN
  B   1892-1907X Thomson
Kemp
  1913-   ROCHDALE B
  1960-   ROCHDALE V
KEMSLEY
  B   1936-   Berry
  V   1945-   Berry
KENDAL
  E   1414-1435X Plantagenet
  E   1418-1509X Beaufort
  E   1446-1485? Foix, De
  B   1644-1682X Rupert
  D   1666-1667X Stuart
  E   1689-1708X George, Prince of
              Denmark
  Dss 1719-1743X Schulenburg
  B   1784-1802X Lowther
KENILWORTH
  B   1937-   Siddeley
KENLIS
  B   1831-   Taylour
KENMARE
  V(I) 1689-   Browne
  E(I) 1800-   Browne
  B   1841-1853X Browne
  B   1856-1952X Browne

86

KENMURE
  V   1633-1847D Gordon
KENNEDY
  L(S) 1452-   Kennedy
Kennedy
  1806-   AILSA B
  1831-   AILSA M
  1502-   CASSILIS E(S)
  1452-   KENNEDY L(S)
KENNET
  B   1935-   Young
KENRY
  B   1866-1926X Wyndham-Quin
KENSINGTON   *
  B   1622-1759X Rich
  B(I) 1776-   Edwardes
  B   1886-   Edwardes
KENSWOOD
  B   1951-   Whitfield
KENT
  E   1067-1096X Odo
  E   1141-1163X Ipre
  E   1226-1243X Burgh
  E   1321-1352X Plantagenet
  E   1360-1407X Holland
  E   1462-1462X Nevill
  E   1465-1741X Grey
  M   1706-1741X Grey
  D   1710-1741X Grey
  D   1799-1820X Guelph
  E   1866-1900X Guelph
  D   1934-   Windsor
KENYON
  B   1788-   Kenyon
Kenyon
  1788-   CREDINGTON B
  1788-   KENYON B
KEPPEL
  V   1782-1786X Keppel
Keppel
  1696-   ALBEMARLE E
  1696-   ASHFORD B
  1696-   BURY V
  1782-1786X KEPPEL V
KER
  L(S) 1701-   Kerr
  B   1821-   Kerr
  E   1722-1804X Ker
KER OF CESSFORD & CAVERTOUN
  L(S) 1616-   Ker

    * See Addenda

Ker
  1707-   BOWMONT & CESSFORD M(S)
  1707-   BROXMOUTH V(S)
  1707-   CESSFORD M(S)
  1707-   KELSO E(S)
  1616-   KER OF CESSFORD & CAVER-
               TOUN L(S)
  1722-1804X KER E
  1600-   ROXBURGHE L(S)
  1616-   ROXBURGHE E(S)
  1707-   ROXBURGHE D(S)
  See also: Kerr
KERDESTON
  B   1332-1361A Kerdeston
Kerdeston
  1332-1361A KERDESTON B
KEREN
  V   1947-1954X Wavell
KERR
  L(S) 1633-   Kerr
Kerr
  1633-   ANCRAM E(S)
  1701-   BRIEN V(S)
  1622-   JEDBURGH L(S)
  1701-   KER L(S)
  1821-   KER B
  1633-   KERR L(S)
  1606-   LOTHIAN E(S)
  1701-   LOTHIAN M(S)
  1821-   LOTHIAN B
  1587-   NEWBOTTLE L(S)
  1940-   TEVIOT B
Kerr Clark Kerr
  1946-1951X INVERCHAPEL B
KERRY
  E(I) 1722-   Fitzmaurice
  B(I) 1264-1697X Fitzmaurice
KERSHAW
  B   1947-   Kershaw
Kershaw
  1947-   KERSHAW B
KESTEVEN
  B   1868-1915X Trollope
  See also: ANCASTER & KESTEVEN
KEYES
  B   1943-   Keyes
Keyes
  1943-   KEYES B
KEYNES
  B   1066/87-1344X Keynes, De
  B   1942-1946X Keynes

87

Keynes
1942-1946X KEYNES B
Keynes, De
1066/87-1344X KEYNES B
Kielmansegg
1722-1730X BRENTFORD Bss(L)
1722-1730X DARLINGTON Css(L)
1721-1730X LEINSTER Css(I)
KILBRACKEN
B   1909-   Godley
KILBURNIE, KINGSBURN & DRUMRY
L(S) 1703-   Lindsay
KILBRANDON
B(L) 1971-   Shaw
KILCONNEL
B(I) 1793-   Trench
KILCOURSIE
V(I) 1647-   Lambart
KILCULLEN
B(I) 1541-1585F Eustace
KILDARE
E(I) 1316-   Fitzgerald
M(I) 1761-   Fitzgerald
B   1870-   Fitzgerald
KILKENNY
B(I) 1619-   Dillon
E   1793-1846X Butler
KILLANIN
B   1900-   Morris
KILLARD
B(I) 1727-   Monckton
KILLARNEY   *
B   1920-1936M Windsor
KILLEARN
B   1943-   Lampson
KILLEEN
B(I) 1449-   Plunkett
KILLULTAGH
V(I) 1626-1683X Conway
See also: CONWAY & KILLULTAGH
KILMAINE
B(I) 1721-1774X O'Hara
B(I) 1789-   Browne
KILMANY
B(L) 1966-   Anstruther-Gray
KILMARNOCK
L(S) 1482-1746F Boyd
E(S) 1661-1746F Boyd
B   1831-   Boyd
KILMAURS
L(S) 1450-1796D Cunynghame
KILMAYDAN
B(I) 1703-1767X St Leger

KILMOREY
V(I) 1625-   Needham
E(I) 1822-   Needham
KILMUIR
B   1954-1967X Fyfe
E   1962-1967X Fyfe
KILPATRICK: See PAISLEY, HAMILTON,
MOUNTCASTELL & KILPATRICK
KILPEC
B   1154/89-1207X Kilpec, De
Kilpec, De
1154/89-1207X KILPEC B
KILSYTH
V(S) 1661-1715F Livingston
KILTARTON
B(I) 1810-   Prendergast-Smyth
KILWARDEN
B(I) 1795-1830X Wolfe
V(I) 1800-1830X Wolfe
B   1798-1830X Wolfe
KILWARLIN
V(I) 1751-   Hill
KILWINNING
L(S) 1614-1636X Balfour
KILWORTH
B(I) 1764-1915X Moore
KIMBERLEY
B   1797-   Wodehouse
E   1866-   Wodehouse
KINALMEAKY
V(I) 1628-   Boyle
KINCARDINE
E(S) 1647-   Bruce
E(S) 1707-   Graham
KINCLEVIN
L(S) 1607-1652X Stewart
KINDERSLEY
B   1941-   Kindersley
Kindersley
1941-   KINDERSLEY B
KING
B   1725-   King
KING OF WARTNABY
B(L) 1983-   King
King   *
1800-   ERRIS B(I)
1642-1647X EYTHEN L(S)
1725-   KING B
1983-   KING OF WARTNABY B(L)
1748-1755X KINGSBOROUGH B(I)
1766-   KINGSBOROUGH V
1821-1869X KINGSTON OF MITCHELS-
                    TOWN B

* See also Addenda

King (Cont'd)
```
  1806-     LORTON V(I)
  1838-     LOVELACE E
  1725-     OCKHAM B
  1838-     OCKHAM V
  See also: Maybray-King
```
KINGARTH
```
  V(S) 1703-     Stuart
```
KING-HALL
```
  B(L) 1966-1966X King-Hall
```
King-Hall
```
  1966-1966X KING-HALL B(L)
```
KINGHORNE
```
  E(S) 1606-     Lyon
  See also: STRATHMORE & KINGHORNE
```
KINGSALE
```
  B(I) 1223-     Coucy, De
  V(I) 1624-1691F Sarsfield
```
KINGSBOROUGH
```
  B(I) 1748-1755X King
  V    1766-     King
```
KINGSBURN: See KILBURNIE, KINGSBURN
  & DRUMRY
KINGSDOWN
```
  B    1858-1867X Pemberton-Leigh
```
KINGSLAND
```
  V    1646-1833D Barnewall
```
KINGS NORTON
```
  B(L) 1965-     Roxbee Cox
```
KINGSTON
```
  E    1628-1680X Pierrepont
  V(S) 1650-1715F Seton
  B    1660-1761X King
  D    1715-1773X Pierrepont
  B(I) 1764-     King
  V(I) 1766-     King
  E(I) 1768-     King
```
KINGSTON OF MITCHELSTOWN
```
  B    1821-1869X King
```
KINGSTON-UPON-THAMES
```
  B    1621-1625X Ramsay
```
KINLOSS
```
  L(S) 1602-     Bruce
```
KINNAIRD
```
  V(S) 1660-     Livingston
  L(S) 1682-     Kinnaird
  B    1860-     Kinnaird
```
Kinnaird
```
  1682-        KINNAIRD L(S)
  1860-        KINNAIRD B
  1831-1878X ROSSIE B
```

KINNEAR
```
  B    1897-1917X Kinnear
```
Kinnear
```
  1897-1917X KINNEAR B
```
KINNOULL
```
  V(S) 1633-     Hay
  E(S) 1633-     Hay
```
KINRARA
```
  E    1876-     Gordon-Lennox
```
KINROSS
```
  B    1902-     Balfour
```
KINTORE
```
  E(S) 1677-     Keith
  B    1838-1966X Keith
```
KINTYRE
```
  L(S) 1626-1660X Campbell
```
KINTYRE & LORNE
```
  M(S) 1701-     Campbell
```
Kirckhoven
```
  1680-1683X BELLAMONT E
  1650-1683X WOTTON B
```
KIRKALDIE
```
  V(S) 1690-     Melville
```
KIRKCUDBRIGHT
```
  L(S) 1633-1832D Maclellan
```
KIRKEBY
```
  B    1294-1294X Kirkeby, De
```
Kirkeby, De
```
  1294-1294X KIRKEBY B
```
KIRKETON
```
  B    1342-1367X Kirketon
```
Kirketon
```
  1342-1367X KIRKETON B
```
KIRKHILL
```
  B(L) 1975-     Smith
```
KIRKLEY
```
  B    1930-1935X Noble
```
KIRKWALL
```
  V(S) 1696-1951D Fitzmaurice
```
KIRKWOOD
```
  B    1951-     Kirkwood
```
Kirkwood
```
  1951-        KIRKWOOD B
```
KISSIN
```
  B(L) 1974-     Kissin
```
Kissin
```
  1974-        KISSIN B(L)
```
KITCHENER OF KHARTOUM
```
  B    1898-1916X Kitchener
  V    1902-     Kitchener
  E    1914-     Kitchener
```

89

```
Kitchener                              KYLSANT
  1914-      BROOME V                     B      1923-1937X Philipps
  1914-      DENTON B                   KYME
  1898-1916X KITCHENER of KHARTOUM B      B      1295-1338A Kyme
  1902-      KITCHENER OF KHARTOUM V    Kyme
  1914-      KITCHENER OF KHARTOUM E      1295-1338A KYME B
Kitson                                 KYNNAIRD
  1907-      AIREDALE B                   V(S) 1660-      Levingston
KNAPTON
  B(I) 1750-      Vesey
KNARESBOROUGH
  B    1905-1929X Meysey-Thompson
Knatchbull
  1880-      BRABOURNE B
KNEBWORTH
  V    1880-      Lytton
Knight
  1762-1772X BARRELLS V
  1762-1772X CATHERLOUGH E(I)
  1746-1772X LUXBOROUGH B(I)
KNIGHTLEY
  B    1892-1895X Knightley
Knightley
  1892-1895X KNIGHTLEY B
KNOLLYS
  B    1603-1632D Knollys
  B    1902-      Knollys
  V    1911-      Knollys
Knollys
  1626-1632D BANBURY E
  1603-1632D KNOLLYS B
  1902-      KNOLLYS B
  1911-      KNOLLYS V
  1616-1632D WALLINGFORD V
KNOVILL
  B    1295-1307X Knovill
Knovill
  1295-1307X KNOVILL B
Knox
  1791-      NORTHLAND V(I)
  1826-      RANFURLY B
  1831-      RANFURLY E(I)
  1781-      WELLES B(I)
KNUTSFORD
  B    1888-      Holland-Hibbert
  V    1895-      Holland-Hibbert
KNYVET
  B    1607-1622X Knyvet          (TITLES are in CAPITALS
Knyvet                              Surnames in smalls)
  1607-1622X KNYVET B
```

90

```
Labouchere                              Lancaster, De
   1859-1869X TAUNTON B                    1299-1334X LANCASTER B
LACI                                    LANE                         *
   B    1066/87-1216/72X Laci, De          B(I) 1676-1724X Lane
Laci, De                                Lane                         *
   1066/87-1216/72X LACI B                1676-1724X LANE B(I)
   1232-1348X LINCOLN E                   1676-1724X LANESBOROUGH V(I)
   1205-1242P ULSTER E(I)               Lane-Fox
LAKE                                       1762-1773X BINGLEY B
   B    1804-1848X Lake                    1933-1947X BINGLEY B
   V    1807-1848X Lake                    1903-1926P FAUCONBERG B
Lake                                    LANERTON
   1804-1848X LAKE B                       B    1874-1880X Howard
   1807-1848X LAKE V                    LANESBOROUGH
Lamb                                       V(I) 1728-     Butler
   1839-1853X BEAUVALE B                   E(I) 1756-     Butler
   1770-1853X MELBOURNE B(I)               V(I) 1676-1724X Lane
   1781-1853X MELBOURNE V(I)            LANG OF LAMBETH
   1815-1853X MELBOURNE B                  B    1942-1945X Lang
   1931-        ROCHESTER B            Lang
LAMBART                                    1942-1945X LANG OF LAMBETH B
   B(I) 1618-        Lambart          LANGDALE
Lambart                                    B    1658-1777X Langdale
   1617-        CAVAN B(I)               B    1836-1851X Bickersteth
   1647-        CAVAN E(I)             Langdale
   1647-        KILCOURSIE V(I)            1658-1777X LANGDALE B
   1618-        LAMBART B(I)          LANGFORD
LAMBERT                                    V(I) 1776-1796X Rowley
   V    1945-        Lambert              B(I) 1800-     Rowley-Conwy
Lambert                                 LANGLEY: See RADCLIFFE & LANGLEY
   1945-        LAMBERT V             LANSDOWNE
LAMBOURNE                                  B    1711-1734X Granville
   B    1917-1928X Lockwood               M    1784-     Petty-Fitzmaurice
LAMBTON                                 LANSLADRON
   V    1833-        Lambton             B    1299-1306X Lansladron, De
Lambton                                 Lansladron, De
   1828-        DURHAM B                  1299-1306X LANSLADRON B
   1833-        DURHAM E              LANVALLEI
   1833-        LAMBTON V                B    1154/89-1217X Lanvallei, De
LAMBURY                                 Lanvallei, De
   B    1962-1967X Lord                   1154/89-1217X LANVALLEI B
LAMINGTON                               LA POER
   B    1880-1951X Cochrane-Baillie       B    1375-        Poer
Lampson                                 LASCELLES
   1943-        KILLEARN B               V    1812-        Lascelles
LANARK                                  Lascelles
   E(S) 1639-        Hamilton             1790-1795X HAREWOOD B
   See also: ARRAN, LANARK & CAMBRIDGE    1796-        HAREWOOD B
LANCASTER                                  1812-        HAREWOOD
   B    1154/89-1272/1307X Tailbois, De    1812-        HAREWOOD E
   E    1267-1321F Plantagenet         LASCELLS
   B    1299-1334X Lancaster, De           B    1295-1297A Lascells, De
   D    1351-1399M Plantagenet    91      * See also Addenda
```

Lascells, De
1295-1297A LASCELLS B
Laszlo, De
1973-   SHARPLES Bss
LATHAM
B   1942-   Latham
Latham
1942-   LATHAM B
LATHOM
E   1880-1930X Bootle-Wilbraham
LATIMER
B   1299-1380A Latimer
B   1432-1577A Nevill
B   1923-   Money-Coutts
V   1673-1964X Osborne
LATIMER OF BRAYBROOKE
B   1299-1411X Latimer
Latimer
1299-1380A LATIMER B
1299-1411X LATIMER OF BRAYBROOKE B
LAUDERDALE
V(S) 1616-   Maitland
E(S) 1624-   Maitland
D(S) 1672-1682X Maitland
B   1806-1863X Maitland
LAUNCESTON
V   1726-1760M Guelph
V   1917-1960X Mountbatten
LAVINGTON
B(I) 1795-1807X Payne
Law
1954-   COLERAINE B
1802-   ELLENBOROUGH B
1844-1871X ELLENBOROUGH E
Lawley
1831-1834X WENLOCK B
1852-1932X WENLOCK B
LAWRENCE
B   1869-   Lawrence
LAWRENCE OF KINGSGATE
B   1923-1927X Lawrence
Lawrence
1869-   LAWRENCE B
1923-1927X LAWRENCE OF KINGSGATE B
1947-   OAKSEY B
1921-   TREVETHIN B
See also: Pethick-Lawrence
LAWSON
B   1950-1965X Lawson
Lawson
1919-1933X BURNHAM V
1950-1965X LAWSON B
See also: Levy-Lawson

Lawson-Johnston
1929-   LUKE B
LAYTON
B   1947-   Layton
Layton
1947-   LAYTON B
LEATHERLAND
B(L) 1964-   Leatherland
Leatherland
1964-   LEATHERLAND B(L)
LEATHERS
B   1941-   Leathers
V   1954-   Leathers
Leathers
1941-   LEATHERS B
1954-   LEATHERS V
Le Blount
1465-1606X MOUNTJOY B
LE BOTILER
B(I) 1192-1299 Le Botiler
Le Botiler
1192-1299 LE BOTILER B(I)
LECALE
V(I) 1624-1687X Cromwell
B(I) 1800-1810X Fitzgerald
LECHMERE
B   1721-1727X Lechmere
Lechmere
1721-1727X LECHMER B
LECONFIELD
B   1859-   Wyndham
LEDET
B   1199/1216-1221X Ledet
Ledet
1199/1216-1221X LEDET B
LEE OF ASHERIDGE
Bss(L) 1970-   Bevan
LEE OF FAREHAM
B   1918-1947X Lee
V   1922-1947X Lee
LEE OF NEWTON
B(L) 1974-1984X Lee
Lee
1918-1947X LEE OF FAREHAM B
1922-1947X LEE OF FAREHAM B
1974-1984X LEE OF NEWTON B(L)
1674-1776X LICHFIELD E
LEEDS
D   1694-1964X Osborne
Leeson
1763-1891D MILLTOWN E(I)
1756-1891D RUSSBOROUGH B(I)
1760-1891D RUSSBOROUGH V(I)

Lefevre: See Shaw-Lefevre
Legge
 1682-   DARTMOUTH B
 1711-   DARTMOUTH E
 1711-   LEWISHAM V
 1760-1820X STAWELL B
Legh
 1892-   NEWTON B
Le Gros
 1100/35-   ? ALANBROOKE Ct
LEICESTER
 E   1103-1204X Beaumont
 E   1206-1264F Montfort, De
 E   1274-1361X Plantagenet
 E   1563-1588X Dudley
 E   1618-1743X Sydney
 E   1744-1759X Coke
 E   1784-1855X Townshend
 E   1837-   Coke
Leicester
 1826-1895X TABLEY, DE B
Leif-Jones
 1932-1939X RHAYADER B
LEIGH
 B   1643-1786X Leigh
 B   1839-   Leigh
Leigh
 1644-1653X CHICHESTER E
 1628-1653X DUNSMORE B
 1643-1786X LEIGH B
 1839-   LEIGH B
 See also: Pemberton-Leigh
LEIGHTON
 B   1896-1896X Leighton
LEIGHTON OF ST MELLONS
 B   1962-   Seager
Leighton
 1896-1896X LEIGHTON B
LEINSTER
 E(I) 1645-1659X Cholmondeley
 D(I) 1691-1719X Schomberg
 Css(I) 1721-30X Kielmansegg
 V   1747-   Fitzgerald
 D(I) 1766-   Fitzgerald
LEITH OF FYVIE
 B   1905-1925X Forbes-Leith
Leith
 1529-   BURGH B
LEITRIM
 B(I) 1583-1583X Burke
 B(I) 1783-1952X Clements
 V(I) 1793-1952X Clements
 E(I) 1795-1952X Clements

Leke
 1624-1736X DEINCOURT B
Lennard
 1611-1786P DACRE B
 1674-1715X SUSSEX E
LENNOX
 E(S) 1154-1425X McArkill
 E(S) 1488-1672X Stewart
 D(S) 1581-1672X Stewart
 D(S) 1675-   Lennox
Lennox
 1675-   DARNLEY E(S)
 1675-   LENNOX D(S)
 1675-   MARCH E
 1675-   METHUEN L(S)
 1675-   RICHMOND D
 1675-   SETTRINGTON B
 1675-   TORBOULTON L(S)
Lennox-Boyd
 1960-   BOYD OF MERTON V
LEONARD
 B(L) 1978-1983X Leonard
Leonard
 1978-1983X LEONARD B(L)
Le Poer
 1673-1704X DECIES V(I)
 1673-1704X TYRONE E(I)
Le Scot
 1231-1246M CHESTER E
LESLIE
 L(S) 1445-   Leslie
 E(S) 1680-   Leslie
LESLIE & BALLENBREICH
 L(S) 1663-   Leslie
Leslie
 1641-   BALGONIE L(S)
 1445-   LESLIE L(S)
 1663-   LESLIE & BALLENBREICH L(S)
 1680-   LESLIE E(S)
 1641-   LEVEN E(S)
 1600-1775X LINDORES L(S)
 1661-1694X NEWARK
 1457-   ROTHES E(S)
L'Espec
 1158-....X ESPEC B
Le Strange
 1299-   STRANGE DE KNOKIN B
LEVEN
 E(S) 1641-   Leslie
LEVER
 B(L) 1975-1977X Lever
LEVER OF MANCHESTER
 B(L) 1979-   Lever

93

Lever
1975-1977X LEVER B(L)
1979-   LEVER OF MANCHESTER B(L)
1917-   LEVERHULME B
1922-   LEVERHULME V
LEVERHULME
B   1917-   Lever
V   1922-   Lever
LEVESON
B   1833-   Leveson-Gower
Leveson-Gower
1846-   BRACKLEY V
1861-   CASTLEHAVEN Bss
1846-   ELLESMERE E
1703-   GOWER B
1746-   GOWER E
1815-   GRANVILLE V
1833-   GRANVILLE E
1833-   LEVESON B
1786-   STAFFORD M
1833-   SUTHERLAND D
1746-   TRENTHAM V
LEVINGSTON
L(S) 1660-   Levingston
Levingston
1660-   KYNNAIRD V(S)
1660-   LEVINGSTON L(S)

LEVINGTON
B   1199/1216-1253X Levington, De
Levington, De
1199/1216-1253X LEVINGTON B
Levy-Lawson
1903-   BURNHAM B
LEWES
E   1876-   Nevill
LEWIN
B(L) 1982-   Lewin
Lewin
1982-   LEWIN B(L)
Lewis
1958-1976X BRECON B
1932-1978X ESSENDON B
1911-   MERTHYR B
LEWISHAM
V   1711-   Legge
LEXINTON
B   1199/1216-1258X Lexinton, De
B   1645-1723X Sutton
Lexinton, De
1199/1216-1258X LEXINTON B

LEY
B   1625-1679X Ley
Ley
1625-1679X LEY B
1626-1679X MARLBOROUGH E
LEYBURN
B   1299-1311X Leyburn
B   1337-1348X Leyburn
Leyburn
1299-1311X LEYBURN B
1337-1348X LEYBURN B
LIBERTON
L(S) 1628-1941D Dalzell
LICHFIELD
E   1645-1672X Stuart
E   1674-1776X Lee
E   1831-   Anson
Liddell
1874-1904X ESLINGTON B
1747-1749X RAVENSWORTH B
1821-   RAVENSWORTH B
1874-1904X RAVENSWORTH E
LIFFORD
B(I) 1768-   Hewitt
V(I) 1781-   Hewitt
LIGONIER
V(I) 1757-1782X Ligonier
B   1763-1782X Ligonier
E   1766-1782X Ligonier
Ligonier
1757-1782X LIGONIER V(I)
1763-1782X LIGONIER B
1766-1782X LIGONIER E
LILFORD
B   1797-   Powys
LIMERICK
E(I) 1685-1715X Dungan
V(I) 1719-1798X Hamilton
V(I) 1800-   Pery
E(I) 1800-   Pery
LIMESI
B   1066/87-1199/1216X Limesi, De
Limesi, De
1066/87-1199/1216X LIMESI B
LINCOLN
E   1100/35-....X Meschines, De
E   1142-....C Romare
E   1216-1217X Gant
E   1217-1232P Blundevil, De
E   1232-1348X Laci, De
E   1349-1399M Plantagenet

94

LINCOLN (Cont'd)
    E   1467-1487X Pole
    E   1525-1545X Brandon
    E   1572-   Clinton, De
LINCOLNSHIRE
    E   1895-1928X Wynn-Carrington
    M   1912-1928X Wynn-Carrington
Lindemann
    1941-1957X CHERWELL B
    1956-1957X CHERWELL V
LINDESEI
    B   1216/72-1248X Lindesei, De
Lindesei, De
    1216/72-1248X LINDESEI B
LINDGREN
    B(L) 1961-1971X Lindgren
Lindgren
    1961-1971X LINDGREN B(L)
LINDLEY
    B(L) 1900-1921X Lindley
Lindley
    1900-1921X LINDLEY B(L)
LINDORES
    L(S) 1600-1775X Leslie
LINDSAY
    L(S) 1113-   Lindsay
    L(S) 1440-   Bethune
    E(S) 1633-   Lindsay
LINDSAY OF BALCARRES
    L(S) 1633-   Lindsay
LINDSAY OF BIRKER
    B   1945-   Lindsay
LINDSAY OF THE BYRES
    L(S) 1445-   Lindsay
LINDSAY & BALNIEL
    L(S) 1651-   Lindsay
Lindsay
    1651-   BALCARRES E(S)
    1398-   CRAWFORD E(S)
    1703-1808D GARNOCK V(S)
    1703-   KILBURNIE, KINGSBURN
              & DRUMRY L(S)
    1113-   LINDSAY L(S)
    1633-   LINDSAY E(S)
    1633-   LINDSAY OF BALCARRES
              L(S)
    1945-   LINDSAY OF BIRKER B
    1445-   LINDSAY OF THE BYRES
              L(S)
    1651-   LINDSAY & BALNIEL L(S)
    1488-1495L MONTROSE D(S)

Lindsay (Cont'd)
    1633-   PARB
    1589-1672? SPYNIE L(S)
    1826-   WIGAN B
    See also: Loyd-Lindsay
LINDSEY
    E   1626-   Bertie
    M   1706-1809X Bertie
LINGEN
    B   1885-1905X Lingen
Lingen
    1885-1905X LINGEN B
LINLEY
    V   1961-   Armstrong-Jones
LINLITHGOW
    E(S) 1600-1716F Livingston
    M   1902-   Hope
LINTON & CABARSTOWN
    L(S) 1683-1861D Stuart
LISBURNE
    V(I) 1685-1691X Loftus
    V(I) 1695-   Vaughan
    E(I) 1776-   Vaughan
LISGAR
    B   1870-1876X Young
L'ISLE
    B   1199/1216-1233X L'Isle, De
    B   1311-1360X L'Isle
    B   1357-1381A L'Isle
    B   1443-....? Talbot
    V   1452-1469X Talbot
    B   1475-1512X Grey
    V   1483-1512X Grey
    V   1513-1523S Brandon
    V   1523-1541X Plantagenet
    B   1541-1553F Dudley
    V   1542-1553F Dudley
    B   1561-1589X Dudley
    V   1605-1743X Sydney
    B(I) 1758-   Lysaght
L'ISLE OF THE ISLE OF WIGHT
    B   1272/1307-1299X L'Isle, De
L'ISLE OF RUGEMONT
    B   1199/1216-1216/72X L'Isle
L'ISLE, DE
    B   1835-   Sidney
    V   1956-   Sidney
L'Isle
    1311-1360X L'ISLE B
    1357-1381X L'ISLE B
    1199/1216-1216/72X L'ISLE OF
              RUGEMONT B

95

L'Isle, De
1199/1216-1233X L'ISLE B
1272/1307-1299X L'ISLE OF THE
            ISLE OF WIGHT B
LISMORE
  B(I) 1785-1898X O'Callaghan
  V(I) 1806-1898X O'Callaghan
  B   1838-1898X O'Callaghan
LISTER
  B   1897-1912X Lister
Lister
  1897-1912X LISTER B
  1797-1925X RIBBLESDALE B
  See also: Cunliffe-Lister
LISTOWEL
  V(I) 1816-   Hare
  E(I) 1822-   Hare
Littleton
  1835-   HATHERTON B
LIVERPOOL
  E   1796-1851X Jenkinson
  E   1905-   Foljambe
LIVINGSTON
  L(S) 1449-1715F Livingston
Livingston
  1641-1716F CALENDAR E(S)
  1661-1716F CAMPSIE L(S)
  1661-1715F KILSYTH V(S)
  1660-   KINNAIRD V(S)
  1600-1716F LINLITHGOW E(S)
  1449-1715F LIVINGSTONE L(S)
  1647-1694X NEWBURGH V(S)
  1660-   NEWBURGH E(S)
  1696-1711X TEVIOT V(S)
LIXNAW
  B(I) 1555-   Fitzmaurice
LIZURES
  B   1100/35-1189/99X Lizures, De
Lizures, De
  1100/35-1189/99X LIZURES B
LLANDAFF
  B(I) 1783-1833X Mathew
  V(I) 1793-1833X Mathew
  E(I) 1797-1833X Mathew
  V   1895-1913X Matthews
LLANOVER
  B   1859-1867X Hall
LLANGATTOCK
  B   1892-1916X Rolls
LLEWELLIN
  B   1945-1957X Llewellin

Llewellin
  1945-1957X LLEWELLIN B
LLEWELYN-DAVIES
  B(L) 1963-   Llewelyn-Davies
LLEWELYN-DAVIES OF HASTOE
  Bss(L) 1967-   Llewelyn-Davies
Llewelyn-Davies
  1963-   LLEWELYN-DAVIES B(L)
  1967-   LLEWELYN-DAVIES OF
           HASTOE Bss(L)
LLOYD
  B   1925-   Lloyd
LLOYD OF HAMPSTEAD
  B(L) 1965-   Lloyd
LLOYD OF KILGERRAN
  B(L) 1973-   Lloyd
Lloyd
  1925-   LLOYD B
  1965-   LLOYD OF HAMPSTEAD B(L)
  1973-   LLOYD OF KILGERRAN B(L)
  1974-   GEOFFREY-LLOYD B(L)
  1976-1978X SELWYN-LLOYD B(L)
  See also: Jones-Lloyd
LLOYD-GEORGE OF DWYFOR
  E   1945-   Lloyd George
Lloyd George
  1945-   GWYNEDD V
  1945-   LLOYD-GEORGE OF DWYFOR E
  1957-   TENBY V
Lloyd Mostyn
  1831-   MOSTYN B
LOCH
  B   1895-   Loch
Loch
  1895-   LOCH B
LOCHEE
  B   1908-1911X Robertson
LOCHINVAR
  L(S) 1633-1847D Gordon
LOCHOW & GLENILLA
  V(S) 1701-   Campbell
LOCKWOOD
  Bss(L) 1977-   Hall
Lockwood
  1917-1928X LAMBOURNE B
Loder
  1934-   WAKEHURST B
LOFTUS
  V(I) 1622-1725X Loftus
  B(I) 1751-1783X Loftus
  V(I) 1756-1783X Loftus

```
LOFTUS (Cont'd)                          LONSDALE
  B(I)  1785-       Tottenham              V    1696-1751X Lowther
  V(I)  1789-       Tottenham              E    1784-1802X Lowther
  B     1801-       Tottenham              B    1797-      Lowther
Loftus                                     V    1797-      Lowther
  1622-1725X ELY V(I)                      E    1807-      Lowther
  1766-1783X ELY E(I)                    Lonsdale
  1685-1691X LISBURNE V(I)                 1918-1924X ARMAGHDALE B
  1622-1725X LOFTUS V(I)                 Lopes
  1751-1783X LOFTUS B(I)                   1897-1922X LUDLOW B
  1756-1783X LOFTUS V(I)                   1938-      ROBOROUGH B
  1685-1690X RATHFARNHAM B(I)            Lord
LONDESBOROUGH                              1962-1967X LAMBURY B
  B     1850-       Denison             LOREBURN
  E     1887-1937X Denison                 B    1906-1923X Reid
LONDONDERRY                                E    1911-1923X Reid
  E(I)  1622-1714X Ridgeway            LORN
  B(I)  1719-1764X Pitt                   L(S) 1439-1470P Stewart
  E(I)  1726-1764X Pitt                LORNE
  B(I)  1789-       Stewart               L(S) 1470-       Campbell
  E(I)  1796-       Stewart               M(S) 1801-       Campbell
  M(I)  1816-       Stewart             See also: KINTYRE & LORNE
LONG                                    Lorraine, De
  V     1921-       Long                   1075-1080X DURHAM E
Long                                    L'ORTI
  1826-1838X FARNBOROUGH B                 B    1299-1341A L'Orti
  1921-      LONG V                     L'Orti
Longespée                                 1299-1341A L'ORTI B
  1196-1261A SALISBURY E               LORTON
Longfield                                 V(I)  1806-      King
  1795-1811X LONGUEVILLE B(I)          LOTHIAN
  1800-1811X LONGUEVILLE V(I)             E(S)  1606-      Ker
LONGFORD                                   E(S)  1631-      Kerr
  B(I)  1621-1704X Aungier                 M(S)  1701-      Kerr
  V(I)  1675-1704X Aungier                 B     1821-      Kerr
  E(I)  1677-1704X Aungier             LOUDOUN
  V(I)  1713-1726F Fleming                 L(S)  1601-      Campbell
  B     1747-       Bouverie, De           E(S)  1633-      Campbell
  B(I)  1756-       Pakenham            LOUGHBOROUGH
  E(I)  1785-       Pakenham               B     1780-1805X Wedderburn
  Css(I) 1785-      Pakenham               B     1795-      Wedderburn
LONGUEVILLE                            LOUGHGUYRE
  V     1690-1799X Yelverton              B(I)  1718-1766X Fane
  B(I)  1795-1811X Longfield           LOUGHNEAGH
  V(I)  1800-1811X Longfield              B(I)  1660-      Clotworthy
Longueville                            LOUNDRES
  1639-1643P GREY DE RUTHYN B             B(I)  1478-      Preston
LONGVILLIERS                           LOUR
  B     1342-1374X Longvilliers           L(S)  1639-      Carnegie
Longvilliers
  1342-1374X LONGVILLIERS B
```

LOUTH
E(I) 1319-1329X Bermingham
B(I) 1541-   Plunkett
E(I) 1759-1799X Bermingham
LOVAINE
B   1199/1216-1294X Lovaine, De
LOVAINE OF ALNWICK
B   1784-   Percy
Lovaine, De
1199/1216-1294X LOVAINE B
LOVAT
L(S) 1458/64-   Fraser
B   1837-   Fraser
LOVEL
V   1483-1487F Lovel
LOVEL OF KARY
B   1348-1351A Lovel
LOVEL OF MINSTER LOVEL
B   1728-1759X Lovel
LOVEL OF TICHMERSH
B   1299-1487F Lovel
LOVEL & HOLLAND
B   1762-   Perceval
Lovel
1373-1487F HOLLAND B
1483-1487F LOVEL V
1348-1351A LOVEL OF KARY B
1728-1759X LOVEL OF MINSTER
              LOVEL B
1299-1487F LOVEL OF TICHMERSH B
1469-1489C MORLEY B
LOVELACE
B   1627-1736X Lovelace
E   1838-   King
Lovelace
1627-1736X LOVELACE B
Low
1962-   ALDINGTON B
Lowe
1880-1892X SHERBROOKE V
LOWRY
B(L) 1979-   Lowry
Lowry
1979-   LOWRY B(L)
Lowry-Corry
1781-   BELMORE B(I)
1789-   BELMORE V(I)
1797-   BELMORE E(I)
1880-1903X ROWTON B
LOWTHER
B   1696-1751X Lowther

LOWTHER (Cont'd)
B   1784-1802X Lowther
V   1784-1802X Lowther
B   1797-   Lowther
V   1797-   Lowther
Lowther
1784-1802X BURGH B
1784-1802X KENDAL B
1696-1751X LONSDALE V
1784-1802X LONSDALE E
1797-   LONSDALE B
1797-   LONSDALE V
1807-   LONSDALE E
1696-1751X LOWTHER B
1784-1802X LOWTHER B
1784-1802X LOWTHER V
1797-   LOWTHER B
1797-   LOWTHER V
1921-   ULLSWATER V
Loyd-Lindsay
1885-1901X WANTAGE B
Lubbock
1900-   AVEBURY B
LUCAN
E(I) 1689-1693X Sarsfield
B(I) 1776-   Bingham
E(I) 1795-   Bingham
LUCAS
B   1644-1705X Lucas
LUCAS OF CHILWORTH
B   1946-   Lucas
LUCAS OF CRUDWELL
B   1663-   Lucas
Lucas
1644-1705X LUCAS B
1946-   LUCAS OF CHILWORTH B
1663-   LUCAS OF CRUDWELL B
Lucie, De
1100/35-1154/89X LUCY B
1189/99-1213X LUCY B
LUCY
B   1100/35-1154/89X Lucie, De
B   1189/99-1213X Lucie, De
B   1264-1304X Lucy, De
LUCY OF EGREMONT
B   1320-1345X Lucy
Lucy
1320-1365X LUCY OF EGREMONT B
Lucy, De
1264-1304X LUCY B

98

LUDLOW
E   1760-1842X Ludlow
B   1831-1842X Ludlow
B   1897-1922X Lopes
V   1748-1801X Herbert
Ludlow
1760-1842X LUDLOW E
1831-1842X LUDLOW B
LUGARD
B   1928-1945X Lugard
Lugard
1928-1945X LUGARD B
LUKE
B   1929-   Lawson-Johnston
LUMLEY
B   1384-1400F Lumley
B   1547-1609X Lumley
V(I) 1628-   Lumley
B   1681-   Lumley
V   1689-   Lumley
Lumley
1384-1400F LUMLEY B
1547-1609X LUMLEY B
1628-   LUMLEY V(I)
1681-   LUMLEY B
1689-   LUMLEY V
1690-   SCARBROUGH E
LUNDIE
L(S) 1642-1660X Campbell
LURGAN
B   1839-   Brownlow
LUTEREL
B   1295-1295X Luterel
Luterel
1295-1295X LUTEREL B
Luttrell
1768-1829X CARHAMPTON B(I)
1781-1829X CARHAMPTON E(I)
1785-1829X CARHAMPTON E(I)
1768-1829X IRNHAM B(I)
LUXBOROUGH
B(I) 1746-1772X Knight
LYELL
B   1914-   Lyell
Lyell
1914-   LYELL B
Lygon
1815-1979X BEAUCHAMP E
1806-1979X BEAUCHAMP OF POWYKE B
1815-1979X ELMLEY V
LYLE
L(S) 1446-....X Lyle

LYLE OF WESTBOURNE
B   1945-1976X Lyle
Lyle
1446-....X LYLE L(S)
1945-1976X LYLE OF WESTBOURNE B
LYMINGTON
V   1720-   Wallop
LYNDHURST
B   1827-1863X Copley
LYNEDOCH
B   1814-1843X Graham
LYNN
B   1723-   Townshend
LYON
L(S) 1606-   Lyon
L(S) 1677-   Lyon
Lyon
1445-   GLAMIS L(S)
1677-   GLAMIS, TANNADYCE,
            SIDLAW & STRATH-
            DICHTIE L(S)
1606-   KINGSHORNE E(S)
1606-   LYON L(S)
1677-   LYON L(S)
1672-   STRATHDICHTIE L(S)
1672-   STRATHMORE E(S)
1672-   SYDLAW L(S)
LYONS
B   1856-1887X Lyons
V   1881-1887X Lyons
LYONS OF BRIGHTON
B(L) 1974-1978X Lyons
Lyons
1939-1963X ENNISDALE B
1856-1887X LYONS B
1881-1887X LYONS V
1974-1978X LYONS OF BRIGHTON B(L)
Lysaght
1758-   L'ISLE B(I)
LYTTELTON
B   1640-1645X Lyttelton
B   1757-1779X Lyttelton
B   1794-   Lyttelton
Lyttelton
1954-   CHANDOS V
1794-   FRANKLEY B
1640-1645X LYTTELTON B
1757-1779X LYTTELTON B
1794-   LYTTELTON B
1776-   WESTCOTE B(I)

99

```
LYTTON                                  McALPINE OF WEST GREEN
  B    1866-      Bulwer-Lytton           B(L) 1984-        McAlpine
  V    1880-      Bulwer-Lytton         McALPINE OF MOFFAT
  E    1880-      Bulwer-Lytton           B(L) 1980-        McAlpine
Lytton                                  McAlpine
  1880-        KNEBWORTH V               1984-       McALPINE OF WEST GREEN B(L)
LYVEDEN                                   1980-       McALPINE OF MOFFAT B(L)
  B    1859-      Vernon                MACANDREW
                                          B    1959-        MacAndrew
                                        MacAndrew
                                          1959-       MACANDREW B
                                        McArkill
                                          1154-1425F LENNOX E(S)
                                        MacCarthy
                                          1628-1691F BLARNEY B
                                        M'Carthy
                                          1556-1597R CLANCARE E(I)
                                          1658-1690F MUSKERRY B(I)
                                          1556-1597R VALENTIA B(I)
                                        McCARTHY
                                          B(L) 1975-        McCarthy
                                        McCarthy
                                          1975-       McCARTHY B(L)
                                        MACARTNEY
                                          B(I) 1776-1806X Macartney
                                          V(I) 1793-1806X Macartney
                                          E(I) 1794-1806X Macartney
                                          B    1796-1806X Macartney
                                        Macartney
                                          1776-1806X MACARTNEY B(I)
                                          1793-1806X MACARTNEY V(I)
                                          1794-1806X MACARTNEY E(I)
                                          1796-1806X MACARTNEY B
                                        M'Carty
                                          1658-1770X CLANCARTY E(I)
                                          1689-....X MOUNT CASHELL V(I)
                                        MACAULAY
                                          B    1857-1859X Macaulay
                                        Macaulay
                                          1857-1859X MACAULAY B
                                        M'Clintock
                                          1868-        RATHDONNELL B(I)
                                        McCLUSKEY
                                          B(L) 1976-        McCluskey
                                        McCluskey
                                          1976-       McCLUSKEY B(L)
                                        McCORQUODALE OF NEWTON
          (TITLES are in CAPITALS         B    1955-1971X McCorquodale
           Surnames in smalls)          McCorquodale
                                          1955-1971X McCORQUODALE OF NEWTON B
                            100
```

MACDERMOTT
B(L) 1947-   MacDermott
MacDermott
1947-   MACDERMOTT B(L)
MACDONALD
B(I) 1776-   Macdonald of
                Macdonald
MACDONALD OF EARNSCLIFFE
B   1891-1920X Macdonald
MACDONALD OF GWAENYSGOR
B   1949-   Macdonald
Macdonald
1476-1493S ISLES, THE L(S)
1891-1920X MACDONALD OF EARNS-
           CLIFFE B
1949-   MACDONALD OF GWAEN-
           YSGOR B
Macdonald of Macdonald
1776-   MACDONALD B(I)
MACDONELL & ARRASS
L(S) 1660-1680X MacDonell
MacDonell
1660-1680X ARRASS L(S)
1660-1680X MACDONELL & ARRASS L(S)
MACDONNELL
B   1908-1925X MacDonnell
MacDonnell
1908-1925X MACDONNELL B
McDonnell
1620-1791X ANTRIM E(I)
1644-1682X ANTRIM M(I)
1785-   ANTRIM E(S)
1789-1791X ANTRIM M(I)
1618-1791X DUNLUCE V(I)
1785-   DUNLUCE V(I)
MACDUFF
V(I) 1759-1912D Duff
E   1900-   Carnegie
M   1889-1912X Duff
MacDuff
1057-1425X FIFE E(S)
MCENTEE
B   1951-1953X McEntee
McEntee
1951-1953X MCENTEE B
MCFADZEAN
B(L) 1966-   McFadzean
McFadzean
1966-   MCFADZEAN B(L)
MCFARLANE OF LLANDAFF
Bss(L) 1979-   McFarlane

McFarlane
1979-   MCFARLANE OF LLANDAFF
McGarel-Hogg   Bss(L)
1887-1957X MAGHERAMORNE B
MCGOWAN
B   1937-   McGowan
McGowan
1937-   MCGOWAN B
MCGREGOR OF DURRIS
B(L) 1978-   McGregor
McGregor
1978-   MCGREGOR OF DURRIS B(L)
MACHANSIRE & POLMONT
L(S) 1643-   Hamilton
MCINTOSH OF HARRINGEY
B(L) 1982-   McIntosh
McIntosh
1982-   MCINTOSH OF HARRINGEY B(L)
MACKAY PF CLASHFERN
B(L) 1979-   Mackay
Mackay
1929-   GLENAPP V
1911-   INCHCAPE B
1924-   INCHCAPE V
1929-   INCHCAPE E
1979-   MACKAY OF CLASHFERN B(L)
1628-   REAY L(S)
1971-   TANLAW B(L)
MACKENZIE
L(S) 1609-1815X Mackenzie
Mackenzie
1929-1983X AMULREE B
1685-1745F CASTLEHAVEN L(S)
1861-   CASTLEHAVEN B
1861-   CROMARTIE E
1703-1745F CROMARTY E(S)
1766-1815X FORTROSE B(I)
1609-1815X MACKENZIE L(S)
1685-1745F MACLEOD L(S)
1861-   MACLEOD B
1623-1815X SEAFORTH E(S)
1771-1781X SEAFORTH E(I)
1797-1815X SEAFORTH B
1685-1746F TARBAT V(S)
1861-   TARBAT V
See also: Muir-Mackenzie
See also: Stewart-Mackenzie
See also: Stuart-Wortley-Mackenzie
MACKIE OF BENSHIE
B(L) 1974-   Mackie

101

Mackie
1981-   JOHN-MACKIE B(L)
1974-   MACKIE OF BENSHIE B(L)
MACKINTOSH OF HALIFAX
  B   1948-   Mackintosh
  V   1957-   Mackintosh
Mackintosh
  1948-   MACKINTOSH OF HALIFAX B
  1957-   MACKINTOSH OF HALIFAX V
McLaren
  1911-   ABERCONWAY B
MACLAY
  B   1922-   Maclay
Maclay
  1922-   MACLAY B
  1963-   MUIRSHIEL V
MACLEAN
  B(L) 1971-   Maclean
Maclean
  1971-   MACLEAN B(L)
MCLEAVY
  B(L) 1967-1976X McLeavy
McLeavy
  1967-1976X MCLEAVY B(L)
MACLEHOSE OF BEOCH
  B(L) 1982-   MacLehose
MacLehose
  1982-   MACLEHOSE OF BEOCH B(L)
Maclellan
  1633-1832D KIRKCUDBRIGHT L(S)
MACLEOD
  L(S) 1685-1745F Mackenzie
  B   1861-   Mackenzie
MACLEOD OF BORVE
  Bss(L) 1971-   Macleod
MACLEOD OF FUINARY
  B(L) 1967-   MacLeod
Macleod
  1971-   MACLEOD OF BORVE Bss(L)
MacLeod
  1967-   MACLEOD OF FUINARY B(L)
MACMILLAN
  B(L) 1930-1952X Macmillan
MACMILLAN OF OVENDEN
  V   1984-   Macmillan
Macmillan
  1930-1952X MACMILLAN B(L)
  1984-   MACMILLAN OF OVENDEN V
  1984-   STOCKTON E

MACNAGHTEN
  B(L) 1887-1913X Macnaghten
Macnaghten
  1887-1913X MACNAGHTEN B(L)
MCNAIR
  B   1955-   McNair
McNair
  1955-   MCNAIR B
McNeill
  1867-1874X COLONSAY B(I)
  1927-1934X CUSHENDUN B
MACPHERSON OF DRUMOCHTER
  B   1851-   Macpherson
Macpherson
  1963-   DRUMALBYN B
  1951-   MACPHERSON OF
             DRUMOCHTER B
  1936-   STRATHCARRON B
MacWilliam
  1129-1222X CAITHNESS E(S)

(TITLES are in CAPITALS
 Surnames in smalls)

102

MABANE
B   1962-1969X Mabane
Mabane
1962-1969X MABANE B
MACCLESFIELD
E   1679-1702X Gerard
B   1716-   Parker
E   1721-   Parker
MADELEY
E   1911-1945X Crewe-Milnes
MADERTY
L(S) 1609-   Drummond
MAELOR
B(L) 1966-1984X Jones
MAENAN
B   1948-1951X Taylor
Maffey
1947-   RUGBY B
MAGENNIS
V(I) 1623-1693X Magennis
Magennis
1623-1693X IVEAGH V(I)
1623-1693X MAGENNIS V(I)
MAGHERAMORNE
B   1887-1957X McGarel-Hogg
MAGUIRE
B(I) 1627-1644F Maguire
Maguire
1627-1644F ENNISKILLEN B(I)
1627-1644F MAGUIRE B(I)
Mahon
1800-1845X HARTLAND B(I)
MAIDSTONE
V   1623-   Finch
MAIS
B(L) 1967-   Mais
Mais
1967-   MAIS B(L)
MAITLAND
V(S) 1624-   Maitland
MAITLAND OF THIRLESTANE
L(S) 1590-   Maitland
Maitland
1624-1624M BOLTOUN L(S)
1674-1682X GUILDFORD E
1616-   LAUDERDALE V(S)
1624-   LAUDERDALE E(S)
1672-1682X LAUDERDALE D(S)
1806-1863X LAUDERDALE B
1624-   MAITLAND V(S)
1590-   MAITLAND OF THIRLE-
             STANE L(S)

Maitland (Cont'd)
1672-1682X MARCH M(S)
1674-1682X PETERSHAM B
1624-   THIRLESTANE & BOULTON L(S)
Major: See Henniker-Major
MAKGILL OF COUSLAND
L(S) 1651-   Makgill
Makgill
1651-   MAKGILL OF COUSLAND L(S)
1651-   OXFUIRD V(S)
Makins
1964-   SHERFIELD B
MALCOLM OF POLTALLOCH
B   1896-1902X Malcolm
Malcolm
1896-1902X MALCOLM OF POLTALLOCH B
MALDEN
V   1661-   Capel
MALET
B   1066/87-1224X Malet
Malet
1066/87-1224X MALET B
Malise
1115-1346R STRATHERN E(S)
MALLOWNE
B(I) 1622-   Mallowne O'Mullan
Mallowne O'Mullan
1622-   MALLOWNE B(I)
MALMESBURY
M   1715-1731X Wharton
B   1788-   Harris
E   1800-   Harris
Malone
1785-1816X SUNDERLIN B(I)
MALPAS
V   1706-   Cholmondeley
MALTON
B   1728-1782X Watson-Wentworth
E   1734-1782X Watson-Wentworth
B&E(I) 1750-82X Wentworth
MALTRAVERS   *
B   1330-1364A Maltravers
B   1556-   Howard
Maltravers
1330-1364A MALTRAVERS B
MALVERN
V   1955-   Huggins
MAMHEAD
B   1931-1945X Newman
MANCHESTER
B   1620-   Montagu
V   1620-   Montagu

103   * See also Addenda

MANCHESTER (Cont'd)
```
  E    1626-       Montagu
  D    1719-       Montagu
MANCROFT
  B    1937-       Mancroft
Mancroft
  1937-       MANCROFT B
MANDEVILLE
  B    1066/87-1135/54X Mandeville,
                       De
  B    1199/1216-1275X Mandeville,
                       De
  V    1620-       Montagu
Mandeville, De
  1135/54-1189X ESSEX E
  1213-1216P GLOUCESTER E
  1066/87-1135/54X MANDEVILLE B
  1199/1216-1275X MANDEVILLE B
MANERS
  B    1309-1309X Maners, De
Maners, De
  1309-1309X MANERS B
MANNERS
  B    1807-       Manners-Sutton
MANNERS OF HADDON
  B    1679-       Manners
Manners
  1703-       GRANBY M
  1679-       MANNERS OF HADDON B
  1896-       ROOS OF BELVOIR B
  1525-       RUTLAND E
  1703-       RUTLAND D
Manners-Sutton
  1835-1941X BOTTESFORD B
  1835-1941X CANTERBURY V
  1807-       MANNERS B
Manningham-Buller
  1954-       DILHORNE B
  1964-       DILHORNE V
MANNY
  B    1347-1399X Manny
Manny
  1347-1399X MANNY B
MANSELL
  B    1711-1750X Mansell
Mansell
  1711-1750X MANSELL B
MANSFIELD
  V    1620-1691X Cavendish
  B    1756-1793X Murray
  E    1776-       Murray
```

Mansfield
```
  1871-       SANDHURST B
  1917-1921X SANDHURST V
MANTON
  B    1922-       Watson
MANVERS
  E    1806-1955X Pierrepont
MAR
  E(S) 1426-1435X Mar, Of
  E(S) 1457-1479X Stewart
  E(S) 1565-       Erskine
Mar, Of
  1295-       GARIOCH L(S)
  1426-1435X MAR E(S)
MARCH
  E(S) 1060-1419D Dunbar
  M(S) 1672-1682X Maitland
  E    1328-1424X Mortimer
  E    1479-1483M Plantagenet
  E(S) 1582-1672X Stewart
  E    1619-1672X Stuart
  E    1675-       Lennox
  E(S) 1697-       Douglas
MARCHAMLEY
  B    1908-       Whiteley
MARCHMONT
  E(S) 1697-1794D Hume
MARCHWOOD
  B    1937-       Penny
  V    1945-       Penny
MARE, DE LA
  B    1299-1315X Mare, De La
Mare, De La
  1299-1315X MARE, DE LA B
MARGADALE
  B    1964-       Morrison
MARGESSON
  V    1942-       Margesson
Margesson
  1942-       MARGESSON V
MARISCHAL
  E(S) 1458-1715F Keith
MARJORIBANKS
  B    1873-1873X Robertson
Marjoribanks
  1881-1935X TWEEDMOUTH B
MARKENFIELD
  B    1782-       Norton
MARKS
  B    1929-1938X Marks
```

MARKS OF BROUGHTON
 B   1961-   Marks
Marks
 1929-1938X MARKS B
 1961-   MARKS OF BROUGHTON B
MARLBOROUGH
 E   1626-1679X Ley
 E   1689-   Churchill
 D   1702-   Churchill
MARLEY
 B   1930-   Aman
MARMION
 B   1264-1264X Marmion
MARMION OF TAMWORTH
 B   1066/87-1292X Marmion
MARMION OF WITRINGHAM
 B   1199/1216-1216/72D Marmion
 B   1313-1335A Marmion
Marmion
 1264-1264X MARMION B
 1066/87-1292X MARMION OF TAMWORTH B
 1199/1216-1216/72D MARMION OF
              WITRINGHAM B
 1313-1335A MARMION OF WITRINGHAM B
MARNEY
 B   1523-1525X Marney
Marney
 1523-1525X MARNEY B
MARPLES
 B(L) 1974-1978X Marples
Marples
 1974-1978X MARPLES B(L)
Marquis
 1956-   WALBERTON V
 1939-   WOOLTON B
 1953-   WOOLTON V
 1956-   WOOLTON E
MARR & GARVIACH
 E(S) 1486-....X Stewart
MARSH
 B(L) 1981-   Marsh
Marsh
 1981-   MARSH B(L)
MARSHAL
 B   1100/35-1199X Marshal
 B   1309-1314A Marshal
Marshal
 1100/35-1199X MARSHAL B
 1309-1314A MARSHAL B
 1189-1245X PEMBROKE E

MARSHALL OF CHIPSTEAD
 B   1921-1936X Marshall
MARSHALL OF LEEDS
 B(L) 1980-   Marshall
Marshall
 1921-1936X MARSHALL OF CHIPSTEAD B
 1980-   MARSHALL OF LEEDS B(L)
MARSHAM
 V   1801-   Marsham
Marsham
 1801-   MARSHAM V
 1716-   ROMNEY B
 1801-   ROMNEY E
MARTIN
 B   1295-1326A Martin
Martin
 1295-1326A MARTIN B
MARTONMERE
 B   1964-   Robinson
Martyn-Hemphill
 1906-   HEMPHILL B
MARYBOROUGH
 B(I) 1821-1863X Wellesley
MASHAM
 B   1711-1776X Masham
 B   1891-1924X Cunliffe-Lister
 B   1935-   Cunliffe-Lister
MASHAM OF ILTON
 Bss(L) 1970-   Cunliffe-Lister
Masham
 1711-1776X MASHAM B
Mason
 1935-   BLACKFORD B
MASSEREENE
 V(I) 1660-   Clotworthy
 E(I) 1756-1816X Skeffington
Massey
 1800-1952X CLARINA B(I)
 1776-   MASSY B(I)
Massue
 1690-1720X GALWAY V(I)
 1692-1720X GALWAY E(I)
 1692-1720X PORTARLINGTON B(I)
MASSY
 B(I) 1776-   Massey
MATHERS
 B   1952-1965X Mathers
Mathers
 1952-1965X MATHERS B

105

Mathew
 1783-1833X LLANDAFF B(I)
 1793-1833X LLANDAFF V(I)
 1797-1833X LLANDAFF E(I)
MATTHEWS
 B(L) 1980-   Matthews
Matthews
 1895-1913X LLANDAFF V
 1980-   MATTHEWS B(L)
MAUCHLIN: See TARRINZEAN & MAUCHLIN
MAUD: See REDCLIFFE-MAUD
MAUDE OF STRATFORD-UPON-AVON
 B(L) 1983-   Maude
Maude
 1791-   HAWARDEN V(I)
 1983-   MAUDE OF STRATFORD-
          UPON-AVON B(L)
 1785-   MONTALT, DE B(I)
 1886-1905X MONTALT, DE E
MAUDUIT
 B   1066/87-1256M Mauduit
 B   1342-1342X Mauduit
Mauduit
 1066/87-1256M MAUDUIT B
 1342-1342X MAUDUIT B
MAUGHAM
 B   1935-1981X Maugham
 V   1939-1981X Maugham
Maugham
 1935-1981X MAUGHAM B
 1939-1981X MAUGHAM V
MAULE
 L(S) 1646-1715F Maule
MAULE OF WHITECHURCH
 V(I) 1743-1782X Maule
Maule
 1646-1715F BRECHIN L(S)
 1646-1715F MAULE L(S)
 1743-1782X MAULE OF WHITECHURCH V(I)
 1646-1874X NAVAR L(S)
 1646-1715X PANMURE E(S)
 1743-1782X PANMURE E(I)
 1831-1874X PANMURE B
MAULEY
 B   1295-1415A Mauley
MAULEY, DE
 B   1838-   Ponsonby
Mauley
 1295-1415A MAULEY B
Maxwell
 1620-1716A CARLYLE L(S)
 1646-....X DIRLETOUN E(S)

Maxwell (Cont'd)
 1646-....X ELBOTTLE L(S)
 1620-1716F ESKDALE L(S)
 1756-   FARNHAM B(I)
 1760-1779X FARNHAM V(I)
 1763-1779X FARNHAM E(I)
 1781-1823X FARNHAM V(I)
 1781-1823X FARNHAM E(I)
 1585-1716F MORTON E(S)
 1620-1716F NITHSDALE E(S)
 1264-   ROS, DE B
 See also: Constable-Maxwell
MAY
 B   1935-   May
May
 1886-1886X FARNBOROUGH B
 1931-   MAY B
MAYBRAY-KING
 B(L) 1971-   Maybray-King
Maybray-King
 1971-   MAYBRAY-KING B(L)
MAYHEW
 B(L) 1981-   Mayhew
Mayhew
 1981-   MAYHEW B(L)
MAYNARD
 B(I) 1620-1775X Maynard
 B   1628-1865X Maynard
 V   1766-1865X Maynard
Maynard
 1620-1775X MAYNARD B(I)
 1628-1865X MAYNARD B
 1766-1865X MAYNARD V
Mayne
 1776-1794X NEWHAVEN B(I)
MAYO
 V(I) 1628-1767D Bourke
 B(I) 1776-   Bourke
 V(I) 1781-   Bourke
 E(I) 1785-   Bourke
Meade
 1766-   CLANWILLIAM V(I)
 1776-   CLANWILLIAM E(I)
 1828-   CLANWILLIAM B
 1766-   GILLFORD B(I)
MEATH
 E(I) 1627-   Brabazon
MEDINA
 E   1917-   Mountbatten
MEDWAY
 B   1892-   Gathorne-Hardy

106

MEINILL
 B   1295-1299X Meinill
 B   1313-1322X Meinill
 B   1336-1778X Meinill
Meinill
 1295-1299X MEINILL B
 1313-1322X MEINILL B
 1336-1778X MEINILL B
MELBOURNE
 B(I) 1770-1853X Lamb
 V(I) 1781-1853X Lamb
 B   1815-1853X Lamb
MELCHETT
 B   1928-   Mond
MELCOMBE
 B   1761-1762X Dodington
MELDRUM
 B   1815-   Gordon
MELFORT
 V(S) 1685-1902D Drummond
 E(S) 1686-1902D Drummond
 D(S) 1686-1694F Drummond
MELGUM
 V(S) 1627-1630X Gordon
MELGUND
 V   1813-   Elliot
Melles
 1932-1962P BURTON B
MELROSE
 L(S) 1609-1625X Ramsay
 E(S) 1619-1627C Hamilton
 B   1827-1858X Hamilton
MELVILLE
 V   1802-   Dundas
MELVILLE OF MONYMAILL
 L(S) 1616-   Melville
 E(S) 1690-   Melville
Melville
 1690-   KIRKALDIE V(S)
 1616-   MELVILLE OF MONYMAILL L(S)
 1690-   MELVILLE OF MONYMAILL E(S)
 1690-   RAITH, MONYMAILL &
              BALWEARIE L(S)
MENDIP
 B   1794-   Ellis
MENTEITH
 E(S) 1258-1425X Menteith
Menteith
 1258-1425X MENTEITH E(S)
MENTMORE
 V   1911-   Primrose

MERE, DE LA
 B   1661-1770X Booth
MEREDYTH
 B   1866-1929X Somerville
MEREWORTH
 B   1926-   Browne
MERIONETH
 E   1947-   Mountbatten
MERIVALE
 B   1925-   Duke
MERLAY
 B   1135/54-1266X Merlay
Merlay
 1135/54-1266X MERLAY B
MERRIMAN
 B   1941-1962X Merriman
Merriman
 1941-1962X MERRIMAN B
MERSEY
 B   1910-   Bigham
 V   1916-   Bigham
MERTHYR
 B   1911-   Lewis
MERTON OF TRAFALGAR
 V   1805-   Nelson
Meschines, De
 1139-....X CAMBRIDGE E
 1119-1231C CHESTER E
 1100/35-....X LINCOLN E
MESTON
 B   1919-   Meston
Meston
 1919-   MESTON B
METCALFE
 B   1845-1846X Metcalfe
Metcalfe
 1845-1846X METCALFE B
METHEL: See ELCHO & METHEL
METHLIC: See HADDO, METHLIC,
 TARVES & KELLIE
METHUEN
 L(S) 1675-   Lennox
 B   1838-   Methuen
Methuen
 1838-   METHUEN B
METHVEN
 L(S) 1528-1584X Stewart
MEXBOROUGH
 E(I) 1766-   Savile
Meysey-Thompson
 1905-1929X KNARESBOROUGH B

107

MICHELHAM
B 1905- Stern
MICKLETHWAIT
B(I) 1724-1733X Micklethwait
V(I) 1727-1733X Micklethwait
Micklethwait
1724-1733X MICKLETHWAIT B(I)
1727-1733X MICKLETHWAIT V(I)
MIDDLESEX
E 1622-1674X Cranfield
E 1675-1843X Sackville
MIDDLETON
E(S) 1660-1695F Middleton
B 1711- Willoughby
Middleton
1805-1813P BARHAM B
1660-1695F CLERMONT & FETTER-
CAIRN L(S)
1660-1695F FETTERCAIRN L(S)
1660-1695F MIDDLETON E(S)
MIDLETON
V(I) 1717-1779X Brodrick
E 1920-1979X Brodrick
MIDLOTHIAN
E 1911- Primrose
MILBROKE
B 1442-1443X Cornwall
MILDMAY OF FLETE
B 1922-1950X Mildmay
Mildmay
1669-1753A FITZWALTER B
1730-1756X FITZWALTER E
1730-1756X HARWICH V
1922-1950X MILDMAY OF FLETE B
MILES
B(L) 1979- Miles
Miles
1979- MILES B(L)
MILFORD
B(I) 1776-1823X Philipps
B 1847-1857X Philipps
MILFORD HAVEN
E 1706-1727M Guelph
M 1917- Mountbatten
Millar
1962- INCHYRA B
Milles
1880- SONDES E
1880- THROWLEY V
MILLS
B 1957- Mills
V 1963- Mills

Mills
1886-1982X HILLINGDON B
1957- MILLS B
1963- MILLS V
MILLTOWN
E(I) 1763-1891D Leeson
MILNE
B 1933- Milne
Milne
1933- MILNE B
MILNER
B 1901-1925X Milner
V 1902-1925X Milner
MILNER OF LEEDS
B 1951- Milner
Milner
1901-1925X MILNER B
1902-1925X MILNER V
1951- MILNER OF LEEDS B
Milnes: See Crewe-Milnes
Milo de Gloucester
1140-1154X HEREFORD E
MILSINGTON
V(S) 1703-1835X Colyear
MILTON
B 1689-1704X Sydney
V(I) 1716- Fitzwilliam
B 1742- Fitzwilliam
V 1746- Fitzwilliam
B(I) 1753-1808X Damer
B 1762-1808X Damer
V 1792-1808X Damer
MILVERTON
B 1947- Richards
MINSTER
B 1821- Conyngham
MINTO
B 1797- Elliot
V 1813- Elliot
E 1813- Elliot
MISHCON
B(L) 1978- Mishcon
Mishcon
1978- MISHCON B(L)
Mitchell-Thomson
1932- SELSDON B
MITCHISON
B(L) 1964-1970X Mitchison
Mitchison
1964-1970X MITCHISON B(L)

108

Mitford
1902-   REDESDALE B
See also: Freeman-Mitford
MOELS
B   1216/72-1272/1307C Moels
B   1299-1337A Moels
Moels
1216/72-1272/1307C MOELS B
1299-1337A MOELS B
MOHUN
B   1066/87-1216/72C Mohun
B   1299-1594A Mohun
MOHUN OF OKEHAMPTON
B   1628-1712X Mohun
Mohun
1066/87-1216/72X MOHUN B
1299-1594A MOHUN B
1628-1712X MOHUN OF OKEHAMPTON B
MOIRA
E   1761-1868X Rawdon
MOLESWORTH
V(I) 1716-   Molesworth
Molesworth
1716-   MOLESWORTH V(I)
1716-   PHILIPSTOWN B(I)
MOLINES
B   1347-....X Molines
B   1445-   Hungerford
Molines
1347-....X MOLINES B
MOLLOY
B(L) 1981-   Molloy
Molloy
1981-   MOLLOY B(L)
MOLSON
B(L) 1961-   Molson
Molson
1961-   MOLSON B(L)
MOLYNEUX
V(I) 1628-1972X Molyneux
Molyneux
1628-1972X MOLYNEUX V(I)
1771-1972X SEFTON E(I)
1831-1972X SEFTON B
MONCK
B   1660-1688X Monck
B(I) 1797-1848X Monck
V(I) 1801-   Monck
B   1866-   Monck
Monck
1660-1688X MONCK B

Monck (Cont'd)
1797-1848X MONCK B(I)
1801-   MONCK V(I)
1866-   MONCK B
1822-1848X RATHDOWNE E
1660-1688X TORRINGTON E
MONCKTON
B   1887-1971X Monckton
MONCKTON OF BRENCHLEY
V   1957-   Monckton
Monckton
1727-   GALWAY V(I)
1727-   KILLARD B(I)
1887-1971X MONCKTON B
1957-   MONCKTON OF BRENCHLEY V
MONCREIFF
B   1873-   Moncreiff
Moncreiff
1873-   MONCREIFF B
Mond
1928-   MELCHETT B
Money-Coutts
1923-   LATIMER B
Monk
1660-1688X ALBEMARLE D
1660-1688X BEAUCHAMP B
MONK BRETTON
B   1884-   Dodson
MONKSWELL
B   1885-   Collier
MONMOUTH
B   1 66/87-1257X Fitzbaderon
E   1626-1660X Carey
D   1660-1685F Scot
E   1689-1814X Mordaunt
MONSELL
V   1935-   Eyres Monsell
MONSLOW
B(L) 1966-1966X Monslow
Monslow
1966-1966X MONSLOW B(L)
MONSON
V(I) 1628-1661F Monson
B   1728-   Monson
Monson
1628-1661F CASTLEMAINE V(I)
1628-1661F MONSON V(I)
1728-   MONSON B
1886-1898X OXENBRIDGE V

109

MONTAGU   *
B   1154/89-1216/72P Montagu
B   1300-1539X Montagu
B   1342-1361X Montagu
B   1357-1471X Montagu
B   1461-1477F Nevill
V   1554-1797X Brown
E   1689-1749X Montagu
M   1705-1749X Montagu
D   1766-1790X Montagu
MONTAGU OF BEAULIEU
B   1885-   Douglas-Scott-
                     Montagu
MONTAGU OF BOUGHTON
B   1621-1749X Montagu
B   1762-1772X Montagu
MONTAGU OF KIMBOLTON
B   1620-   Montagu
MONTAGU OF ST NEOTS
B   1660-   Montagu
Montagu
    1700-1772X HALIFAX B
    1714-1715X HALIFAX E
    1715-1772X HALIFAX E
    1660-   HINCHINGBROKE V
    1620-   MANCHESTER B
    1620-   MANCHESTER V
    1626-   MANCHESTER E
    1719-   MANCHESTER D
    1620-   MANDEVILLE V
    1154/89-1216/72P MONTAGU B
    1342-1361X MONTAGU B
    1357-   MONTAGU B
    1689-1749X MONTAGU E
    1705-1749X MONTAGU M
    1766-1790X MONTAGU D
    1621-1749X MONTAGU OF BOUGHTON B
    1762-1772X MONTAGU OF BOUGHTON B
    1620-   MONTAGU OF KIMBOLTON B
    1660-   MONTAGU OF ST NEOTS B
    1689-1749X MONTHERMER V
    1705-1749X MONTHERMER M
    1337-1400F SALISBURY E
    1409-1428C SALISBURY E
    1660-   SANDWICH E
    1907-   SWAYTHLING B
    See also: Douglas-Scott-Montagu
Montague
    1947-   AMWELL B
MONTALT
B   1154/89-1216/72P Montalt, De
B   1295-1329X Montalt, De
        * See also Addenda   110

MONTALT, DE
B(I) 1785-   Maude
E   1886-1905X Maude
Montalt, De
    1154/89-1216/72P MONTALT B
    1295-1329X MONTALT B
MONTBEGON
B   1135/54-1216/72X Montbegon, De
Montbegon, De
    1135/54-1216/72X MONTBEGON B
MONTEAGLE
B   1514-1686P Stanley
B   1605-1686A Parker
B(I) 1760-   Browne
B   1806-   Browne
MONTEAGLE OF BRANDON
B   1839-   Spring Rice
MONTEITH & AIRTH
E(S) 1427-1694D Graham
MONTFICHET
B   1066/87-1268X Montfichet, De
Montfichet, De
    1066/87-1268X MONTFICHET B
MONTFORT
B   1066/87-1216/72P Montfort, De
B   1295-1367A Montfort, De
B   1741-1851X Bromley
Montfort, De
    1264-1265F CHESTER E
    1206-1264F LEICESTER E
    1066/87-1216/72P MONTFORT B
    1295-1367A MONTFORT B
MONTGOMERIE
L(S) 1449-   Montgomerie
Montgomerie
    1806-   ARDROSSAN B
    1508-   EGLINTON E(S)
    1449-   MONTGOMERIE L(S)
    1859-   SETON & TRANENT B
    1859-   WINTON E
MONTGOMERY
B   1342-1342X Montgomery
E   1605-   Herbert
V(I) 1622-1757X Montgomery
MONTGOMERY OF ALAMEIN
V   1946-   Montgomery
Montgomery
    1342-1342X MONTGOMERY B
    1622-1757X MONTGOMERY V(I)
    1946-   MONTGOMERY OF ALAMEIN V
    1622-1757X MOUNT ALEXANDER V(I)
    1661-1757X MOUNT ALEXANDER E(I)

Montgomery, De
  1071-1102F SHREWSBURY E
MONTHERMER
  B   1309-1471F Monthermer
  B   1337-1337X Monthermer
  V   1689-1749X Montagu
  M   1705-1749X Montagu
  M   1766-1790X Brudenell
Monthermer
  1299-1306L GLOUCESTER & HERTFORD E
  1309-1471F MONTHERMER B
  1337-1337X MONTHERMER B
MONTJOY
  B   1465-1606X Blount
  B(I) 1616-1681X Blount
  B   1627-1681X Blount
MONTJOY OF THE ISLE OF WIGHT
  B   1711-1758X Windsor
Montmorency, De
  1816-1917X FRANKFORT DE MONTMOR-
            ENCY V(I)
  1756-1951X MOUNTMORRES B(I)
  1763-1951X MOUNTMORRES V(I)
MONTROSE
  D(S) 1488-1495L Lindsay
  E(S) 1505-   Graham
  M(S) 1644-   Graham
  D(S) 1707-   Graham
MONYMAILL: See RAITH, MONYMAILL &
          BALWEARIE
MONYPENNY
  L(S) 1464-....X Monypenny
Monypenny
  1464-....X MONYPENNY L(S)
MOORE
  B(I) 1616-   Moore
  V(I) 1621-   Moore
  B(I) 1715-1764X Moore
  B   1801-1892X Moore
  B   1954-   Moore
Moore
  1758-1764X CHARLEVILLE E(I)
  1661-   DROGHEDA E(I)
  1791-1892X DROGHEDA M(I)
  1764-1915X KILWORTH B(I)
  1616-   MOORE B(I)
  1621-   MOORE E(I)
  1715-1764X MOORE B(I)
  1801-1892X MOORE B
  1954-   MOORE B
  1766-1915X MOUNT CASHELL V(I)
  1781-1915X MOUNT CASHELL E(I)

Moore-Brabazon
  1942-   BRABAZON OF TARA B
MORAN
  B   1943-   Wilson
MORAY
  E(S) 1130-1130X Angus
  E(S) 1312-1455F Randolph
  E(S) 1562-   Stuart
Moray
  1225-1336A BOTHWELL L(S)
  1343-1346M STRATHERN E(S)
Morcar
  1066-   NORTHUMBERLAND E
MORDAUNT
  V   1659-1814X Mordaunt
Mordaunt
  1689-1814X MONMOUTH E
  1659-1814X MORDAUNT V
  1628-1814X PETERBOROUGH B
MORDINGTON
  L(S) 1641-1791X Douglas
MORETON
  B   1720-   Moreton
Moreton
  1068-1104F CORNWALL E
  1720-1770X DUCIE B
  1763-   DUCIE B
  1837-   DUCIE E
  1720-   MORETON B
Morgan
  1981-   ELYSTAN-MORGAN B(L)
  1859-1962X TREDEGAR B
  1905-1913X TREDEGAR V
  1926-1949X TREDEGAR V
  See also: Vaughan-Morgan
MORLEY
  B   1299-1442C Morley
  B   1469-1489C Lovel
  B   1523-1686A Parker
  E   1815-   Parker
MORLEY OF BLACKBURN
  V   1908-1923X Morley
Morley
  1299-1442C MORLEY B
  1908-1923X MORLEY OF BLACKBURN V
  See also: Hope-Morley
MORNE: See NEWRY & MORNE
MORNINGTON
  B(I) 1746-   Wesley
  E(I) 1760-   Wesley
Morres
  1800-1917X FRANKFORT B(I)

111

```
MORRIS                              Morton
 B(L) 1889-1901X Morris               1947-1973X MORTON B(L)
 B   1918-      Morris              MORVERN: See INVERARAY, MILL, MORVERN
MORRIS OF BORTH-Y-GEST                & TIRY
 B(L) 1960-     Morris              Morvic
MORRIS OF GRASMERE                    1154/89-1261X MORWICK B
 B(L) 1967-     Morris              MORVILL
MORRIS OF KENWOOD                     B   1154/89-1189/99P Morvill, De
 B   1950-      Morris              B   1319-1319X Morvill, De
Morris                              Morvill, De
 1900-          KILLANIN B            1154/89-1189/99P MORVILL B
 1889-1901X MORRIS B(L)               1319-1319X MORVILL B
 1918-          MORRIS B            MORWICK
 1960-          MORRIS OF BORTH-Y-    B   1154/89-1261X Morvic, De
                GEST B(L)          Mosley
 1967-          MORRIS OF GRASMERE    1916-1933X ANSLOW B
                B(L)                  1911-          RAVENSDALE B
 1950-          MORRIS OF KENWOOD B MOSTYN
 1934-1963X NUFFIELD B                B   1831-      Lloyd Mostyn
 1938-1963X NUFFIELD V              MOTTISTONE
MORRISON                              B   1933-      Seely
 B   1945-      Morrison           MOULTON
MORRISON OF LAMBETH                   B(L) 1912-1921X Moulton
 B(L) 1959-1965X Morrison          Moulton
Morrison                              1912-1921X MOULTON B(L)
 1959-          DUNROSSIL V        Mounsell
 1964-          MARGADALE B          1874-1932X EMLY B
 1945-          MORRISON B         MOUNT ALEXANDER
 1959-1965X MORRISON OF LAMBETH       V(I) 1622-1757X Montgomery
                B(L)                  E(I) 1661-1757X Montgomery
MORTIMER                           MOUNTBATTEN OF BURMA
 B   1295-1461M Mortimer              V   1945-      Mountbatten
 B   1296-1296X Mortimer              E   1947-      Mountbatten
 E   1711-1853X Harley             Mountbatten
MORTIMER OF CHIRKE                    1917-          ALDERNEY V
 B   1307-1336A Mortimer              1917-1960X BERKHAMSTED E
MORTIMER OF RICHARD'S CASTLE          1917-1960X CARISBROOKE M
 B   1299-1304A Mortimer              1947-          EDINBURGH D
Mortimer                              1947-          GREENWICH B
 1328-1424X MARCH E                   1917-1960X LAUNCESTON V
 1295-1461M MORTIMER B                1917-          MEDINA E
 1296-1296X MORTIMER B                1947-          MERIONETH E
 1307-1336A MORTIMER OF CHIRKE B      1917-          MILFORD HAVEN M
 1299-1304A MORTIMER OF RICHARD'S     1945-          MOUNTBATTEN OF BURMA V
                CASTLE B              1947-          MOUNTBATTEN OF BURMA E
 1368-1461M ULSTER E(I)               1947-          ROMSEY B
MORTON                             MOUNT CASHELL
 E(S) 1458-     Douglas               V(I) 1689-....X M'Carty
 E(S) 1585-1716F Maxwell              V(I) 1706-1719X Davys
MORTON OF HENRYTON                    V(I) 1766-1915X Moore
 B(L) 1947-1973X Morton               E(I) 1781-1915X Moore
```

MOUNTCASTELL: See PAISLEY, HAMILTON,
MOUNTCASTELL & KILPATRICK
MOUNTCASTLE
L(S) 1606-   Hamilton
B(I) 1701-   Hamilton
MOUNT CHARLES
B(I) 1753-1781X Conyngham
V(I) 1797-   Conyngham
E(I) 1816-   Conyngham
MOUNT EAGLE
B(I) 1760-   Browne
MOUNT-EARL
V(I) 1816-   Quin
See also: DUNRAVEN & MOUNT-EARL
MOUNT EDGCUMBE
E   1789-   Edgcumbe
MOUNT EDGCUMBE & VALLETORT
V   1781-   Edgcumbe
MOUNTEVANS
B   1945-   Evans
MOUNTFLORENCE
B(I) 1760-   Cole
MOUNTGARRET
V(I) 1550-   Butler
B   1911-   Butler
MOUNTJOY
B   1465-1606X Le Blount
V(I) 1682-1769X Stewart
B(I) 1785-1829X Gardiner
V(I) 1795-1829X Gardiner
V   1796-   Stuart
MOUNTMORRES
B(I) 1756-1951X Montmorency, De
V(I) 1763-1951X Montmorency, De
MOUNTNORRIS
B(I) 1628-   Annesley
E(I) 1793-1844X Annesley
MOUNTRATH
E(I) 1660-1802X Coote
MOUNT ROYAL: See STRATHCONA &
  MOUNT ROYAL
MOUNT SANDFORD
B   1800-1846X Sandford
MOUNT STEPHEN
B   1891-1921X Stephen
MOUNT STUART OF WORTLEY
B   1761-   Stuart
MOUNT STUART, CUMBRAE & INCH-
  MARNOCK
L(S) 1703-   Stuart

MOUNT TEMPLE
B   1932-1939X Ashley
MOUNT-TEMPLE
B   1880-1888X Cowper-Temple
MOWBRAY
B   1066/87-1216/72P Albini, De
B   1295-1383A A Mowbray
Mowbray
  1295-1383A MOWBRAY B
  1396-1475X NORFOLK D
  1377-1475X NOTTINGHAM E
  1451-1475X WARREN E
Mowbray, De
  1081-1095M NORTHUMBERLAND E
MOYLE
B(L) 1966-1974X Moyle
Moyle
  1966-1974X MOYLE B(L)
MOYNE
B   1932-   Guinness
MOYNIHAN
B   1929-   Moynihan
Moynihan
  1929-   MOYNIHAN B
MOYOLA
B(L) 1971-   Chichester-Clark
Muff
  1945-   CALVERLEY B
MUGDOCK: See ABERUTHVEN, MUGDOCK
  & FINTRIE
MUIR-MACKENZIE
B   1915-1930X Muir-Mackenzie
Muir-Mackenzie
  1915-1930X MUIR-MACKENZIE B
MUIRSHIEL
V   1963-   Maclay
MULGRAVE
E   1626-1735X Sheffield
B(I) 1767-   Phipps
B   1790-1792X Phipps
B   1794-   Phipps
V   1812-   Phipps
E   1812-   Phipps
Mulholland
  1892-   DUNLEATH B
MULL: See INVERARY, MULL, MORVERN
  & TIRY
MULLEY
B(L) 1984-   Mulley
Mulley
  1984-   MULLEY B(L)

113

Mullins
  1800-   VENTRY B(I)
MULTON OF EGREMONT
  B   1216/72-1294P Multon
  B   1297-1334A Multon
MULTON OF GILLESLAND
  B   1100/35-1272/1307P Multon
  B   1307-1313C Multon
Multon
  1216/72-1294P MULTON OF EGREMONT B
  1297-1334A MULTON OF EGREMONT B
  1100/35-1272/1307P MULTON OF GILL-
                 ESLAND B
MUNARD
  L(S) 1697-   Douglas
MUNCASTER
  B   1783-1917X Pennington
MUNCHENSI
  B   1066/87-1216/72P Munchensi
  B   1264-1289X Munchensi
Munchensi
  1066/87-1216/72P MUNCHENSI B
  1264-1289X MUNCHENSI B
MUNCY
  B   1299-....X Muncy, De
Muncy, De
  1299-....X MUNCY B
Munro
  1934-1955X ALNESS B
Munro-Ferguson
  1920-1934X NOVAR V
MUNSTER
  Dss(I) 1716-1743X Schulenburg
  E(I) 1789-1830M Guelph
  E   1831-   Fitz-Clarence
MURRAY   *
  E(S) 1360-1455F Dunbar
  E(S) 1501-1544M Stewart
  L(S) 1696-1724L Murray
MURRAY OF BLAIR, MOULIN & TILLIMET
  L(S) 1686-   Murray
MURRAY OF ELIBANK
  B   1912-1920X Murray
MURRAY OF GARVESEND
  B(L) 1976-   Murray
MURRAY OF LOCHMABEN
  L(S) 1622-1658X Murray
MURRAY OF NEWHAVEN
  B(L) 1964-   Murray
MURRAY OF STANLEY
  B   1786-1957X Stewart-Murray

MURRAY OF TULLIBARDINE
  L(S) 1604-   Murray
MURRAY, BALVENIE & GASK
  L(S) 1676-   Murray
Murray   *
  1622-1658X ANNAND V(S)
  1624-1658X ANNANDALE E(S)
  1661-   ANNANDALE E(S)
  1457-   ATHOLL E(S)
  1676-   ATHOLL M(S)
  1703-   ATHOLL D(S)
  1641-1776M BALVAIRD L(S)
  1703-   BALWHIDDER, GLENALMOND
             & GLENLYON V(S)
  1674-1698X BAYNING Vss
  1674-1698X BEAUCHAMP Vss
  1905-1942X DUNEDIN B
  1926-1942X DUNEDIN V
  1686-   DUNMORE E(S)
  1831-   DUNMORE B
  1911-1962X ELIBANK V
  1686-   FINCASTLE V(S)
  1696-1724L GLENALMOND V(S)
  1643-   HUNTINGTOWER L(S)
  1670-   HUNTINGTOWER L(S)
  1605-   MANSFIELD B
  1756-1793X MANSFIELD B
  1776-   MANSFIELD E
  1696-1724L MURRAY L(S)
  1686-   MURRAY OF BLAIR, MOULIN
             & TILLIMET L(S)
  1912-1920X MURRAY OF ELIBANK B
  1976-   MURRAY OF GRAVESEND
  1622-1658X MURRAY OF LOCHMABEN L(S)
  1964-   MURRAY OF NEWHAVEN B(L)
  1604-   MURRAY OF TULLIBARDINE
             L(S)
  1676-   MURRAY, BALVENIE & GASK
             L(S)
  1605-   SCONE L(S)
  1621-   STORMONT V(S)
  1703-   STRATHTAY & STRATHARDALE
             E(S)
  1606-   TULLIBARDINE E(S)
  1703-   TULLIBARDINE M(S)
  See also: Erskine-Murray
  See also: Stewart-Murray
MURTON OF LINDISFARNE
  B(L) 1979-   Murton
Murton
  1979-   MURTON OF LINDISFARNE B(L)

114   *See also Addenda

```
MUSARD                              NAAS
  B    1066/87-1300X Musard           B(I) 1776-      Bourke
Musard                              NAIRNE
  1066/87-1300X MUSARD B              L(S) 1681-      Nairne
MUSCHAMP                            Nairne
  B    1100/35-1249X Muschamp, De    1681-    NAIRNE L(S)
Muschamp, De                       Nall-Cain
  1100/35-1249X MUSCHAMP B           1933-    BROCKET B
MUSGRAVE                            NANSLADRON
  B    1350-1373X Musgrave           B    1299-....X Nansladron
Musgrave                           Nansladron
  1350-1373X MUSGRAVE B              1299-....X NANSLADRON B
MUSKERRY                           NAPIER
  B(I) 1658-1690F M'Carthy           L(S) 1627-      Napier
  B(I) 1781-       Deane           NAPIER OF MAGDALA
                                     B    1868-      Napier
                                   Napier
                                     1872-    ETTRICK B
                                     1627-    NAPIER L(S)
                                     1868-    NAPIER OF MAGDALA B
                                   Nassau
                                     1695-1830X ENFIELD B
                                     1698-1754X GRANTHAM E
                                     1695-1830X ROCHFORD E
                                     1695-1830X TUNBRIDGE V
                                   Nassau, De
                                     1698-1754X ALFORD B
                                     1698-1754X BOSTON V
                                   NATHAN
                                     B    1940-      Nathan
                                   Nathan
                                     1940-    NATHAN B
                                   NAVAN
                                     B(I) 1628-1885X Jones
                                   NAVAR
                                     L(S) 1481-1504X Stewart
                                     L(S) 1646-1874X Maule
                                   Neave
                                     1979-    AIREY OF ABINGDON Bss(L)
                                   Needham
                                     1625-    KILMOREY V(I)
                                     1822-    KILMOREY E(I)
                                     1822-    NEWRY & MORNE V(I)
                                   NELSON OF THE NILE
                                     B    1798-1805X Nelson
                                   NELSON OF THE NILE & OF HILLBOROUGH
          (TITLES are in CAPITALS    B    1801-      Nelson
           Surnames in smalls)      V    1801-1805X Nelson
                                   NELSON OF TRAFALGAR
                                     E    1805-      Nelson

                        115
```

NELSON OF STAFFORD
    B   1960-   Nelson
Nelson
    1805-   MERTON OF TRAFALGAR V
    1798-1805X NELSON OF THE NILE B
    1801-   NELSON OF THE NILE &
                    OF HILLBOROUGH B
    1801-1805V NELSON OF THE NILE &
                    OF HILLBOROUGH V
    1805-   NELSON OF TRAFALGAR E
    1960-   NELSON OF STAFFORD B
NEMPHLAR: See INGLISBERRY & NEMPHLAR
NEREFORD
    B   1294-1297X Nereford
Nereford
    1294-1297X NEREFORD B
NETHERTHORPE
    B   1959-   Turner
NETTERVILLE
    V   1622-1882X Netterville
Netterville
    1622-1882X NETTERVILLE V
NEVILL
    B   1342-....X Nevill
    V   1784-   Nevill
NEVILL OF ESSEX
    B   1311-1358X Nevill
NEVILL OF MONTAGU
    B   1460-1471F Nevill
NEVILL OF RABY
    B   1154/89-1216/72P Nevill
    B   1294-1570F Nevill
Nevill
    1450-   ABERGAVENNY B
    1784-   ABERGAVENNY E
    1876-   ABERGAVENNY M
    1469-1477D BEDFORD D
    1429-1462A FAUCONBERG B
    1406-1442P FURNIVAL B
    1462-1462X KENT E
    1432-1577A LATIMER B
    1876-   LEWES E
    1461-1477F MONTAGU B
    1470-1477F MONTAGU M
    1342-....X NEVILL B
    1784-   NEVILL V
    1311-1358X NEVILL OF ESSEX
    1460-1471F NEVILL OF MONTAGU
    1154/89-1216/72P NEVILL OF RABY B
    1294-1570F NEVILL OF RABY
    1464-1470R NORTHUMBERLAND E

Nevill (Cont'd)
    1442-1471F SALISBURY E
    1449-1471F WARWICK E
    1397-1570F WESTMORLAND E
NEWALL
    B   1946-   Newall
Newall
    1946-   NEWALL B
NEWARK
    V   1627-1773X Pierrepont
    L(S) 1661-1694X Leslie
    V   1796-1955X Pierrepont
NEWBOROUGH
    B(I) 1714-   Cholmondeley
    B(I) 1776-   Wynn
NEWBOTTLE
    L(S) 1587-   Kerr
NEWBURGH
    V(S) 1647-1694X Livingston
    E(S) 1660-   Livingston
    B   1716-   Cholmondeley
Newburgh
    1066-1242C WARWICK E
NEWCASTLE
    E   1623-1624X Stuart
    E   1628-1691X Cavendish
    M   1643-1691X Cavendish
    D   1664-1691X Cavendish
    D   1694-1711X Holles
    D   1715-1768X Holles
NEWCASTLE-UNDER-LYNE
    D   1756-   Holles
NEWCOMEN
    B(I) 1800-1825X Newcomen
    V(I) 1803-1825X Newcomen
Newcomen
    1800-1825X NEWCOMEN B(I)
    1803-1825X NEWCOMEN V(I)
NEWHAVEN
    V(S) 1681-1738X Cheyne
    B(I) 1776-1794X Mayne
NEWLANDS
    B   1898-1929X Hozier
NEWLISTON
    L(S) 1703-   Dalrymple
Newman
    1931-1945X MAMHEAD B
NEWMARCH
    B   1264-....X Newmarch
Newmarch
    1264-....X NEWMARCH B

116

NEWMARSH
  B   1628-1695X Wentworth
NEWPORT
  E   1628-1681X Blount
  B   1642-1762X Newport
  V   1675-1762X Newport
  B(I) 1743-   Jocelyn
  V   1815-   Bridgeman
Newport
  1694-1762X BRADFORD E
  1642-1762X NEWPORT B
  1675-1762X NEWPORT V
  1716-1719X TORRINGTON B
NEWRY & MORNE
  V(I) 1822-   Needham
NEWTON
  B   1892-   Legh
Newton
  1934-1942X ELTISLEY B
NEWTOWN
  B(I) 1718-1784X Child
NEWTOWN BUTLER
  B(I) 1715-   Butler
Nicholls: See Harmar-Nicholls
NICHOLSON
  B   1912-1918X Nicholson
Nicholson
  1912-1918X NICHOLSON B
NICOL
  Bss(L) 1982-   Nicol
Nicol
  1982-   NICOL Bss(L)
Nicolson
  1916-   CARNOCK B
NIDDRY
  B   1814-   Hope
NIEDPATH
  B   1814-   Wemyss
NITH
  V(S) 1684-   Scott
NITH, THORTHORWALD & ROSS
  V(S) 1684-   Scott
NITHSDALE
  E(S) 1620-1716F Maxwell
Nivison
  1922-   GLENDYNE B
Noble
  1974-1984X GLENKINGLAS B(L)
  1930-1935X KIRKLEY B
NOEL
  B   1617-1798X Noel
  B   1841-   Noel

NOEL OF TITCHFIELD
  B   1681-1798X Noel
Noel
  1813-   BARHAM B
  1841-   CAMPDEN V
  1682-1798X GAINSBOROUGH E
  1841-   GAINSBOROUGH E
  1617-1798X NOEL B
  1841-   NOEL B
  1681-1798X NOEL OF TITCHFIELD B
NOEL-BAKER
  B(L) 1977-1982X Noel-Baker
Noel-Baker
  1977-1982X NOEL-BAKER B(L)
NOEL-BUXTON
  B   1930-   Buxton
Noel-Paton
  1958-   FERRIER B(L)
NONSUCH
  Bss 1679-1774X Villiers
NORBURY
  B(I) 1800-   Toler
  E(I) 1827-   Toler
NORFOLK
  E   1066-....F Wayher
  E   1135-1307X Bigod
  E   1312-1338X Plantagenet
  D   1396-1475X Mowbray
  Dss 1397-1399X Plantagenet
  D   1483-   Howard
  E   1644-   Howard
NORMAN
  B   1944-1950X Norman
Norman
  1944-1950X NORMAN B
NORMANBROOK
  B   1963-1967X Brook
NORMANBY
  M   1694-1735X Sheffield
  V   1812-   Phipps
  M   1838-   Phipps
NORMAND
  B(L) 1947-1962X Normand
Normand
  1947-1962X NORMAND B(L)
NORMANTON
  E(I) 1806-   Agar
NORREYS OF RYCOTE
  B   1572-   Bertie
NORRIE
  B   1957-   Norrie

117

Norrie
  1957-   NORRIE B
Norris
  1620-1623X BERKSHIRE E
  1620-1623X THAME V
NORTH
  B   1554-1942A North
North
  1673-1734X GREY OF ROLLESTON B
  1752-   GUILFORD E
  1554-1942A NORTH B
NORTHALLERTON
  V   1706-1727M Guelph
  V   1917-1981X Cambridge
NORTHAMPTON
  E   1066-1184X St Liz
  E   1337-1372X Bohun, De
  M   1557-1571X Parr
  E   1604-1614X Howard
  E   1618-   Compton
  M   1812-   Compton
NORTHBOURNE
  B   1884-   James
NORTHBROOK
  B   1866-   Baring
  E   1876-1929X Baring
NORTHCHURCH
  Bss(L) 1963-   Davidson
NORTHCLIFFE
  B   1905-   Harmsworth
  V   1917-1922X Harmsworth
NORTHCOTE
  B   1900-1911X Northcote
Northcote
  1885-   IDDESLEIGH E
  1900-1911X NORTHCOTE B
NORTHESK
  E(S) 1647-   Carnegie
NORTHFIELD
  B(L) 1975-   Chapman
NORTHINGTON
  E   1764-1786X Henly
  B   1885-   Eden
NORTHLAND
  V(I) 1791-   Knox
NORTHUMBERLAND
  E   1066-....X Morcar
  E   1068-1068X Copsi
  E   1068-1069X Comyn
  E   1069-1072F Gospatrick
  E   1072-1076F Waltheof

NORTHUMBERLAND (Cont'd)
  E   1076-1080R Walcher
  E   1080-1081R Alberic, or Aubrey
  E   1081-1095M Mowbray, De
  E   1139-1152X Henry, Prince of
                Scotland
  E   1152-1157X William, Prince of
                Scotland
  E   1189-1195S Pudsey, De
  E   1377-1461X Percy
  E   1464-1470R Nevill
  D   1551-1553F Dudley
  E   1557-1670X Percy
  E   1674-1716X Fitzroy
  D   1683-1716X Fitzroy
  E   1749-   Seymour
  D   1766-   Percy
NORTHWICK
  B   1797-1887X Rushout
NORTHWODE
  B   1313-1416A Northwode
Northwode
  1313-1416A NORTHWODE B
NORTON
  B   1878-   Adderley
Norton
  1782-   GRANTLEY B
  1782-   MARKENFIELD
  1916-   RATHCREEDAN B
  See also Hill-Norton
NORWICH
  E   1154-....X Bigod
  B   1342-1374X Norwich
  E   1626-1630X Denny
  E   1645-1672X Goring
  E   1672-1777X Howard
  E   1784-1836X Gordon
  V   1952-   Cooper
Norwich
  1342-1374X NORWICH B
NORWOOD
  B(I) 1797-   Toler
NOTTINGHAM
  E   1377-1475X Mowbray
  E   1476-1483X Plantagenet
  E   1483-1491X Berkeley
  E   1525-1536X Fitzroy
  E   1597-1681X Howard
  E   1681-   Finch
NOVANT
  B   1066/87-1154/89X Novant, De

Novant, De
1066/87-1154/89X NOVANT B
NOVAR
V   1920-1934X Munro-Ferguson
NUFFIELD
B   1934-1963X Morris
V   1938-1963X Morris
NUGENT
B(I) 1689-   Nugent
B(I) 1767-1788X Nugent
E(I) 1776-1889X Nugent
B   1960-1973X Nugent
NUGENT OF GUILDFORD
B(L) 1966-   Nugent
Nugent
1767-1788X CLARE V(I)
1486-   DELVIN B(I)
1689-   NUGENT B(I)
1767-1788X NUGENT B(I)
1776-1889X NUGENT E(I)
1960-1973X NUGENT B
1966-   NUGENT OF GUILDFORD
             B(L)
1621-   WESTMEATH E(I)
1822-1871X WESTMEATH M
Nugent-Temple-Grenville
1799-1822M TEMPLE OF STOWE E
NUNBURNHOLME
B   1906-   Wilson
NUNEHAM
V   1749-1830X Harcourt
B   1917-   Harcourt

(TITLES are in CAPITALS
Surnames in smalls)

OAKLEY
B   1831-   Cadogan
OAKSEY
B   1947-   Lawrence
OAKSHOTT
B(L) 1959-1975X Oakshott
Oakshott
1959-1975X OAKSHOTT B(L)
O'BRIEN
V(I) 1662-1764X O'Brien
B   1900-1914X O'Brien
O'BRIEN OF LOTHBURY
B(L) 1973-   O'Brien
O'Brien
1543-   INCHIQUIN B(I)
1654-1855X INCHIQUIN E
1662-1764F O'BRIEN V(I)
1891-1914X O'BRIEN B
1973-   O'BRIEN OF LOTHBURY B(L)
1918-1930X SHANDON B
1826-1846X TADCASTER B
1540-1741D THOMOND E(I)
1756-1774X THOMOND E(I)
1800-1855X THOMOND M(I)
See also Wyndham-O'Brien
O'Bryen
1714-1741X TADCASTER D
1801-1808X THOMOND B
O'Callaghan
1785-1898X LISMORE B(I)
1806-1898X LISMORE V(I)
1838-1898X LISMORE B
O'CARROLL
B(I) 1552-....? O'Carroll
O'Carroll
1552-....? O'CARROLL B(I)
See also: C
OCHILTRIE
L(S) 1543-1615S Stewart
L(S) 1615-1675X Stewart
OCKHAM
B   1725-   King
V   1838-   King
O'Dempsey
1550-1714X CLANMALIER B(I)
1631-1714X CLANMALIER V(I)
1599-1714X PHILIPSTOWN B(I)
Odo
1067-1096X KENT E
O'Donnell
1603-1642X TYRCONNELL E(I)

119

```
OFFALEY                             O'Hara
  Bss(I) 1620-1658L Digby alias       1721-1774X KILMAINE B(I)
                   Fitzgerald         1706-1774X TYRAWLEY B(I)
OFFALY                              OLDACSTLE
  B(I)   1203-      Fitzgerald        B    1409-1417X Oldcastle
  E(I)   1761-      Fitzgerald      Oldcastle
OGILVIE OF CULLEN                     1409-1417F COBHAM B
  L(S) 1698-        Ogilvie           1409-1417X OLDCASTLE B
OGILVIE OF DESKFORD & CULLEN        OLIPHANT
  L(S) 1701-        Ogilvie           L(S) 1456-1751X Oliphant
Ogilvie                            Oliphant
  1698-      OGILVIE OF CULLEN L(S)    1456-1751X OLIPHANT L(S)
  1701-      OGILVIE OF DESKFORD &   OLIVIER
             CULLEN L(S)              B    1924-1943X Olivier
  1701-      REIDHAVEN V(S)           B(L) 1970-        Olivier
  1698-      SEAFIELD V(S)          Olivier
  1701-      SEAFIELD E(S)            1924-1943X OLIVIER B
Ogilvie-Grant                        1970-        OLIVIER B(L)
  1858-1884X STRATHSPEY B           Olmius
OGILVY OF AIRLIE                      1762-1787X WALTHAM B(I)
  L(S) 1491-        Ogilvy          O'MALLAN: See GLEAN-O'MALLAN
OGILVY OF ALYTH & LINTRATHEN        O'Mallan: See Mallowne O'Mullan
  L(S) 1639-        Ogilvy          O'Mullane
OGILVY OF DESKFORD                    1622-....L GLEAN-O'MALLAN B(I)
  L(S) 1616-1811P Ogilvy           O'NEILL
Ogilvy                               B(I) 1793-1855X O'Neill
  1639-      AIRLIE E(S)             V(I) 1795-1855X O'Neill
  1642-1803D BANFF L(S)             E(I) 1800-1841X O'Neill
  1638-1811X FINDLATER E(S)          B    1868-        O'Neill
  1491-      OGILVY OF AIRLIE L(S)  O'NEILL OF THE MAINE
  1639-      OGILVY OF ALYTH &        B(L) 1970-        O'Neill
             LINTRATHEN L(S)        O'Neill
  1616-1811P OGILVY OF DESKFORD       1542-1612X DUNCANNON B(I)
             L(S)                     1793-1855X O'NEILL B(I)
OGLE                                  1795-1855X O'NEILL V(I)
  B    1461-1597A Ogle                1800-1841X O'NEILL E(I)
  B    1620-1691A Ogle                1868-        O'NEILL B
  V(I) 1645-1670X Ogle                1970-        O'NEILL OF THE MAINE B(L)
Ogle                                  1953-        RATHCAVAN B
  1461-1597A OGLE B                   1800-1855X RAYMOND V(I)
  1620-1691A OGLE B                   1542-1608F TYRONE E(I)
  1645-1670X OGLE V(I)             ONGLEY
OGMORE                               B    1776-1877X Ongley
  B    1950-      Rees-Williams     Ongley
O'GRADY                              1776-1877X ONGLEY B
  B(I) 1831-1955X O'Grady          ONSLOW
O'Grady                              B    1716-        Onslow
  1831-1955X GUILLAMORE V(I)        E    1801-        Onslow
  1831-1955X O'GRADY B(I)          Onslow
O'HAGAN                              1776-        CRANLEY B
  B    1870-      Strachey          1801-        CRANLEY V
                    120
```

Onslow (Cont'd)
  1716-   ONSLOW B
  1801-   ONSLOW E
ORAM
  B(L) 1975-   Oram
Oram
  1975-   ORAM B(L)
ORANMORE & BROWNE
  B(I) 1836-   Browne
ORANSAY
  L(S) 1706-   Campbell
Orde-Powlett
  1707-   BOLTON B
ORFORD
  E   1697-1727X Russell
  E   1742-1797X Walpole
  E   1806-1931X Walpole
ORIEL
  Bss(I) 1790-1831X Foster
  B   1821-   Foster
ORKNEY
  E(S) 1066/87-1470P Sinclair
  D(S) 1567-1567F Hepburn
  E(S) 1581-1614F Stewart
  E(S) 1696-1951D Hamilton
ORMATHWAITE
  B   1868-1984X Walsh
ORMELIE
  L(S) 1681-   Campbell
  E   1831-1862X Campbell
  E   1885-1922X Campbell
  See also: GLENORCHY, BENEDARA-
    LOCH, ORMELIE & WEICK
ORMOND OF ROCHFORD
  B   1495-1515A Butler
ORMONDE
  E(I) 1328-   Butler
  E(S) 1445-1455F Douglas
  M(S) 1481-1504X Stewart
  E(I) 1527-1538A Boleyn
  E(I) 1603-1613X Butler
  M(I) 1642-1715F Butler
  E(S) 1651-1715P Douglas
  D(I) 1661-1715F Butler
  D   1681-1715F Butler
  M(I) 1816-1820X Butler
  B   1821-   Butler
  M(I) 1825-   Butler
Ormsby-Gore
  1876-   HARLECH B
Orr
  1949-1971X BOYD-ORR B

ORREBY
  B   1309-1317X Orreby
Orreby
  1309-1317X ORREBY B
ORRERY
  E(I) 1660-   Boyle
ORR-EWING
  B(L) 1971-   Orr-Ewing
Orr-Ewing
  1971-   ORR-EWING B(L)
ORWELL
  B(I) 1762-1783X Vernon
OSBORNE
  B   1673-1964X Osborne
Osborne
  1689-1964X CARMARTHEN M
  1674-1964X DANBY E
  1832-1859M GODOLPHIN
  1673-1964X LATIMER V
  1696-1964X LEEDS D
  1673-1964X OSBORNE B
Osmund
  1066/87-....X DORSET E
OSSINGTON
  V   1872-1873X Denison
OSSORY
  E(I) 1527-   Butler
  See also UPPER OSSORY
OSSULSTON
  B   1682-   Bennet
OSWALDESTRE
  B   1627-   Howard
Otway Cave
  1839-1862A BRAYE B
OVERSLEY
  B   1628-1695X Wentworth
OVERSTONE
  B   1850-   Jones-Lloyd
OVERTOUN
  B   1893-1908X White
OXENBRIDGE
  V   1886-1898X Monson
OXENFOORD
  B   1841-   Dalrymple
OXFORD
  E   1155-1338F Vere
  E   1392-1461F Vere
  E   1464-1702X Vere
  E   1711-1853X Harley
OXFORD & ASQUITH
  E   1925-   Asquith

OXFUIRD
  V(S) 1651-   Makgill
OXMANTOWN
  B(I) 1681-1764X Parsons
  B(I) 1792-   Parsons

(TITLES are in CAPITALS
 Surnames in smalls)

Page
  1978-   WHADDON B(L)
PAGANELL
  B   1066/87-1294X Paganell
Paganell
  1066/87-1294X PAGANELL B
PAGET
  B   1550-   Paget
PAGET OF NORTHAMPTON
  B(L) 1974-   Paget
Paget
  1815-   ANGLESEY M
  1711-1769X   BURTON B
  1550-   PAGET B
  1974-   PAGET OF NORTHAMPTON
                 B(L)
  1918-1949X   QUEENBOROUGH B
  1714-1769X   UXBRIDGE E
  1784-   UXBRIDGE E
PAINTLAND: See TAY & PAINTLAND
PAISLEY
  L(S) 1587-   Hamilton
PAISLEY, HAMILTON, MOUNTCASTELL
  & KILPATRICK L(S
  L(S) 1606-   Hamilton
PAKENHAM
  B(I) 1756-   Pakenham
  B   1945-   Pakenham
Pakenham
  1756-   LONGFORD B(I)
  1785-   LONGFORD Css(I)
  1785-   LONGFORD E(I)

Pakenham (Cont'd)
  1756-   PAKENHAM B(I)
  1945-   PAKENHAM B
  1821-   SILCHESTER B
Pakington
  1874-   HAMPTON B
Palk
  1880-1939X HALDON B
PALMER
  B(I) 1661-1705X Palmer
  B   1933-   Palmer
Palmer
  1661-1705X CASTLEMAINE E(I)
  1661-1705X PALMER B(I)
  1933-   PALMER B
  1945-1977X RUSHOLME B
  1872-   SELBORNE B
  1882-   SELBORNE E
  1882-   WOLMER V
PALMERSTON
  V(I) 1722-1865X Temple
PANMURE
  L(S) 1180-1219X Valonis, De
  E(S) 1646-1715F Maule
  E(I) 1743-1782X Maule
  B   1831-1874X Maule
PANNELL
  B(L) 1974-   Pannell
Pannell
  1974-   PANNELL B(L)
PANTULF
  B   1066/87-1216/72X Pantulf
Pantulf
  1066/87-1216/72X PANTULF B
PARBROATH
  L(S) 1633-   Lindsay
PARGITER
  B(L) 1966-   Pargiter
Pargiter
  1966-   PARGITER B(L)
Parke
  1856-1868X WENSLEYDALE B
PARKER
  B   1716-   Parker
  V   1721-   Parker
  B(L) 1913-1918X Parker
PARKER OF WADDINGTON
  B(L) 1958-1972X Parker
Parker
  1784-   BORINGDON B
  1815-   BORINGDON V

122

Parker (Cont'd)
```
1716-        MACCLESFIELD B
1721-        MACCLESFIELD E
1605-1686A   MONTEAGLE B
1523-1686A   MORLEY B
1815-        MORLEY E
1716-        PARKER B
1721-        PARKER V
1913-1918X   PARKER B(L)
1958-1972X   PARKER OF WADDINGTON
             B(L)
```
Parkinson-Fortescue
```
1874-1898X   CARLINGFORD B
1852-1898X   CLERMONT B(I)
```
Parkyns
```
1795-1850X   RANCLIFFE B
```
PARMOOR
```
B    1914-        Cripps
```
Parnell
```
1841-        CONGLETON B
```
PARR OF HORTON
```
B    1543-1546X Parr
```
PARR OF KENDAL
```
B    1538-1553F Parr
```
Parr
```
1543-1571X   ESSEX E
1557-1571X   NORTHAMPTON M
1543-1546X   PARR OF HORTON B
1538-1553F   PARR OF KENDAL B
```
PARRY
```
B(L) 1975-        Parry
```
Parry
```
1975-        PARRY B(L)
```
Parsons
```
1681-1764X   OXMANTOWN B(I)
1792-        OXMANTOWN B(I)
1681-1764X   ROSSE V(I)
1718-1764X   ROSSE E(I)
1806-        ROSSE E(I)
```
Partington
```
1917-1949X   DOVERDALE B
```
PASSFIELD
```
B    1929-1947X Webb
```
Paston
```
1673-1732X   YARMOUTH V
1679-1732X   YARMOUTH E
```
PATESHULL
```
B    1342-1349X Pateshull
```
Pateshull
```
1342-1349X PATESHULL B
```
Paton: See Noel-Paton

Patrick
```
1541-1697S UPPER OSSORY B(I)
```
Patten: See Wilson-Patten
PAULET
```
B    1717-1754X Paulet
```
Paulet
```
1689-1794X   BOLTON D
1717-1754X   PAULET B
1539-        ST JOHN OF BASING B
1550-        WILTSHIRE E
1551-        WINCHESTER M
```
PAUNCEFOTE
```
B    1899-1902X Pauncefote
```
Pauncefote
```
1899-1902X PAUNCEFOTE
```
Payne
```
1795-1807X LAVINGTON B(I)
```
PAYNELL
```
B    1189/99-1216/72X Paynell
B    1216/72-1272/1307X Paynell
B    1299-1318X Paynell
```
PAYNELL OF OTLEY
```
B    1317-....X Paynell
```
PAYNELL OF TRACINGTON
```
B    1303-1317X Paynell
```
Paynell
```
1189/99-1216/72X PAYNELL B
1216/72-1272/1307X PAYNELL B
1299-1318X PAYNELL B
1317-....X PAYNELL OF OTLEY B
1303-1317X PAYNELL OF TRACINGTON B
```
Peachey
```
1794-1838X SELSEY B
```
Peake
```
1956-        INGLEBY V
```
PEARCE
```
B(L) 1962-        Pearce
```
Pearce
```
1962-        PEARCE B(L)
```
PEARSON
```
B(L) 1965-        Pearson
```
Pearson
```
1910-        COWDRAY B
1917-        COWDRAY V
1965-        PEARSON B(L)
```
PEART
```
B(L) 1976-        Peart
```
Peart
```
1976-        PEART B(L)
```
Pease
```
1923-        DARYNGTON B
```

Pease
  1917-   GAINFORD B
  1936-   WARDINGTON B
PECHE OF BRUNNE
  B   1299-1323X Peche
PECHE OF WORMLEIGHTON
  B   1321-1339A Peche
Peche
  1299-1323X PECHE OF BRUNNE B
  1321-1339A PECHE OF WORMLEIGH-
           TON B
PECKOVER
  B   1907-1919X Peckover
Peckover
  1907-1919X PECKOVER B
PEDDIE
  B(L) 1961-1978X Peddie
Peddie
  1961-1978X PEDDIE B(L)
PEEBLES
  V(S) 1697-   Douglas
PEEL
  V   1895-   Peel
  E   1929-   Peel
Peel
  1929-   CLANFIELD V
  1825-   PEEL V
  1929-   PEEL E
PELHAM
  B   1706-1768X Holles
PELHAM OF STANMER
  B   1762-   Pelham
Pelham
  1801-   CHICHESTER E
  1762-   PELHAM OF STANMER B
  See also Anderson-Pelham
Pellew
  1814-   EXMOUTH B
  1816-   EXMOUTH V
Pemberton-Leigh
  1858-1867X KINGSDOWN B
PEMBROKE
  E   1138-1245X Clare
  E   1189-1245X Marshal
  E   1247-1323X Valence
  E   1339-1391X Hastings
  E   1414-1446X Plantagenet
  E   1446-1450F Pole
  E   1452-1461F Tudor
  E   1468-1472S Herbert

PEMBROKE (Cont'd)
  E   1479-1483M Plantagenet
  E   1485-1495X Tudor
  Mss 1532-1533M Boleyn
  E   1551-   Herbert
PENDER
  B   1937-   Denison-Pender
Pennant
  1783-1808X PENRHYN B(I)
  See also: Douglas-Pennant
PENNEY
  B(L) 1967-   Penney
Penney
  1967-   PENNEY B(L)
Pennington
  1783-1917X MUNCASTER B
PENNOCK
  B(L) 1982-   Pennock
Pennock
  1982-   PENNOCK B(L)
Penny
  1937-   MARCHWOOD B
  1945-   MARCHWOOD V
PENRHYN
  B(I) 1783-1808X Pennant
  B   1866-   Douglas-Pennant
PENSHURST
  B   1825-1869X Smythe
PENTLAND
  B   1909-1984X Sinclair
PENZANCE
  B   1869-1899X Wilde
Pepys
  1836-   COTTENHAM B
  1850-   COTTENHAM E
  1850-   CROWHURST V
PERCEVAL
  B(I) 1715-   Perceval
  V(I) 1722-   Perceval
Perceval
  1770-   ARDEN B(I)
  1733-   EGMONT E(I)
  1762-   HOLLAND OF ENMORE B
  1762-   LOVEL & HOLLAND B
  1715-   PERCEVAL B(I)
  1722-   PERCEVAL V(I)
PERCY
  B   1066/87-1272/1307X Percy
  B   1299-1571X Percy
  B   1557-1670X Percy

PERCY (Cont'd)
B   1723-   Seymour
E   1766-   Smithson
PERCY OF ALNWICK
B   1643-1652X Percy
PERCY OF NEWCASTLE
B   1953-1958X Percy
Percy
1790-   BEVERLEY E
1449-1460X EGREMONT B
1784-   LOVAINE OF ALNWICK B
1377-1461X NORTHUMBERLAND E
1557-1670X NORTHUMBERLAND E
1766-   NORTHUMBERLAND D
1066/87-1272/1307X PERCY B
1299-1571X PERCY B
1557-1670X PERCY B
1766-   PERCY E
1643-1652X PERCY OF ALNWICK B
1953-1958X PERCY OF NEWCASTLE B
1446-1670X POYNINGS B
1816-1865X PRUDHOE B
1397-1404X WORCESTER E
PERROT
B   1297-1297X Perrot
Perrot
1297-1297X PERROT B
PERRY
B   1938-1956X Perry
PERRY OF WALTON
B(L) 1979-   Perry
Perry
1938-1956X PERRY B
1979-   PERRY OF WALTON B(L)
PERTH
E(S) 1605-   Drummond
L(S) 1797-1800X Drummond
PERY
V(I) 1785-1806X Pery
Pery
1815-   FOXFORD B
1790-   GLENTWORTH B(I)
1800-   LIMERICK V(I)
1803-   LIMERICK E(I)
1785-1806X PERY V(I)
Pestell: See Wells-Pestell
PETERBOROUGH
B   1628-1814X Mordaunt
PETERSFIELD
Bss 1673-1734L Querouaille

PETERSHAM
B   1674-1682X Maitland
V   1742-   Stanhope
PETHICK-LAWRENCE
B   1945-1961X Pethick-Lawrence
Pethick-Lawrence
1945-1961X PETHICK-LAWRENCE B
PETRE
B   1603-   Petre
Petre
1913-1920P FURNIVAL B
1603-   PETRE B
Petty
1719-1751X DUNKERRON V(I)
1688-1696L SHELBURN Bss & B(I)
1699-   SHELBURN B(I)
1719-1751X SHELBURNE E(I)
Petty-Fitzmaurice
1784-   CALNE & CALSTONE V
1751-   DUNKERRON B(I)
1751-   FITZMAURICE V(I)
1784-   LANSDOWNE M
1753-   SHELBURNE E(I)
1760-   WYCOMBE B
1784-   WYCOMBE E
PEVENSEY
V   1730-1743X Compton
V   1816-1909X Holroyd
PEVEREL
B   1066/87-1154/89X Peverel
PEVEREL OF BRUNNE
B   1100/35-....X Peverel
PEVEREL OF DOVER
B   1066/87-1100/35X Peverel
Peverel
1066/87-1154/89X PEVEREL B
1100/35-....X PEVEREL OF BRUNNE B
1066/87-1100/35X PEVEREL OF DOVER
PEYTON OF YEOVIL
B(L) 1983-   Peyton
Peyton
1983-   PEYTON OF YEOVIL B(L)
PEYVRE
B   1299-1299X Peyvre
Peyvre
1299-1299X PEYVRE B
Philipps
1923-1937X KYLSANT B
1776-1823X MILFORD B(I)
1847-1857X MILFORD B

Philipps (Cont'd)
1908-   ST DAVIDS B
1918-   ST DAVIDS V
PHILIPSTOWN
B(I) 1599-1714X O'Dempsey
B(I) 1716-   Molesworth
PHILLIMORE
B   1918-   Phillimore
Phillimore
1918-   PHILLIMORE B
PHILLIPS
Bss(L) 1964-   Phillips
Phillips
1964-   PHILLIPS Bss(L)
Phipps
1767-   MULGRAVE B(I)
1794-   MULGRAVE B
1812-   MULGRAVE V
1812-   MULGRAVE E
1790-1792X MULGRAVE B
1812-   NORMANBY V
1838-   NORMANBY M
Pickford
1918-1923X STERNDALE B
PIERCY
B   1945-   Piercy
Piercy
1945-   PIERCY B
PIERREPONT
B   1627-1773X Pierrepont
B(I) 1703-1715X Pierrepont
B   1714-1715X Pierrepont
B   1796-1955X Pierrepont
Pierrepont
1644-1680X DORCHESTER M
1706-1773X DORCHESTER M
1628-1680X KINGSTON E
1715-1773X KINGSTON D
1806-1955X MANVERS E
1627-1773X NEWARK V
1796-1955X NEWARK V
1627-1773X PIERREPONT B
1703-1715X PIERREPONT B(I)
1714-1715X PIERREPONT B
1796-1955X PIERREPONT B
PIGOT
B   1766-1777X Pigot
Pigot
1766-1777X PIGOT B
PIKE
Bss(L) 1974-   Pike

Pike
1974-   PIKE Bss(L)
PILKINGTON
B(L) 1968-1984X Pilkington
Pilkington
1968-1984X PILKINGTON B(L)
Pincerna
1216/72-1303X BOTELER OF WARRINGTON B
PINKNEY
B   1299-1301X Pinkney
Pinkney
1299-1301X PINKNEY B
PIPARD
B   1299-1309X Pipard
Pipard
1299-1309X PIPARD B
PIRBRIGHT
B   1895-1903X Worms, De
PIRRIE
B   1906-1924X Pirrie
V   1921-1924X Pirrie
Pirrie
1906-1924X PIRRIE B
1921-1924X PIRRIE V
PITT OF HAMPSTEAD
B(L) 1975-   Pitt
Pitt
1784-1804X CAMELFORD B
1761-1835X CHATHAM Bss
1766-1835X CHATHAM E
1719-1764X LONDONDERRY B(I)
1726-1764X LONDONDERRY E(I)
1975-   PITT OF HAMPSTEAD B(L)
1776-1828X RIVERS OF STRATFIELD-SAY
1802-1880X RIVERS OF SUDELEY CASTLE
PITTENWEEM
L(S) 1606-1625D Stewart
PLANT
B(L) 1978-   Plant
Plant
1978-   PLANT B(L)
Plantagenet
1385-1397X ALBEMARLE D
1397-1399F ALBEMARLE D
1411-1421X ALBEMARLE E
1414-1435X BEDFORD D
1377-1397X BUCKINGHAM E
1362-1461M CAMBRIDGE E
1253-1253S CHESTER E
1362-1368X CLARENCE D
1411-1421X CLARENCE D

126

Plantagenet (Cont'd)
1461-1477F CLARENCE D
1226-1300X CORNWALL E
1330-1336X CORNWALL E
1337-   CORNWALL D
1337-1399M DERBY E
1176-1199X GLOUCESTER E
1385-1399X GLOUCESTER D
1414-1446X GLOUCESTER D
1461-1483M GLOUCESTER D
1397-1399M HEREFORD D
1414-1435X KENDALL E
1321-1352F KENT E
1267-1321F LANCASTER E
1351-1399M LANCASTER D
1274-1361X LEICESTER E
1349-1399M LINCOLN E
1522-1541X L'ISLE V
1479-1483M MARCH E
1312-1338X NORFOLK E
1397-1399X NORFOLK Dss
1476-1483X NOTTINGHAM E
1414-1446X PEMBROKE E
1479-1483M PEMBROKE E
1342-1372S RICHMOND E
1414-1435X RICHMOND E
1472-1477F SALISBURY E
1477-1484X SALISBURY E
1513-1541F SALISBURY Css
1163-1347C SURREY E
1352-1461M ULSTER E(I)
1477-1483X WARREN E
1472-1477F WARWICK E
1320-1407A WOODSTOCK B
1385-1461M YORK D
1474-1483X YORK D
PLATT
  B(L) 1967-1978X Platt
  Bss(L) 1981-   Platt
Platt
  1967-1978X PLATT B(L)
  1981-   PLATT Bss(L)
PLAYFAIR
  B   1892-1939X Playfair
Playfair
  1892-1939X PLAYFAIR B
PLAYZ
  1294-1297A Playz, De
  1317-1360A Playz, De
Playz, De
  1294-1297A PLAYZ B
  1317-1360A PLAYZ B

PLENDER
  B   1931-1946X Plender
Plender
  1931-1946X PLENDER B
PLESSETS
  B   1299-1299X Plessets
Plessets
  1299-1299X PLESSETS B
  1246-1268P WARWICK E
PLEYDELL-BOUVERIE
  B   1765-   Bouverie, De
PLOWDEN
  B(L) 1959-   Plowden
Plowden
  1959-   PLOWDEN B(L)
PLUKENET
  B   1295-1327X Plukenet
Plukenet
  1295-1327X PLUKENET B
PLUMER
  B   1919-1944X Plumer
  V   1929-1944X Plumer
Plumer
  1919-1944X PLUMER B
  1929-1944X PLUMER V
PLUMMER
  B(L) 1965-1972X Plummer
PLUMMER OF ST MARYLEBONE
  B(L) 1981-   Plummer
Plummer
  1965-1972X PLUMMER B(L)
  1981-   PLUMMER OF ST MARYLEBONE
           B(L)
Plumptre
  1924-1932X FITZWALTER B
PLUNKET
  B   1827-   Plunket
Plunket
  1827-   PLUNKET B
  1895-1919X RATHMORE B
Plunkett
  1439-   DUNSANY B(I)
  1449-   KILLEEN B(I)
  1541-   LOUTH B(I)
  1628-1984X FINGALL E(I)
  1831-1984X FINGALL B
PLURENDEN
  B(L) 1975-1978X Sternberg
PLYMOUTH
  E   1675-1680X Fitzcharles
  E   1682-1843X Windsor
  E   1905-   Windsor-Clive

127

Poer
1375-   LA POER B
POER, DE LA
B(I) 1375-   Poer, De La
Poer, De La
1375-   POER, DE LA B
Poer Beresford, De La
1812-   DECIES B(I)
POINTZ
B   1295-1340X Pointz
Pointz
1295-1340X POINTZ B
Pole   *
1467-1487X LINCOLN E
1533-1539F MONTAGU B
1446-1450F PEMBROKE E
1385-1503F SUFFOLK E
1448-1503F SUFFOLK D
POLE, DE LA
B   1356-1503F Pole, De La
Pole, De La
1356-1503F POLE, DE LA B
POLLINGTON
B(I) 1753-   Savile
V(I) 1766-   Savile
Pollock
1926-   HANWORTH B
1936-   HANWORTH V
POLMONT: See MACHANSIRE & POLMONT
POLTIMORE
B   1831-   Bampfylde
POLWARTH
L(S) 1450-   Hepburne-Scott
POMERAI
B   1066/87-1272/1307X Pomerai, De
Pomerai, De
1066/87-1272/1307X POMERAI B
Pomeroy
1783-   HARBERTON B(I)
1791-   HARBERTON V(I)
POMFRET
B   1674-1716X Fitzroy
E   1721-1867X Fermor
PONSONBY
B   1806-1866X Ponsonby
V   1839-1855X Ponsonby
PONSONBY OF SHULBREDE
B   1930-   Ponsonby
PONSONBY OF SYSONBY
B   1749-   Ponsonby

Ponsonby
1721-   BESSBOROUGH B(I)
1739-   BESSBOROUGH E(I)
1937-   BESSBOROUGH E
1722-   DUNCANNON V(I)
1834   DUNCANNON B
1838-   MAULEY, DE B
1806-1866X PONSONBY B
1839-1855X PONSONBY V
1930-   PONSONBY OF SHUL-
            BREDE B
1749-   PONSONBY OF SYS-
            ONBY B
1935-   SYSONBY B
PONTYPRIDD
B   1912-1927X Thomas
POOLE
B   1958-   Poole
Poole
1958-   POOLE B
Pope
1628-1668X DOWNE E(I)
POPPLEWELL
B(L) 1966-1977X Popplewell
Popplewell
1966-1977X POPPLEWELL B(L)
PORCHESTER
B   1780-   Herbert
PORRITT
B(L) 1973-   Porritt
Porritt
1973-   PORRITT B(L)
PORT
B   1154/89-....X Port, De
PORT OF BASING
B   1066/87-1189/99X Port, De
Port, De
1154/89-....X PORT B
1066/87-1189/99X PORT OF BASING B
PORTAL
B   1935-1949X Portal
V   1945-1949X Portal
PORTAL OF HUNGERFORD
B   1945-1971X Portal
V   1946-1971X Portal
Portal
1935-1949X PORTAL B
1945-1949X PORTAL V
1945-1971X PORTAL OF HUNGERFORD B
1946-1971X PORTAL OF HUNGERFORD V

*See also Addenda   128

PORTARLINGTON
 B(I) 1692-1720X Massue
 E(I) 1785-   Dawson
PORTER
 B(L) 1938-1956X Porter
Porter
 1938-1956X PORTER B(L)
PORTLAND
 E   1633-1688X Weston
 E   1689-   Bentinck
 D   1716-   Bentinck
PORTLESTER
 B(I) 1462-1585F Eustace
PORTMAN
 B   1837-   Portman
 V   1873-   Portman
Portman
 1837-   PORTMAN B
 1873-   PORTMAN V
PORTMORE
 L(S) 1699-1835X Colyear
 E(S) 1703-1835X Colyear
PORTSEA
 B   1934-1948X Falle
PORTSMOUTH
 Dss 1673-1734X Querouaille
 E   1743-   Wallop
POULETT
 B   1627-1973X Poulett
 E   1706-1973X Poulett
Poulett
 1706-1973X HINTON V
 1627-1973X POULETT B
 1706-1973X POULETT E
Powell: See Baden-Powell
Power
 1620-1642X VALENTIA V(I)
POWERSCOURT
 V(I) 1618-1634X Wingfield
 V(I) 1665-1718X Wingfield
 V(I) 1743-   Wingfield
 B   1885-   Wingfield
POWIS
 B   1794-   Clive
 E   1804-   Clive
Powlett
 1754-1891X BARNARD V
 1797-1866X BAYNING B
 1797-1810X BEAUCHAMP B
 1754-1891X DARLINGTON E
 See also: Orde-Powlett

POWIS
 B   1629-1748X Herbert
 E   1674-1748X Herbert
 M   1687-1748X Herbert
 B   1748-1801X Herbert
 E   1748-1801X Herbert
Powys
 1797-   LILFORD B
Poynder: See Dickson-Poynder
POYNINGS
 B   1337-1446P Poynings
 B   1446-1670X Percy
 B   1545-1547X Poynings
Poynings
 1337-1446P POYNINGS B
 1545-1547X POYNINGS B
Pratt
 1786-   BAYHAM V
 1812-   BRECKNOCK E
 1765-   CAMDEN B
 1786-   CAMDEN E
 1794-   CAMDEN M
Prendergast Smyth
 1810-   KILTARTON B(I)
PRESTON
 V(S) 1681-1739X Graham
Preston
 1609-1715 DINGWALL L(S)
 1370-   GORMANSTON B(I)
 1478-   GORMANSTON V(I)
 1868-   GORMANSTON B
 1478-   LOUNDRES B(I)
 1650-1674X TARA V(I)
 1800-1821X TARA B(I)
Primrose
 1700-   DALMENY & PRIMROSE L(S)
 1911-   EPSOM B
 1703-   INVERKEITHING L(S)
 1911-   MENTMORE V
 1911-   MIDLOTHIAN E
 1700-   ROSEBERY V(S)
 1703-   ROSEBERY E(S)
 1828-   ROSEBERY B
PRITCHARD
 B(L) 1975-   Pritchard
Pritchard
 1975-   PRITCHARD B(L)
Prittie
 1800-   DUNALLEY B(I)
PROBY
 B(I) 1752-   Proby

129

Proby
1752-1909X CARYSFORT B(I)
1789-1909X CARYSFORT E(I)
1801-1909X CARYSFORT B
1752-   PROBY B(I)
Prothero
1919-1937X ERNLE B
PRUDHOE
B   1816-1865X Percy
PRYS-DAVIES
B(L) 1982-   Prys-Davies
Prys-Davies
1982-   PRYS-DAVIES B(L)
Pudsey, De
1189-1195S NORTHUMBERLAND E
PULTENEY
V   1742-1764X Pulteney
Pulteney
1742-1764X BATH E
1792-1808X BATH Bss
1803-1808X BATH Css
1742-1764X HEDON B
1742-1764X PULTENEY V
PURBECK
V   1619-1657X Villiers

QUEENSBOROUGH
B   1918-1949X Paget
QUEENSBERRY
E(S) 1633-   Douglas
M(S) 1682-   Douglas
D(S) 1684-   Scott
QUENINGTON
V   1915-   Hicks-Beach
Querouaille
1673-1734X FAREHAM Css
1673-1734X PETERSFIELD Bss
1673-1734X PORTSMOUTH Dss
QUIBELL
B   1945-1962X Quibell
Quibell
1945-1962X QUIBELL B
QUICKSWOOD
B   1941-1956X Gascoyne-Cecil
Quin
1800-   ADARE B(I)
1822-   ADARE V(I)
1822-   DUNRAVEN & MOUNT-EARL
           E(I)
1816-   MOUNT-EARL V(I)
1822-   MOUNT-EARL E(I)
See also: Wyndham-Quin
Quincy
1207-1264X WINCHESTER E
QUINTON
B(L) 1982-   Quinton
Quinton
1982-   QUINTON B(L)

(TITLES are in CAPITALS
Surnames in smalls)

RABY
B   1640-1799X Wentworth
B   1833-1891X Vane
RADCLIFFE
B   1949-1977X Radcliffe
V   1962-1977X Radcliffe
RADCLIFFE & LANGLEY
V   1688-1716F Radcliffe
Radcliffe
  1688-1716F DERWENTWATER E
  1949-1977X RADCLIFFE B
  1962-1977X RADCLIFFE V
  1688-1716F RADCLIFFE & LANGLEY V
  1688-1716F TYNDALE B
RADNOR
E   1679-1757X Robartes
E   1765-   Bouverie, De
RADSTOCK
B(I) 1800-1953X Waldegrave
RAGLAN
B   1852-   Somerset
RAGLEY
B   1750-   Conway
RAINCLIFFE
V   1887-1937X Denison
RAITH, MONYMAILL & BALWEARIE
L(S) 1690-   Melville
RAMALTON
B(I) 1682-1769X Stuart
RAMSAY
L(S) 1606-1625X Ramsay
B   1875-   Ramsay
RAMSAY OF DALHOUSIE
L(S) 1618-   Ramsay
RAMSAY & CARRINGTON
L(S) 1633-   Ramsay
Ramsay
  1486-1500F BOTHWELL L(S)
  1633-   DALHOUSIE E(S)
  1815-1860X DALHOUSIE B
  1838-1860X DALHOUSIE M
  1600-1625X EASTBARNS L(S)
  1606-1625X HADDINGTON V(S)
  1621-1625X HOLDERNESSE E
  1621-1625X KINGSTON-UPON-THAMES B
  1609-1625X MELROSE L(S)
  1606-1625X RAMSAY L(S)
  1875-   RAMSAY B
  1618-   RAMSAY OF DALHOUSIE L(S)
  1633-   RAMSAY & CARRINGTON L(S)

Ramsbotham
  1941-   SOULBURY B
  1954-   SOULBURY V
RAMSDEN
B   1945-1955X Ramsden
Ramsden
  1945-1955X RAMSDEN B
RAMSEY OF CANTERBURY
B(L) 1974-   Ramsey
Ramsey
  1974-   RAMSEY OF CANTERBURY
                   B(L)
RAMSEY, DE
B   1887-   Fellowes
RANCLIFFE
B   1795-1850X Parkyns
Randolph
  1312-1455F MORAY E(S)
RANELAGH
B(I) 1715-1754X Cole
RANFURLY
B   1826-   Knox
E(I) 1831-   Knox
RANK
B   1957-1972X Rank
Rank
  1957-1972X RANK B
RANKEILLOUR
B   1932-   Hope
RANKSBOROUGH
B   1914-1921X Brocklehurst
Ratcliffe
  1485-1495F FITZWALTER B
  1525-1641X FITZWALTER V
  1529-1641X SUSSEX E
RATENDONE
V   1931-   **Freeman-Thomas**
RATHCAVAN
B   1953-   O'Neill
RATHCREEDAN
B   1916-   Norton
RATHDONNELL
B(I) 1868-   M'Clintock
RATHDOWN
B(I) 1717-   **Chetwynd**
RATHDOWNE
E   1822-1848X Monck
RATHFARNHAM
B(I) 1685-1690X Loftus
E(I) 1715-1731X Wharton

131

RATHMORE
B   1895-1919X Plunket
RATHWIER
B(I) 1475-....X Daniel
RATOATH
B(I) 1468-....X Bould
RAVENSDALE
B   1911-   Mosley
RAVENSWORTH
B   1747-1749X Liddell
B   1821-   Liddell
E   1874-1904X Liddell
RAWDON
B(I) 1750-1868X Rawdon
B   1783-1868X Rawdon
E   1816-1868X Rawdon
Rawdon
1750-1868X RAWDON B(I)
1783-1868X RAWDON B
1816-1868X RAWDON E
Rawdon-Hastings
1816-1868X HASTINGS M
RAWLINSON
B   1919-1925X Rawlinson
RAWLINSON OF EWELL
B(L) 1978-   Rawlinson
Rawlinson
1919-1925X RAWLINSON B
1978-   RAWLINSON OF EWELL
                    B(L)
Rawson
1541-1560L CLONTARFE V(I)
RAYLEIGH
B   1821-   Strutt
RAYMOND
B   1731-1753X Raymond
V(I) 1800-1855X O'Neill
Raymond
1731-1753X RAYMOND B
RAYNE
B(L) 1976-   Rayne
Rayne
1976-   RAYNE B(L)
RAYNER
B(L) 1983-   Rayner
Rayner
1983-   RAYNER B(L)
RAYNHAM
V   1682-   Townshend
REA
B   1937-   Rea

Rea
1937-   REA B
READING
B   1914-   Isaacs
V   1916-   Isaacs
E   1917-   Isaacs
M   1926-   Isaacs
REAY
L(S) 1628-   Mackay
B   1881-1921X Reay
Reay
1881-1921X REAY B
REDCLIFFE-MAUD
B(L) 1967-1982X Redcliffe-Maud
Redcliffe-Maud
1967-1982X REDCLIFFE-MAUD B(L)
REDESDALE
B   1802-1886X Freeman-Mitford
E   1877-1886X Freeman-Mitford
B   1902-   Mitford
REDLYNCH
B   1747-   Fox-Strangways
REDMAYNE
B(L) 1966-1983X Redmayne
Redmayne
1966-1983X REDMAYNE B(L)
Redvers, De
11 /35-1293X DEVON E
Rees-Williams
1950-   OGMORE B
REEDE, DE
B   1644-....X Reede, De
Reede, De
1644-....X REEDE, DE B
REID
B(L) 1948-1975X Reid
Reid
1906-1923X LOREBURN B
1911-1923X LOREBURN E
1948-1975X REID B(L)
REIDHAVEN
V(S) 1701-   Ogilvie
REIGATE
B(L) 1970-   Vaughan-Morgan
REILLY
B(L) 1978-   Reilly
Reilly
1978-   REILLY B(L)
REITH
B   1940-   Reith
Reith
1940-   REITH B

132

REMNANT
  B   1928-   Remnant
Remnant
  1928-   REMNANT B
RENDEL
  B   1894-1913X Rendel
Rendel
  1894-1913X RENDEL B
RENDLESHAM
  B(I) 1806-   Thellusson
RENFREW
  B   1404-   Stewart
RENNELL
  B   1933-   Rodd
RENTON
  B(L) 1979-   Renton
Renton
  1979-   RENTON B(L)
RENWICK
  B   1964-   Renwick
Renwick
  1964-   RENWICK B
REVELSTOKE
  B   1885-   Baring
RHAYADER
  B   1932-1939X Leif-Jones
RHODES
  B(L) 1964-   Rhodes
Rhodes
  1964-   RHODES B(L)
RHONDDA
  B   1916-1918X Thomas
  V   1918-1958X Thomas
RHYL
  B(L) 1970-1981X Birch
Rhys
  1780-   DYNEVOR B
RIBBLESDALE
  B   1797-1925X Lister
RICCARTOUN
  V(S) 1697-1810X Hamilton
Rice: See Spring Rice
RICH
  B   1547-1759X Rich
Rich
  1624-1756X HOLLAND B
  1622-1759X KENSINGTON
  1776-   KENSINGTON B(I)
  1547-1759X RICH B
  1618-1759X WARWICK E

Richards
  1947-   MILVERTON B
RICHARDSON
  B(L) 1979-   Richardson
RICHARDSON OF DUNTISBOURNE
  B(L) 1983-   Richardson
Richardson
  1628-1735X CRAMOND L(S)
  1979-   RICHARDSON B(L)
  1983-   RICHARDSON OF DUNTIS-
           BOURNE B(L)
RICHMOND
  E   1066/87-1230P Alan, or Fergaunt
  E   1230-1399F Dreux, De
  E   1342-1372S Plantagenet
  E   1414-1435X Plantagenet
  E   1452-1485M Tudor
  D   1525-1536X Fitzroy
  E   1613-1624X Stuart
  D   1623-1624X Stuart
  D   1641-1672X Stuart
  D   1675-   Lennox
RIDDELL
  B   1920-1934X Riddell
Riddell
  1920-1934X RIDDELL B
RIDELL
  B   1100/35-1199/1216X Ridell
Ridell
  1100/35-1199/1216X RIDELL B
RIDEAU
  B   1952-   Alexander
RIDGEWAY
  B(I) 1616-1714X Ridgeway
Ridgeway
  1616-1714X GALLEN RIDGEWAY B(I)
  1622-1714X LONDONDERRY E(I)
  1616-1714X RIDGEWAY B(I)
RIDLEY
  V   1900-   Ridley
Ridley
  1900-   RIDLEY V
  1900-   WENSLEYDALE B
RIE
  B   1066/87-1199/1216X Rie, De
Rie, De
  1066/87-1199/1216X RIE B
RINGRONE
  B(I) 1181-   Courcy, De
RIPARIIS
  B   1299-1399X Ripariis, or Rivers

RIPON
  E   1833-   Robinson
  M   1871-1923X Robinson
RIPPON
  B   1708-1778X Douglas
RITCHIE OF DUNDEE
  B   1905-   Ritchie
Ritchie
  1905-   RITCHIE OF DUNDEE B
RITCHIE-CALDER
  B(L) 1966-1972X Calder
RIVERDALE
  B   1935-   Balfour
RIVERS
  B   1448-1491X Widvile
  E   1466-1491X Widvile
  E   1626-1728X Savage
  Css 1641-1650L Savage
RIVERS OF STRATFIELD-SAY
  B   1776-1828X Pitt
RIVERS OF SUDELEY CASTLE
  B   1802-1880X Pitt
Rivers: See Ripariis
RIVERSDALE
  B   1783-1861X Tonson
ROBARTES
  B   1625-1764X Robartes
  B   1869-1974X Agar-Robartes
Robartes
  1679-1757X BODMIN V
  1679-1757X RADNOR E
  1625-1764X ROBARTES B
ROBBINS
  B(L) 1959-1984X Robbins
Robbins
  1959-1984X ROBBINS B(L)
ROBENS OF WOLDINGHAM
  B(L) 1961-   Robens
Robens
  1961-   ROBENS OF WOLDINGHAM
           B(L)
ROBERTHALL
  B(L) 1969-   Roberthall
Roberthall
  1969-   ROBERTHALL B(L)
ROBERTS
  B   1892-1914X Roberts
  E   1901-1955X Roberts
Roberts
  1919-   CLWYD B
  1974-1981X GORONWY-ROBERTS B(L)

Roberts (Cont'd)
  1892-1914X ROBERTS B
  1901-1955X ROBERTS E
  1901-1955X ST PIERRE V
ROBERTSON
  B(L) 1899-1909X Robertson
ROBERTSON OF OAKRIDGE
  B   1961-   Robertson
Robertson
  1908-1911X LOCHEE B
  1873-1873X MARJORIBANKS B
  1899-1909X ROBERTSON B(L)
  1961-   ROBERTSON OF OAKRIDGE B
ROBINS
  B   1958-1962X Robins
Robins
  1958-1962X ROBINS B
ROBINSON
  B   1947-1952X Robinson
Robinson
  1827-1923X GODERICH V
  1770-1923X GRANTHAM B
  1816-1923X GREY OF WREST, DE E
  1964-   MARTONMERE B
  1823-   RIPON E
  1871-1923X RIPON M
  1947-1952X ROBINSON B
  1777-1883X ROKEBY B(I)
  1896-1933X ROSMEAD B
ROBOROUGH
  B   1938-   Lopes
ROBSART
  B   1425-1431L Robsart
Robsart
  1425-1431L ROBSART B
ROBSON
  B   1910-1918X Robson
ROBSON OF KIDDINGTON
  Bss(L) 1974-   Robson
Robson
  1910-1918X ROBSON B
  1974-   ROBSON OF KIDDINGTON
           Bss(L)
ROCHDALE
  B   1913-   Kemp
  V   1960-   Kemp
ROCHE
  B   1299-1306A Roche, De La
  V(I) 1490-1703? Roche
  B(L) 1935-1956X Roche

Roche
1490-1703? FERMOY V(I)
1856- FERMOY B(I)
1490-1703? ROCHE V(I)
1935-1956X ROCHE B(L)
Roche, De La
1299-1306A ROCHE B
ROCHESTER
V 1611-1645X Carr
E 1652-1681X Wilmot
E 1682-1753X Hyde
B 1931- Lamb
ROCHFORD
B 1495-1515X Butler
V 1525-1538X Boleyn
V 1621-1677X Carey
E 1695-1830X Nassau
Rochfort
1737-1814X BELLFIELD B(I)
1751-1814X BELLFIELD V(I)
1756-1814X BELVEDERE E(I)
ROCKINGHAM
B 1645-1782X Watson
V 1714-1782X Watson
M 1746-1782X Watson
ROCKLEY
B 1934- Cecil
ROCKSAVAGE
E 1815- Cholmondeley
Rodd
1933- RENNELL B
RODEN
E(I) 1771- Jocelyn
RODNEY
B 1782- Rodney
Rodney
1782- RODNEY B
ROE
B 1917-1923X Roe
Roe
1917-1923X ROE B
Rogers
1871-1889X BLACHFORD B
ROKEBY
B(I) 1777-1883X Robinson
Rolfe
1850-1868X CRANWORTH B
ROLL OF IPSDEN
B(L) 1977- Roll
Roll
1977- ROLL OF IPSDEN B(L)

ROLLE
B 1748-1750X Rolle
B 1796-1842X Rolle
Rolle
1748-1750X ROLLE B
1796-1842X ROLLE B
ROLLO
L(S) 1651- Rollo
B 1869- Rollo
Rollo
1869- DUNNING B
1651- ROLLO L(S)
1869- ROLLO B
Rolls
1892-1916X LLANGATTOCK B
Romare
1142-....C LINCOLN E
ROMER
B(L) 1938-1944X Romer
Romer
1938-1944X ROMER B
ROMILLY
B 1866-1883X Romilly
Romilly
1866-1883X ROMILLY B
ROMNEY
E 1694-1704X Sydney
B 1716- Marsham
E 1801- Marsham
ROMSEY
B 1947- Mountbatten
RONALDSHAY
E 1892- Dundas
ROOKWOOD
B 1892-1902X Selwin-Ibbetson
ROOS (or ROS), DE
B 1100/35-1216/72P Roos, De
B 1264- Roos, De
ROOS OF WERKE, DE
B 1295-1295F Roos, De
ROOS OF KENDALL, DE
B 1272/1307-....X Roos, De
ROOS OF NOTTINGHAMSHIRE, DE
B 1332-1338X Roos, De
ROOS OF BELVOIR
B 1896- Manners
Roos, De
1100/35-1216/72P ROOS, DE B
1264- ROOS, DE B
1295-1295F ROOS OF WERKE, DE
1272/1307-....X ROOS OF KENDALL, DE

Roos, De (Cont'd)
1332-1338X ROOS OF NOTTINGHAMSHIRE,
                DE B
ROOTES
  B   1959-   Rootes
Rootes
  1959-   ROOTES B
Roper
  1627-1676X BALTINGLASS V(I)
  1627-1676X BANTRY B(I)
  1786-1819P DACRE B
  1616-   TEYNHAM B
  See also: Trevor-Roper
ROS, DE: See ROOS, DE
ROSCOMMON
  E(I) 1622-1850D Dillon
Rose
  1866-1885X STRATHNAIRN B
ROSEBERRY
  V(S) 1700-   Primrose
  E(S) 1703-   Primrose
  B   1828-   Primrose
ROSENHEIM
  B(L) 1970-1972X Rosenheim
Rosenheim
  1970-1972X ROSENHEIM B(L)   *
ROSMEAD
  B   1896-1933X Robinson
ROSS
  E(S) 1165-1461F Ross
  D(S) 1488-1504X Stewart
  L(S) 1490-1754X Ross
  E(I) 1772-1802X Gore
  B   1815-1890X Boyle
ROSS OF MARNOCK
  B(L) 1979-   Ross
ROSS: See also NITH, THORTHORWALD
  & ROSS
Ross
  1165-1461F ROSS E(S)
  1490-1754X ROSS L(S)
  1979-   ROSS OF MARNOCK B(L)
ROSSE
  V(I) 1681-1764X Parsons
  E(I) 1718-1764X Parsons
  E(I) 1806-   Parsons
ROSSIE
  B   1831-1878X Kinnaird
ROSSLYN
  E   1801-   Wedderburn

        * See Addenda

ROSSMORE
  B(I) 1796-   Cuninghame
  B   1838-   Westenra
ROTHERHAM
  B   1910-1950X Holland
ROTHERMERE
  B   1914-   Harmsworth
  V   1919-   Harmsworth
ROTHERWICK
  B   1939-   Cayzer
ROTHES
  E(S) 1457-   Leslie
ROTHESAY
  D(S) 1398-   Stewart
ROTHSCHILD
  B   1885-   Rothschild
Rothschild
  1885-   ROTHSCHILD B
ROUNDWAY
  B   1916-1944X Colston
ROUS
  B   1796-   Rous
Rous
  1821-   DUNWICH V
  1796-   ROUS B
  1821-   STRADBROKE E
ROWALLAN
  B   1911-   Corbett
ROWLEY
  B(L) 1966-1968X Henderson
Rowley
  1776-1796X LANGFORD V(I)
  1766-   SUMMERHILL B(I)
Rowley-Conwy
  1800-   LANGFORD B(I)
ROWTON
  B   1880-1903X Lowry-Corry
Roxbee Cox
  1965-   KINGS NORTON B(L)
ROXBURGHE
  L(S) 1600-   Ker
  E(S) 1616-   Ker
  D(S) 1707-   Ker
ROYDEN
  B   1944-1950X Royden
Royden
  1944-1950X ROYDEN B
ROYLE
  B(L) 1964-1975X Royle
Royle
  1964-1975X ROYLE B(L)

Royle (Cont'd)
1983-   FANSHAWE OF RICHMOND
               B(L)
ROYSTON
    V   1754-   Yorke
RUFFSIDE
    V   1951-1958X Brown
RUGBY
    B   1947-   Maffey
RUGLEN
    E(S) 1697-1810X Hamilton
RUNCIMAN
    B   1933-   Runciman
RUNCIMAN OF DOXFORD
    V   1937-   Runciman
Runciman
    1933-   RUNCIMAN B
    1937-   RUNCIMAN OF DOXFORD V
RUNCORN
    B(L) 1964-1968X Vosper
Rupert
    1644-1682X CUMBERLAND D
    1644-1682X HOLDERNESS E
    1644-1682X KENDAL B
RUSHCLIFFE
    B   1935-1949X Betterton
RUSHOLME
    B   1945-1977X Palmer
Rushout
    1797-1887X NORTHWICK B
RUSSBOROUGH
    B(I) 1756-1891D Leeson
    V(I) 1760-1891D Leeson
RUSSELL
    B   1539-   Russell
    E   1861-   Russell
RUSSELL OF KILLOWEN
    B(L) 1894-1900X Russell
    B(L) 1929-1946X Russell
    B(L) 1975-   Russell
RUSSELL OF LIVERPOOL
    B   1919-   Russell
RUSSELL OF THORNHAUGH
    B   1603-1627M Russell
Russell
    1861-   AMBERLEY V
    1881-   AMPTHILL B
    1697-1727X BARFLEUR V
    1550-   BEDFORD E
    1694-   BEDFORD D
    1299-   CLIFFORD, DE B

Russell (Cont'd)
    1695-   HOWLAND B
    1697-1727X ORFORD E
    1539-   RUSSELL B
    1861-   RUSSELL E
    1894-1900X RUSSELL OF KILLOWEN B(L)
    1929-1946X RUSSELL OF KILLOWEN B(L)
    1975-   RUSSELL OF KILLOWEN B(L)
    1919-   RUSSELL OF LIVERPOOL
    1603-1627M RUSSELL OF THORNHAUGH B
    1697-1727X SHINGAY B
    1694-   TAVISTOCK M
    See also: Hamilton-Russell
RUTHERFORD
    L(S) 1661-1724? Rutherford
RUTHERFORD OF NELSON
    B   1931-1937X Rutherford
Rutherford
    1661-1724? RUTHERFORD L(S)
    1931-1937X RUTHERFORD OF NELSON B
    1661-1724A TEVIOT L(S)
RUTHVEN
    B   1487-1600F Ruthven
    L(S) 1639-1651X Ruthven
RUTHVEN OF CANBERRA
    V   1945-   Ruthven
RUTHVEN OF GOWRIE
    B   1919-   Ruthven
RUTHVEN OF FREELAND
    L(S) 1651-   Ruthven
Ruthven
    1642-1651X FORTH E(S)
    1581-1600F GOWRIE E(S)
    1935-   GOWRIE B
    1945-   GOWRIE E
    1487-1600F RUTHVEN B
    1639-1651X RUTHVEN L(S)
    1945-   RUTHVEN OF CANBERRA V
    1651-   RUTHVEN OF FREELAND L(S)
    1919-   RUTHVEN OF GOWRIE B
Ruthven or Ruthyn
    1644-1651X BRENTFORD E
RUTLAND
    E   1525-   Manners
    D   1703-   Manners
RYDER OF EATON HASTINGS
    B(L) 1975-   Ryder
RYDER OF WARSAW
    Bss(L) 1978-   Cheshire
Ryder
    1776-   HARROWBY B
    1809-   HARROWBY E

137

Ryder (Cont'd)
1975-   RYDER OF EATON HASTINGS
             B(L)
1809-   SANDON V
RYTHRE
B   1299-1307X Rythre
Rythre
1299-1307X RYTHRE B

SACKVILLE
V   1782-1843X Sackville
B   1876-   Sackville-West
Sackville
1782-1843X BOLEBROOKE B
1567-1843X BUCKHURST B
1864-   BUCKHURST B
1675-1843X CRANFIELD B
1603-1843X DORSET E
1720-1843X DORSET D
1675-1843X MIDDLESEX E
1782-1843X SACKVILLE V
Sackville-West
1876-   SACKVILLE B
SAINSBURY
B(L) 1962-   Sainsbury
Sainsbury
1962-   SAINSBURY B(L)
ST ALBANS
V   1621-1626X Bacon
E   1628-1659X Burgh
E   1660-1683X Jermyn
D   1684-   Beauclerk
ST ALDWYN
V   1906-   Hicks-Beach
E   1915-   Hicks-Beach
ST AMAND
B   1299-1312X St Amand
B   1313-1508A Beauchamp
St Amand
1299-1312X ST AMAND B
ST ANDREWS
D   1789-1830M Guelph
E   1934-   Windsor
ST ASAPH
V   1730-1924X Ashburnham
St Aubyn
1887-   ST LEVAN B
ST AUDRIES
B   1911-1971X Fuller-Acland-Hood
ST BRIDES
B(L) 1977-   James
St Clair
1488-   SINCLAIR L(S)
ST COLME
L(S) 1611-   Stuart
ST DAVIDS
B   1908-   Philipps
V   1918-   Philipps
ST GEORGE
B   1715-1775X St George

(TITLES are in CAPITALS
   Surnames in smalls)

138

St George
1715-1775X ST GEORGE B
ST GERMANS
E   1815-   Eliot
ST HELENS
B(I) 1791-1839X Fitzherbert
B   1801-1839X Fitzherbert
B   1964-   Hughes-Young
ST HELIER
B   1905-1905X Jeune
ST JOHN OF BASING
B   1299-1337? St John
B   1539-   Paulet
ST JOHN OF BATTERSEA
B   1716-   St John
ST JOHN OF BLETSO
B   1559-   St John
ST JOHN OF LAGEHAM
B   1100/35-1154/89P St John
B   1264-1343? St John
ST JOHN OF LYDIARD TREGOZE
B   1712-   St John
St John
1624-1711X BOLINGBROKE E
1712-   BOLINGBROKE V
1299-1337? ST JOHN OF BASING B
1716-   ST JOHN OF BATTERSEA
             B
1559-   ST JOHN OF BLETSO B
1100/35-1154/89P ST JOHN OF
             LAGEHAM B
1264-1343? ST JOHN OF LAGEHAM B
1712-   ST JOHN OF LYDIARD
             TREGOZE B
1626-1629X TREGOZ OF HIGHWORTH
             B
ST JUST
B   1935-1984X Grenfell
ST LAWRENCE
V(I) 1767-1909X St Lawrence
St Lawrence
1461-1909X HOWTH B(I)
1767-1909X HOWTH E(I)
1881-1909X HOWTH B
1767-1909X ST LAWRENCE V(I)
St Leger
1703-1767X DONERAILE V(I)
1776-   DONERAILE B(I)
1785-   DONERAILE V(I)
1703-1767X KILMAYDAN B(I)

ST LEONARDS
B   1852-   Sugden
ST LEVAN
B   1887-   St Aubyn
ST LIZ
B   1663-   Feilding
St Liz
1068-1237M HUNTINGDON E
1066-1184X NORTHAMPTON E
ST MAUR
B   1314-1625A St Maur
E   1863-1885X St Maur
St Maur
1314-1625A ST MAUR B
1863-1885X ST MAUR E
ST OSWALD
B   1885-   Winn
ST PHILIBERT
B   1299-1359X St Philibert
St Philibert
1299-1359X ST PHILIBERT B
ST PIERRE
V   1901-1955X Roberts
ST QUINTIN
B   1294-1302L St Quintin
St Quintin
1294-1302L ST QUINTIN B
ST VALERIE
B   1066/87-1189/99X St Valerie, De
St Valerie, De
1066/87-1189/99X ST VALERIE B
ST VINCENT
E   1797-1823X Jervis
V   1801-   Jervis
SALFORD
V   1897-1909X Egerton
SALISBURY
B   1100/35-1154/89X Saresbury, De
E   1135/54-1189/99X Devereux
E   1196-1261A Longespee
E   1337-1400F Montagu
E   1409-1428C Montagu
E   1442-1471F Nevill
E   1472-1477F Plantagenet
E   1477-1484X Plantagenet
Css 1513-1541F Plantagenet
E   1605-   Cecil
M   1780-   Cecil
SALMON
B(L) 1972-   Salmon

139

Salmon
1972-   SALMON B(L)
SALTER
  B   1953-1975X Salter
Salter
  1953-1975X SALTER B
SALTERSFORD
  B   1796-   Stopford
SALTOUN
  L(S) 1445-   Fraser
SAMPSON
  B   1299-1299X Sampson
Sampson
  1299-1299X SAMPSON B
SAMUEL
  V   1937-   Samuel
SAMUEL OF WYCH CROSS
  B(L) 1972-   Samuel
Samuel
  1921-   BEARSTED B
  1925-   BEARSTED V
  1937-   SAMUEL V
  1972-   SAMUEL OF WYCH CROSS
                   B(L)
Sanders
  1929-1940X BAYFORD B
SANDERSON
  B   1905-1923X Sanderson
  B   1930-1939X Furniss
SANDERSON OF AYOT
  B   1960-   Sanderson
Sanderson
  1905-1923X SANDERSON B
  1960-   SANDERSON OF AYOT B
SANDFORD
  B   1891-1893X Sandford
  B   1945-   Edmondson
Sandford
  1800-1846X MOUNT SANDFORD B
  1891-1893X SANDFORD B
SANDHURST   *
  V   1917-1921X Mansfield
Sandilands
  1647-1681X ABERCROMBIE L(S)
  1564-   TORPHICHEN L(S)
SANDON
  V   1809-   Ryder
SANDWICH
  E   1660-   Montagu
SANDYS
  B   1743-1797X Sandys

       * See also Addenda

SANDYS (Cont'd)
  B   1802-   Hill
SANDYS OF THE VINE
  B   1529-1700A Sandys
Sandys
  1743-1797X SANDYS B
  1529-1700A SANDYS OF THE VINE B
  See also: Duncan-Sandys
SANKEY
  B   1929-1948X Sankey
  V   1932-1948X Sankey
Sankey
  1929-1948X SANKEY B
  1932-1948X SANKEY V
SANQUHAR: See DRUMLANRIG & SANQUHAR
SANTRY
  B(I) 1661-1751X Barry
Saresbury, De
  1100/35-1154/89X SALISBURY B
SARSFIELD
  B(I) 1624-1691F Sarsfield
  V(I) 1624-1691F Sarsfield
Sarsfield
  1624-1691F SARSFIELD B(I)
  1624-1691F SARSFIELD V(I)
  1689-1693X LUCAN E(I)
SAUMAREZ, DE
  B   1831-   Saumarez
Saumarez
  1831-   SAUMAREZ, DE B
SAUNDERS
  B(I) 1758-   Gore
SAUNDERSON
  B   1714-1723X Saunderson
Saunderson
  1627-1723X CASTLETON V(I)
  1716-1723X CASTLETON V
  1720-1723X CASTLETON E
  1714-1723X SAUNDERSON B
SAUNZAVER
  B   1294-1294X Saunzaver
Saunzaver
  1294-1294X SAUNZAVER B
SAVAGE
  V   1626-1728X Savage
  Css(L) 1641-1650X Savage
Savage
  1621-1728X COLCHESTER V
  1626-1728X RIVERS E
  1641-1650L RIVERS Css
  1626-1728X SAVAGE V
  1641-1650X SAVAGE Css(L)

140

SAVERNAKE
V   1821-   Bruce
SAVILE
B   1628-1671X Savile
V(I) 1628-1671X Savile
B   1888-   Savile
SAVILE OF ELAND
B   1668-1700X Savile
Savile
  1628-1671X CASTLEBAR B(I)
  1668-1700X HALIFAX V
  1679-1700X HALIFAX E
  1682-1700X HALIFAX M
  1766-   MEXBOROUGH E(I)
  1753-   POLLINGTON B(I)
  1766-   POLLINGTON V(I)
  1628-1671X SAVILE B
  1628-1671X SAVILE V(I)
  1888-   SAVILE B
  1668-1700X SAVILE OF ELAND B
  1644-1671X SUSSEX E
SAY
B   1066/87-1272/1307P Say, De
B   1313-1375A Say, De
SAY OF CLUN
B   1135/54-....X Say, De
SAY OF RICHARDS CASTLE
B   1154/89-1199/1216X Say, De
SAYE & SELE
B   1447-   Fienes
V   1624-1781X Fienes
Say, De
  1066/87-1272/1307P SAY B
  1313-1375A SAY B
  1135/54-....X SAY OF CLUN B
  1154/89-1199/1216X SAY OF
            RICHARDS CASTLE B
SCALES
B   1066/87-1216/72X Scales, De
B   1299-1462C Scales, De
B   1462-1473A Widvile
Scales, De
  1066/87-1216/72X SCALES B
  1299-1462C SCALES B
SCANLON
B(L) 1979-   Scanlon
Scanlon
  1979-   SCANLON B(L)
SCARBROUGH
E   1690-   Lumley

Scarlett
  1835-   ABINGER B
SCARMAN
B(L) 1977-   Scarman
Scarman
  1977-   SCARMAN B(L)
SCARSDALE
E   1645-1736X Seke
B   1761-   Curzon
V   1911-   Curzon
SCHOMBERG
D   1689-1719X Schomberg
Schomberg
  1691-1719X BANGOR E(I)
  1689-1719X BRENTFORD E
  1689-1719X HARWICH M
  1691-1719X LEINSTER D(I)
  1689-1719X SCHOMBERG D
  1691-1719X TARAGH B(I)
SCHON
B(L) 1976-   Schon
Schon
  1976-   SCHON B(L)
Schulenburg   *
  1716-1743X DUNDALK Bss(I)
  1716-1743X DUNGANNON Css(I)
  1716-1743X DUNGANNON Mss(I)
  1719-1743X FEVERSHAM Css
  1719-1743X GLASTONBURY Bss
  1719-1743X KENDAL Dss
  1716-1743X MUNSTER Dss(I)
  1722-1778X WALSINGHAM Css
SCHUSTER
B   1944-1956X Schuster
Schuster
  1944-1956X SCHUSTER B
Sclater-Booth
  1887-   BASING B
SCONE
L(S) 1605-   Murray
Scot
  1660-1685F MONMOUTH D
SCOTENI
B   1154/89-1216/72X Scoteni, De
Scoteni, De
  1154/89-1216/72X SCOTENI B
SCOTT OF BUCCLEUCH
L(S) 1606-   Scott
SCOTT OF GOLDIELANDS
L(S) 1706-1807X Scott

* See also Addenda

141

SCOTT OF TYNEDALE
B   1663-   Scott
SCOTT OF WHITCHESTER & ESKDAILL
L(S) 1619-   Scott
SCOTT OF WHITCHURCH
L(S) 1663-1685F Scott
Scott
1619-   BUCCLEUCH E(S)
1663-   BUCCLEUCH D(S)
1789-1935X CLONMELL V(I)
1793-1935X CLONMELL E(I)
1673-1685F DALKEITH E(S)
1706-1807X DELORAINE E(S)
1663-1685F DONCASTER V
1663-1685F DONCASTER E
1743-   DONCASTER E
1706-   DOUGLAS OF KINMONT,
            MIDDLEBIE & DORNOCH L(S)
1684-   DRUMLANRIG &
            SANQUHAR E(S)
1684-   DUMFRIESSHIRE M(S)
1784-1935X EARLSFORT B(I)
1799-   ELDON B
1821-   ELDON E
1821-   ENCOMBE V
1706-1807X HERMITAGE V(S)
1684-   NITH V(S)
1684-   NITH, THORTHORWALD
            & ROSS V(S)
1684-   QUEENSBERRY D(S)
1606-   SCOTT OF BUCCLEUCH L(S)
1706-1807X SCOTT OF GOLDIELANDS
            L(S)
1663-   SCOTT OF TYNEDALE B
1619-   SCOTT OF WHITCHESTER
            & ESKDAILL L(S)
1663-1685F SCOTT OF WHITCHURCH
            L(S)
1821-1836X STOWELL B
1660-1693X TARRAS E(S)
1663-   TYNEDALE B
See also: Douglas-Scott-Montagu
SCROPE OF BOLTON
B   1272/1307-1307/27P Scrope, Le
B   1327-1627D Scrope, Le
SCROPE OF MASHAM
B   1350-1517A Scrope, Le
Scrope, Le
1272/1307-1307/27P SCROPE B
1327-1627D SCROPE B

Scrope
1627-1630X SUNDERLAND E
1397-1399F WILTSHIRE E
SCRYMGEOUR
L(S) 1641-   Scrymgeour
Scrymgeour
1641-   DUDHOPE V(S)
1660-   DUNDEE E(S)
1954-   GLASSARY B
1660-   INVERKEITHING L(S)
1641-   SCRYMGEOUR L(S)
SCUDAMORE
V(I) 1628-1716X Scudamore
Scudamore
1628-1716X DROMORE B(I)
1628-1716X SCUDAMORE V(I)
SEAFIELD
V(S) 1698-   Ogilvie
E(S) 1701-   Ogilvie
SEAFORD
B   1826-   Ellis
SEAFORTH
E(S) 1623-1815X Mackenzie
E(I) 1771-1781X Mackenzie
B   1797-1815X Mackenzie
B   1921-1923X Stewart-Mackenzie
Seager
1962-   LEIGHTON OF
            ST MELLONS B
SEAHAM
V   1823-   Stewart
SEATON
B   1839-1955X Colborne-Vivian
SEEAR
Bss(L) 1971-   Seear
Seear
1971-   SEEAR Bss(L)
SEEBOHM
B(L) 1972-   Seebohm
Seebohm
1972-   SEEBOHM B(L)
Seely
1933-   MOTTISTONE B
1941-1970X SHERWOOD B
SEFTON
E(I) 1771-1972X Molyneux
B   1831-1972X Molyneux
SEFTON OF GARSTON
B(L) 1978-   Sefton
Sefton
1978-   SEFTON OF GARSTON B(L)

142

SEGAL
  B(L) 1964-   Segal
Segal
  1964-   SEGAL B(L)
SEGRAVE
  B   1264-....A Segrave, De
  B   1295-1322X Segrave, De
  B   1831-1857X Berkeley
Segrave, De
  1264-....A SEGRAVE B
  1295-1322X SEGRAVE B
Seke
  1645-1736X SCARSDALE E
SELBORNE
  B   1872-   Palmer
  E   1882-   Palmer
SELBY
  V   1905-   Gully
SELE
  V   1624-   Fienes
SELKIRK
  E(S) 1646-   Douglas
SELSDON
  B   1932-   Mitchell-
                  Thomson
SELSEY
  B   1794-1838X Peachey
Selwin-Ibbetson
  1892-1902X ROOKWOOD B
SELWYN-LLOYD
  B(L) 1976-1978X Lloyd
SEMPILL
  L(S) 1489-   Sempill
Sempill
  1489-   SEMPILL L(S)
SEROTA
  Bss(L) 1967-   Serota
Serota
  1967-   SEROTA Bss(L)
SETON
  L(S) 1448-1715F Seton
SETON & TRANENT
  L(S) 1600-1715F Seton
  B   1859-   Montgomerie
Seton
  1605-1694X DUNFERMLINE E(S)
  1598-1715F FYVIE L(S)
  1650-1715F KINGSTON V(S)
  1448-1715F SETON L(S)
  1600-1715F SETON & TRANENT L(S)

Seton (Cont'd)
  1600-1715F TRANENT L(S)
  1600-1716F WINTOUN E(S)
SETTRINGTON
  B   1613-1672X Stuart
  B   1675-   Lennox
SEYMOUR
  B   1547-1552F Seymour
  B   1660-   Seymour
SEYMOUR OF SUDLEY
  B   1547-1549F Seymour
SEYMOUR OF TROWBRIDGE
  B   1641-1750X Seymour
Seymour
  1882-1895X ALCESTER B
  1536-1552F BEAUCHAMP V
  1750-   BEAUCHAMP V
  1559-1750X BEAUCHAMP OF HACHE B
  1749-1845X COCKERMOUTH B
  1703-   CONWAY OF RAGLEY B
  1712-   CONWAY & KILLULTAGH B(I)
  1749-   EGREMONT E
  1537-1552F HERTFORD E
  1559-1750X HERTFORD E
  1640-1750X HERTFORD M
  1750-   HERTFORD E
  1793-   HERTFORD M
  1749-   NORTHUMBERLAND E
  1723-   PERCY B
  1547-1552F SEYMOUR B
  1660-   SEYMOUR B
  1547-1549F SEYMOUR OF SUDLEY B
  1641-1750X SEYMOUR OF TROWBRIDGE B
  1547-1552F SOMERSET D
  1660-   SOMERSET D
  1749-   WARKWORTH B
  1793-   YARMOUTH E
SHACKLETON
  B(L) 1958-   Shackleton
Shackleton
  1958-   SHACKLETON B(L)
SHAFTESBURY
  E   1672-   Ashley-Cooper
SHAND
  B   1892-1904X Shand
Shand
  1892-1904X SHAND B
SHANDON
  B   1918-1930X O'Brien
SHANNON
  V(I) 1660-1740X Boyle
  E(I) 1756-   Boyle

143

SHARP
  Bss(L) 1966-   Sharp
Sharp
  1966-   SHARP Bss(L)
SHARPLES
  Bss(L) 1973-   Laszlo, De
SHAUGHNESSY
  B   1916-   Shaughnessy
Shaughnessy
  1916-   SHAUGHNESSY B
Shaunde, De
  1485-15..X BATH E
Shaw
  1929-   CRAIGMYLE B
  1971-   KILBRANDON B(L)
SHAWCROSS
  B(L) 1959-   Shawcross
Shawcross
  1959-   SHAWCROSS B(L)
Shaw-Lefevre
  1906-1928X EVERSLEY B
  1857-1888X EVERSLEY OF HECKFIELD B
SHEFFIELD
  B   1547-1735X Sheffield
  B(I) 1781-1909X Holroyd
  B(I) 1783-   Holroyd
  B   1802-1909X Holroyd
  E   1816-1909X Holroyd
Sheffield
  1703-1735X BUCKINGHAM D
  1626-1735X MULGRAVE E
  1694-1735X NORMANBY M
  1547-1735X SHEFFIELD B
SHELBURN
  Bss & B(I) 1688-1696L Petty
  B(I) 1699-   Petty
SHELBURNE
  E(I) 1719-1751X Petty
  E(I) 1753-   Petty-Fitzmaurice
SHEPEY
  Css(L) 1680-1686L Bayning
SHEPHERD
  B   1946-   Shepherd
Shepherd
  1946-   SHEPHERD B
SHERARD
  B(I) 1627-1931X Sherard
  V   1718-1732X Sherard
Sherard
  1719-1859X HARBOROUGH E
  1627-1931X SHERARD B(I)

Sherard (Cont'd)
  1714-1859X SHERARD B
  1718-1732X SHERARD V
SHERBORNE
  B   1784-   Dutton
SHERBROOKE
  V   1880-1892X Lowe
SHERFIELD
  B   1964-   Makins
SHERWOOD
  B   1941-1970X Seely
SHINGAY
  B   1697-1727X Russell
SHINWELL
  B(L) 1970-   Shinwell
Shinwell
  1970-   SHINWELL B(L)
SHIPBROOKE
  E(I) 1762-1783X Vernon
Shirley
  1711-   FERRERS E
  1677-1741A FERRERS OF CHARTLEY B
  1711-   TAMWORTH V
Shore
  1797-1981X TEIGNMOUTH B(I)
SHORTCLEUCH: See DAER & SHORTCLEUCH
SHREWSBURY
  E   1071-1102F Montgomery, De
  E   1442-   Talbot
  D   1694-1718X Talbot
SHULDHAM
  B(I) 1776-1798X Shuldham
Shuldham
  1776-1798X SHULDHAM B(I)
SHUTE
  B   1880-   Barrington
SHUTTLEWORTH
  B   1902-   Kay-Shuttleworth
Siddeley
  1937-   KENILWORTH B
SIDLAW: See GLAMIS, TANNADYCE,
  SIDLAW & STRATHDICHTIE
Sidley
  1686-1692X DARLINGTON Bss
  1686-1692X DORCHESTER Css
SIDMOUTH
  V   1805-   Addington
Sidney
  1835-   L'ISLE, DE B
  1956-   L'ISLE, DE V
144

SIEFF
  B(L) 1966-1972X Sieff
SIEFF OF BRIMPTON
  B(L) 1980-   Sieff
Sieff
  1966-1972X SIEFF B(L)
  1980-   SIEFF OF BRIMPTON B(L)
SILCHESTER
  B(L 1821-   Pakenham
SILKIN
  B   1950-   Silkin
Silkin
  1950-   SILKIN B
SILSOE
  B   1963-   Eve
Silverstone
  1974-1977X ASHDOWN B(L)
SIMEY
  B(L) 1965-1969X Simey
Simey
  1965-1969X SIMEY B(L)
SIMON
  V   1940-   Simon
SIMON OF GLAISDALE
  B(L) 1971-   Simon
Simon
  1940-   SIMON V
  1971-   SIMON OF GLAISDALE
            B(L)
SIMONDS
  B   1952-   Simonds
  V   1954-1971X Simonds
  B(L) 1944-1971X Simonds
Simonds
  1952-   SIMONDS B
  1954-1971X SIMONDS V
  1944-1971X SIMONDS B(L)
SINCLAIR
  L(S) 1488-   St Clair
  L(S) 1677-   Campbell
SINCLAIR OF CLEEVE
  B   1957-   Sinclair
Sinclair
  1592-   BERRIEDALE L(S)
  1866-1889X BARROGILL B
  1455-   CAITHNESS E(S)
  1066/87-1470P ORKNEY E(S)
  1909-1984X PENTLAND B
  1957-   SINCLAIR OF CLEEVE B
  1952-   THURSO V

SINHA
  B   1919-   Sinha
Sinha
  1919-   SINHA B
Skeffington
  1756-1816X MASSAREENE E(I)
SKELMERSDALE
  B   1828-   Bootle-Wilbraham
SKENE
  B   1857-1912X Duff
SKRIMSHIRE OF QUARTER
  Bss(L) 1979-1979X Harvie-Anderson
SLAINS
  L(S) 1452-   Hay
SLANE
  B(I) 1185-1726L Fleming
  V   1816-   Conyngham
SLATER
  B(L) 1970-1977X Slater
Slater
  1970-1977X SLATER B(L)
SLIGO
  M(I) 1800-   Browne
SLIM
  V   1960-   Slim
Slim
  1960-   SLIM V
SMITH
  B(L) 1978-   Smith
Smith
  1938-   BICESTER B
  1919-   BIRKENHEAD B
  1921-   BIRKENHEAD V
  1922-   BIRKENHEAD E
  1643-1706X CARRINGTON B
  1917-   COLWYN B
  1916-   DUDLEY B
  1922-   FURNEAUX V
  1891-   HAMBLEDON V
  1975-   KIRKHILL B(L)
  1978-   SMITH B(L)
  1897-1914X STRATHCONA & MOUNT
            ROYAL B
  1900-   STRATHCONA & MOUNT
            ROYAL B
  See also: Buchanan-Smith
            Delacourt-Smith
            Hornsby-Smith
            Walker-Smith
Smyth: See Prendergast-Smyth

145

Smythe
  1825-1869X PENSHURST B
  1628-1869X STRANGFORD V
SNELL
  B   1931-1944X Snell
Snell
  1931-1944X SNELL B
SNOW
  B(L) 1964-   Snow
Snow
  1964-   SNOW B(L)
  1970-   BURNTWOOD B(L)
SNOWDEN
  V   1931-1937X Snowden
Snowden
  1931-1937X SNOWDEN V
SNOWDON
  E   1961-   Armstrong-Jones
SOAMES
  B(L) 1978-   Soames
Soames
  1978-   SOAMES B(L)
SOBERTON
  B   1806-   Anson
SOLWAY
  E(S) 1706-1778P Douglas
  B   1833-1837X Douglas
SOMERHILL
  B   1624-1659X Burgh
  B   1826-1916X Burgh-Canning, De
Somerie
  1308-1322X DUDLEY B
SOMERLEYTON
  B   1916-   Crossley
SOMERS
  B   1697-1716X Somers
  B   1784-1883X Cocks
  E   1821-1883X Somers-Cocks
Somers
  1697-1716X SOMERS B
Somers-Cocks
  1821-1883X EASTNOR V
  1821-1883X SOMERS E
SOMERSET
  E   1397-1471X Beaufort
  M   1397-1471X Beaufort
  D   1443-1444X Beaufort
  D   1448-1471F Beaufort
  D   1496-1499X Tudor
  D   1525-1536X Fitzroy
  D   1547-1552X Seymour

SOMERSET (Cont'd)
  E   1613-1645X Carr
  V(I) 1626-1651X Somerset
  D   1660-   Seymour
Somerset
  1682-   BEAUFORT D
  1506-   CHEPSTOW B
  1644-   GROSMONT V
  1852-   RAGLAN B
  1626-1651X SOMERSET V(I)
  1514-   WORCESTER E
  1642-   WORCESTER M
SOMERTON
  B(I) 1795-   Agar
  V(I) 1800-   Agar
  B   1873-   Agar
SOMERVELL OF HARROW
  B(L) 1954-1960X Somervell
Somervell
  1954-1960X SOMERVELL OF HARROW
                    B(L)
SOMERVILLE
  B   1430-1870X Somerville
Somerville
  1863-1929X ATHLUMNEY B(I)
  1866-1929X MEREDYTH B
  1430-1870X SOMERVILLE B
SONDES
  V   1676-1709X Sondes
  B   1760-   Watson
  E   1880-   Milles
Sondes
  1676-1709X FEVERSHAM E
  1676-1709X SONDES V
  1676-1709X THROWLEY B
SOPER
  B(L) 1965-   Soper
Soper
  1965-   SOPER B(L)
SORENSEN
  B(L) 1964-1971X Sorensen
Sorensen
  1964-1971X SORENSEN B(L)
Soskice
  1966-1979X STOW HILL B(L)
Sotheran-Estcourt
  1903-1915X ESTCOURT B
SOULBURY
  B   1941-   Ramsbotham
  V   1954-   Ramsbotham
Souter
  1313-   AUDLEY B

146

SOUTHAMPTON
E   1537-1543X Fitzwilliam
E   1547-1667X Wriothesley
Css 1670-1774X Villiers
D   1674-1774X Fitzroy
B   1780-   FitzRoy
SOUTHBOROUGH
B   1917-   Hopwood
SOUTHESK
E(S) 1633-   Carnegie
SOUTHWARK
B   1910-1929X Causton
SOUTHWELL
B(I) 1717-   Southwell
V(I) 1776-   Southwell
Southwell
1717-   SOUTHWELL B(I)
1776-   SOUTHWELL V(I)
SOUTHWOOD
B   1937-1946X Elias
V   1946-1946X Elias
SPENCER
B   1603-   Spencer
B   1761-   Spencer
V   1761-   Spencer
E   1765-   Spencer
Spencer
1815-   CHURCHILL B
1902-   CHURCHILL V
1603-   SPENCER B
1761-   SPENCER B
1761-   SPENCER V
1765-   SPENCER E
1643-   SUNDERLAND E
1685-1694X TEVIOT V(S)
SPENCER-CHURCHILL
Bss(L) 1965-1977X Spencer-
                 Churchill
Spencer-Churchill
1965-1977X SPENCER-CHURCHILL
           Bss(L)
SPENS
B   1959-   Spens
Spens
1959-   SPENS B
Spring Rice
1839-   MONTEAGLE OF
           BRANDON B
SPYNIE
L(S) 1589-1672? Lindsay

STAFFORD
B   1299-1521F Stafford
E   1337-1521F Stafford
B   1547-1640X Stafford
B   1640-   Fitzherbert
V   1640-1678F Howard
Css 1688-1693X Howard
E   1688-1762X Howard
M   1786-   Leveson-Gower
STAFFORD OF CLIFTON
B   1371-1381? Stafford
STAFFORD OF SOUTHWYCK
B   1461-1469X Stafford
Stafford
1403-1521F BUCKINGHAM E
1444-1483F BUCKINGHAM D
1469-1469X DEVON E
1299-1521F STAFFORD B
1337-1521F STAFFORD E
1547-1640X STAFFORD B
1371-1381? STAFFORD OF CLIFTON B
1461-1469X STAFFORD OF SOUTHWYCK B
1470-1499X WILTSHIRE E
1509-1523X WILTSHIRE E
STAIR
V(S) 1690-   Dalrymple
E(S) 1703-   Dalrymple
STALLARD
B(L) 1983-   Stallard
Stallard
1983-   STALLARD B(L)
STALYBRIDGE
B   1886-1949X Grosvenor
STAMFORD
E   1625-1976X Grey
STAMFORDHAM
B   1911-1931X Bigge
STAMP
B   1938-   Stamp
Stamp
1938-   STAMP B
STANHOPE
E   1718-1967X Stanhope
STANHOPE OF HARRINGTON
B   1605-1675X Stanhope
STANHOPE OF SHELFORD
B   1616-1952D Stanhope
Stanhope
1628-1967X CHESTERFIELD E
1730-   HARRINGTON B

147

Stanhope (Cont'd)
```
1742-      HARRINGTON E
1742-      PETERSHAM V
1718-1967X STANHOPE E
1616-1952D STANHOPE OF SHELFORD B
1605-1675X STANHOPE OF HARRING-
           TON B
1906-1923X WEARDALE B
```
STANLEY
```
B    1456-1960A Stanley
```
STANLEY OF ALDERLEY
```
B    1839-      Stanley
```
STANLEY OF BICKERSTAFFE
```
B    1832-      Stanley
```
STANLEY OF PRESTON
```
B    1886-      Stanley
```
Stanley
```
1920-1948X ASHFIELD B
1485-      DERBY E
1848-      EDDISBURY B
1514-1686P MONTEAGLE B
1456-1960A STANLEY B
1839-      STANLEY OF ALDERLEY B
1832-      STANLEY OF BICKER-
           STAFFE B
1886-      STANLEY OF PRESTON B
1482-1594A STRANGE OF KNOKYN B
1628-      STRANGE B
```
STANMORE
```
B    1893-1957X Hamilton-Gordon
V    1942-      Benn
B    1313-....A Stapleton
```
Stapleton
```
1840-      BEAUMONT B
1788-1831M DESPENCER B
1313-....A STAPLETON B
```
Stapleton-Cotton
```
1814-      COMBERMERE B
1826-      COMBERMERE V
```
Starsfield
```
1624-1691F KINGSALE V(I)
```
STAVORDALE
```
See ILCHESTER & STAVORDALE
```
STAWELL
```
B    1683-1755X Stawell
B    1760-1820X Legge
```
Stawell
```
1683-1755X STAWELL B
```
STEDMAN
```
Bss(L) 1974-      Stedman
```

Stedman
```
1974-      STEDMAN Bss(L)
```
STENTON: See BELHAVEN & STENTON
Stephen
```
1891-1921X MOUNT STEPHEN B
```
Stern
```
1905-      MICHELHAM B
1895-1912X WANDSWORTH B
```
Sternberg
```
1975-1978X PLURENDEN B(L)
```
STERNDALE
```
B    1918-1923X Pickford
```
STEVENSON
```
B    1924-1926X Stevenson
```
Stevenson
```
1924-1926X STEVENSON B
```
STEWART
```
B(I) 1682-1769X Stewart
B(I) 1789-      Stewart
B    1814-      Stewart
```
STEWART OF ALVECHURCH
```
Bss(L) 1974-      Stewart
```
STEWART OF GARLIES
```
B    1796-      Stewart
```
STEWART OF OCHILTREE
```
L(S) 1542-1615P Stewart
```
Stewart
```
1398-1425F ALBANY D(S)
1452-1523X ALBANY D(S)
1565-1567X ALBANY D(S)
1600-1649F ALBANY D(S)
1660-1685M ALBANY D(S)
1481-1504X ARDMANACH L(S)
1581-1585F ARRAN E(S)
1457-1595R ATHOLL E(S)
1595-1625R ATHOLL E(S)
1580-1672X AUBIGNY L(S)
1469-      AUCHTERHOOSE L(S)
1581-1585F AVANE L(S)
1459-1543R AVONDALE L(S)
1500-1543R AVONDALE L(S)
1606-      BLANTYRE L(S)
1745-1769X BLESINTON E(I)
1587-1624F BOTHWELL E(S)
1481-1504X BRECHIN L(S)
1374-1425M BUCHAN E(S)
1469-      BUCHAN E(S)
1371-1437F CAITHNESS E(S)
1390-....M CARRICK E(S)
1630-1652X CARRICK E(S)
```

148

Stewart (Cont'd)
1580-1672X DALKEITH L(S)
1460-1576X DARNLEY L(S)
1581-1672X DARNLEY E(S)
1644-1667X DAUNTSEY B
1667-1671X DAUNTSEY B
1460-1576X DERNELEY L(S)
1790-1857X DOUGLAS OF DOUGLAS
           CASTLE L(S)
1488-1504X EDIRDALE E(S)
1623-   GALLOWAY E(S)
1607-   GARLIES L(S)
1581-1672X HAMILTON L(S)
1488/1513-   ISLES, THE L(S)
1607-1652X KINCLEVIN L(S)
1488-1672X LENNOX E(S)
1581-1672X LENNOX D(S)
1439-1470P LORN L(S)
1457-1479X MAR E(S)
1582-1672X MARCH E(S)
1486-....X MARR & GARVIACH E(S)
1528-1584X METHVEN L(S)
1682-1769X MOUNTJOY V(I)
1501-1544M MURRAY E(S)
1481-1504X NAVAR L(S)
1615-1675X OCHILTREE L(S)
1581-1614F ORKNEY E(S)
1481-1504X ORMONDE M(S)
1606-1625D PITTENWEEM L(S)
1404-   RENFREW B
1488-1504X ROSS D(S)
1398-   ROTHESAY D(S)
1682-1769X STEWART B(I)
1789-   STEWART B(I)
1814-   STEWART
1974-   STEWART OF ALVECHURCH
           Bss(L)
1706-   STEWART OF GARLIES B
1542-1615P STEWART OF OCHILTREE
           L(S)
1358-1437F STRATHERN E(S)
See also: STUART
See also: VANE-TEMPEST-STEWART
Stewart-Mackenzie
1912-1923X SEAFORTH B
Stewart-Murray
1821-1957X GLENLYON B
1786-1957X MURRAY OF STANLEY B
1786-1957X STRANGE E
STIRLING
V(S) 1630-1739? Alexander
E(S) 1633-1739? Alexander

STOCKS
  B(L) 1966-1975X Stocks
Stocks
  1966-1975X STOCKS B(L)
STOCKTON
  E   1984-   Macmillan
STODART OF LEASTON
  B(L) 1981-   Stodart
Stodart
  1981-   STODART OF LEASTON B(L)
STODDART OF SWINDON
  B(L) 1983-   Stoddart
Stoddart
  1983-   STODDART OF SWINDON
        B(L)
STOKES
  B(L) 1969-   Stokes
Stokes
  1969-   STOKES B(L)
STONE
  B(L) 1976-   Stone
Stone
  1976-   STONE B(L)
STONEHAM
  B(L) 1958-1971X Collins
STONEHAVEN
  B   1925-   Baird
  V   1938-   Baird
Stonor
  1839-   CAMOYS B
STOPFORD
  V(I) 1762-   Stopford
STOPFORD OF FALLOWFIELD
  B(L) 1958-1961X Stopford
Stopford
  1758-   COURTOWN B(I)
  1762-   COURTOWN E(I)
  1796-   SALTERSFORD B
  1762-   STOPFORD V(I)
  1958-1961X STOPFORD OF FALLOW-
        FIELD B(L)
Storey
  1966-1978X BUCKTON B(L)
STORMONT
  V(S) 1621-   Murray
STOURTON
  B   1448-   Stourton
Stourton
  1448-   STOURTON B
STOWELL
  B   1821-1836X Scott

149

```
STOW HILL                              Stratford (Cont'd)
  B(L) 1966-1979X Soskice                1777-       AMIENS V(I)
STRABANE                                 1763-1875X BALTINGLASS B(I)
  B(I) 1617-       Hamilton            STRATHALLAN
  V(I) 1701-       Hamilton             V(S) 1686-       Drummond
STRABOLGI                              STRATHALMOND
  B    1318-       Strabolgi, De        B    1955-       Fraser
Strabolgi, De                         STRATHARDLE: See STRATHTAY
  1318-       STRABOLGI B                         & STRATHARDLE
S'trachey                             Strathbogie
  1870-       O'HAGAN B                 1115-1375A ATHOLL E(S)
Strachey                              STRATHCARRON
  1911-1973X STRACHIE B                 B    1936-       Macpherson
STRACHIE                              STRATHCLYDE
  B    1911-1973X Strachey              B    1917-1928X Ure
STRADBROKE                             B    1955-       Galbraith
  E    1821-       Rous               STRATHCONA & MOUNT ROYAL
STRAFFORD                               B    1897-1914X Smith
  E    1640-1641F Wentworth             B    1900-       Smith
  E    1662-1695X Wentworth           STRATHDICHTIE
  E    1711-1799X Wentworth             L(S) 1672-       Lyon
  B    1835-       Byng                 See also: GLAMIS, TANNADYCE,
  E    1847-       Byng                  SIDLAW & STRATHDICHTIE
  B    1875-       Byng               STRATHEARN: See
STRANGE OF KNOKYN                        ABERNETHY & STRATHEARN
  B    1154/89-1216/72P Strange, Le    CONNAUGHT & STRATHEARN
  B    1299-1477C Strange, Le         STRATHEDEN
  B    1482-1594A Stanley               B    1836-       Campbell
STRANGE                               STRATHERN
  B    1628-       Stanley              E(S) 1115-1346R Malise
  E    1786-1957X Stewart-Murray        E(S) 1343-1346R Moray
STRANGE OF BLACKMERE                    E(S) 1358-1437F Stewart
  B    1308-1616A Strange, Le           E(S) 1427-1427P Graham
STRANGE OF ELLESMERE                  STRATHMORE
  B    1295-....X Strange, Le           E(S) 1672-       Lyon
Strange, Le                          STRATHMORE & KINGHORNE
  1154/89-1216/72P STRANGE OF           E    1937-       Bowes-Lyon
                KNOKYN B              STRATHNAIRN
  1299-1477C STRANGE OF KNOKYN B        B    1866-1885X Rose
  1308-1616A STRANGE OF BLACKMERE B   STRATHNAVER
  1295-....X STRANGE OF ELLESMERE B     L(S) 1573-       Sutherland
STRANGFORD                            STRATHSPEY
  V    1628-1869X Smythe                B    1858-1884X Ogilvie-Grant
STRANGWAYS                            STRATHTAY & STRATHARDLE
  B    1741-       Fox-Strangways       E(S) 1703-       Murray
STRANRAER: See GLENLUCE & STRANRAER  Strauss
STRATFORD DE REDCLIFFE                 1955-1974X CONESFORD B
  V    1852-1880X Canning             STRICKLAND
Stratford                              B    1928-1940X Strickland
  V(I) 1776-1875X ALDBOROUGH V(I)     Strickland
  E(I) 1777-1875X ALDBOROUGH E(I)       1928-1940X STRICKLAND B
                    150
```

STRIVELYN
  B   1371-1378D Strivelyn
Strivelyn
1371-1378D STRIVELYN B
Strutt
1856-   BELPER B
1821-   RAYLEIGH B
STUART
  B   1638-1861D Stuart
STUART OF CASTLE STUART
  B   1796-   Stuart
STUART OF FINDHORN
  V   1959-   Stuart
STUART OF LEIGHTON BROMSWALD
  B   1619-1672X Stuart
STUART OF WORTLEY
  B   1917-1926X Stuart-Wortley
STUART DE DECIES
  B   1839-1874X Villiers-Stuart
STUART DE ROTHESAY
  B   1828-1845X Stuart
Stuart
1562-   ABERNETHY & STRATH-
          EARN L(S)
1330-   ANGUS E(S)
1622-   AYR V(S)
1469-....X BUCHAN E(S)
1703-   BUTE E(S)
1796-   BUTE M
1644-1660X CAMBRIDGE E
1661-1661X CAMBRIDGE D
1664-1667X CAMBRIDGE E
1664-1667X CAMBRIDGE D
1667-1671X CAMBRIDGE D
1677-1677X CAMBRIDGE D
1766-   CARDIFF B
1619-   CASTLE STEWART B(I)
1793-   CASTLE STEWART V(I)
1800-   CASTLE STEWART E(I)
1581-   DOUNE L(S)
1659-1660X GLOUCESTER D
1689-1700X GLOUCESTER D
1666-1667X KENDAL D
1703-   KINGARTH V(S)
1645-1672X LICHFIELD E
1683-1861D LINTON & CABARSTOWN
          L(S)
1619-1672X MARCH E
1562-   MORAY E(S)
1796-   MOUNTJOY V
1761-   MOUNT STUART OF
          WORTLEY B

Stuart (Cont'd)
1703-   MOUNT STUART, CUMRAE &
         INCHMARNOCK L(S)
1623-1624X NEWCASTLE E
1682-1769X RAMALTON B(I)
1613-1624X RICHMOND E
1623-1624X RICHMOND D
1641-1672X RICHMOND D
1611-   ST COLME L(S)
1613-1672X SETTRINGTON B
1638-1861D STUART B
1796-   STUART OF CASTLE STUART B
1959-   STUART OF FINDHORN V
1619-1672X STUART OF LEIGHTON
         BROMSWALD B
1828-1845X STUART DE ROTHESAY B
1581-1672X TORBOLTON L(S)
1633-1861D TRAQUAIR E
1659-1685M ULSTER E(I)
1796-   WINDSOR E
1605-1625M YORK D
1643-1685M YORK D
See also: Villiers-Stuart
Stuart-Wortley
1917-1926X STUART OF WORTLEY B
Stuart-Wortley-Mackenzie
1876-   CARLTON V
1826-   WHARNCLIFFE B
1876-   WHARNCLIFFE E
Sturt
1876-1940X ALINGTON B
STUTEVILLE
  B   1066/87-1216/72X Stuteville, De
  B   1189/99-1305X Stuteville, De
Stuteville, De
1066/87-1216/72X STUTEVILLE B
1189/99-1305X STUTEVILLE B
SUDBURY
  B   1672-   FitzRoy
SUDELEY
  B   1066/87-1216/72P Sudeley, De
  B   1299-1473X Sudeley, De
  B   1441-1473X Boteler
  B   1838-   Hanbury-Tracy
Sudeley, De
1066/87-1216/72P SUDELEY B
1299-1473X SUDELEY B
SUDLEY
  V(I) 1758-   Gore
  B   1884-   Gore
Suenson-Taylor
1953-   GRANTCHESTER B

151

```
SUFFIELD
  B    1786-        Harbord
SUFFOLK
  E    1337-1382X Ufford
  E    1385-1503F Pole
  M    1444-1503F Pole
  D    1448-1503F Pole
  D    1514-1551X Brandon
  D    1551-1554F Grey
  E    1603-        Howard
Sugden
  1852-        ST LEONARDS B
SUIRDALE
  V(I) 1800-        Hutchinson
SUMMERHILL
  B(I) 1766-        Rowley
SUMMERSKILL
  Bss(L) 1961-      Summerskill
SUMNER
  B(L) 1913-1934X Hamilton
  V    1927-1934X Hamilton
SUNDERLAND
  E    1627-1630X Scrope
  E    1643-        Spencer
SUNDERLIN
  B(I) 1785-1816X Malone
SUNDON
  B(I) 1735-1752X Clayton
SUNDRIDGE
  B    1766-        Campbell
SURREY
  E    1088-1148P Warenne, De
  E    1148-1160   Blois
  E    1163-1347C Plantagenet
  E    1347-1397F Fitz-Alan
  D    1397-1400X Holland
  E    1400-1475X Fitz-Alan
  E    1483-        Howard
SUSSEX
  E    1155-1243R Albini, De
  E    1282-1347X Plantagenet
  E    1529-1641X Ratcliffe
  E    1644-1671X Savile
  E    1674-1715X Lennard
  E    1717-1799X Yelverton
  D    1801-1843X Guelph
SUTHERLAND
  E(S) 1214-        Sutherland
  D    1833-        Leveson-Gower
Sutherland
  1573-        STRATHNAVER L(S)
  1214-        SUTHERLAND E(S)

SUTTON
  B    1332-1360A Sutton, De
Sutton
  1645-1723X LEXINTON B
  See also: Manners-Sutton
Sutton, De
  1332-1360A SUTTON B
  1342-1643P DUDLEY B
SWANBOROUGH
  Bss(L) 1958-1971X Isaacs
SWANN
  B(L) 1981-        Swann
Swann
  1981-        SWANN B(L)
SWANSEA
  B    1893-        Vivian
SWAYTHLING
  B    1907-        Montagu
Swift
  1627-1634X CARLINGFORD V(I)
SWILLINGTON
  B    1326-....X Swillington
Swillington
  1326-....X SWILLINGTON B
SWINFEN
  B    1919-        Eady
SWINTON
  V    1935-        Cunliffe-Lister
  E    1955-        Cunliffe-Lister
SWORDS
  V(I) 1622-1702X Beaumont
SWYNNERTON
  B    1337-....X Swynnerton
Swynnerton
  1337-....X SWYNNERTON B
SYDENHAM
  B    1840-1841X Thomson
SYDENHAM OF COMBE
  B    1913-1933X Clarke
SYDLAW
  L(S) 1672-        Lyon
SYDNEY
  B(I) 1768-1774X Cosby
  B    1783-1890X Townshend
  B    1789-1890X Townshend
  E    1874-1890X Townshend
SYDNEY OF PENSHURST
  B    1603-1743X Sydney
SYDNEY OF SHEPPEY
  V    1689-1704X Sydney
Sydney
  1618-1743X LEICESTER E
```
152

Sydney (Cont'd)
1605-1743X L'ISLE V
1689-1704X MILTON B
1694-1704X ROMNEY E
1603-1743X SYDNEY OF PENSHURST B
1689-1704X SYDNEY OF SHEPPEY V
SYSONBY
B   1935-   Ponsonby

TAAFFE
V(I) 1628-1919F Taaffe
Taaffe
1628-1919F BALLYMOTE B
1662-1738X CARLINGFORD E(I)
1628-1919F TAAFFE V(I)
TABLEY, DE
B   1826-1895X Leicester
TADCASTER
D   1714-1741X O'Bryen
B   1826-1846X O'Brien
Tailbois, De
1154/89-1272/1307X LANCASTER B
TALBOT
B   1066/87-1272/1307P Talbot
B   1331-1777A Talbot
TALBOT OF HENSOL
B   1733-   Talbot
E   1761-1782X Talbot
E   1784-   Chetwynd-Talbot
TALBOT OF MALAHIDE
B(I) 1831-   Talbot
TALBOT DE MALAHIDE
B   1856-1973X Talbot
TALBOT OF RICHARDS CASTLE
B   1325-1388X Talbot
Talbot
1694-1718X ALTON M
1685-1691F BALTINGLASS V(I)
1442-1616A FURNIVAL B
1839-1849X FURNIVALL B
1443-....? L'ISLE B
1452-1469X L'ISLE V
1442-   SHREWSBURY E
1694-1718X SHREWSBURY D
1066/87-1272/1307P TALBOT B
1331-1777A TALBOT B
1733-   TALBOT OF HENSOL B
1761-1782X TALBOT OF HENSOL E
1831-   TALBOT OF MALAHIDE B(I)
1856-1973X TALBOT DE MALAHIDE B
1325-1388X TALBOT OF RICHARDS
                CASTLE B
1685-1691F TALBOTSTOWN B(I)
1622-1691F TYRCONNELL B(I)
1685-1691F TYRCONNELL E(I)
1689-1691F TYRCONNELL M(I)
1689-1691F TYRCONNELL D(I)
1446-   WATERFORD E(I)
1446-   WEXFORD E(I)
TALBOTSTOWN
B(I) 1685-1691F Talbot

(TITLES are in CAPITALS
Surnames in smalls)

153

TALBOYS
  B   1529-1539X Talboys
Talboys
  1529-1539X TALBOYS B
TAMWORTH
  V   1711-   Shirley
TANGLEY
  B(L) 1963-1973X Herbert
TANI
  B   1066/87-1272/1307X Tani, De
Tani, De
  1066387-1272/1307X TANI B
TANKERVILLE
  E   1418-1459A Grey
  E   1695-1701X Grey
  E   1714-   Bennet
TANLAW
  B(L) 1971-   Mackay
TANNADYCE: See GLAMIS, TANNADYCE,
  SIDLAW & STRATHDICHTIE
TARA
  V(I) 1650-1674X Preston
  B(I) 1800-1821X Preston
TARAGH
  B(I) 1691-1719X Schomberg
TARBAT
  V(S) 1685-1746F Mackenzie
  V   1861-   Mackenzie
TARRAS
  E(S) 1660-1693X Scott
TARRINZEAN & MAUCHLIN
  L(S) 1633-   Campbell
TARVES
  L(S) 1682-   Gordon
  See also: HADDO, METHLIC,
  TARVES & KELLIE
Tatem
  1918-1942X GLANELY B
TATTESHALL
  B   1066/87-1272/1307P Tatteshall
  B   1295-1306A Tatteshall
Tatteshall
  1066/87-1272/1307P TATTESHALL B
  1295-1306A TATTESHALL B
TAUNTON
  B   1859-1869X Labouchere
TAVISTOCK
  M   1694-   Russell
TAY & PAINTLAND
  V   1677-   Campbell
TAYLOR
  B(L) 1958-   Taylor

TAYLOR OF BLACKBURN
  B(L) 1978-   Taylor
TAYLOR OF GRYFE
  B(L) 1968-   Taylor
TAYLOR OF HADFIELD
  B(L) 1982-   Taylor
TAYLOR OF MANSFIELD
  B(L) 1966-

Taylor
  1982-   INGROW B(L)
  1948-1951X MAENAN B
  1958-   TAYLOR B(L)
  1978-   TAYLOR OF BLACKBURN
              B(L)
  1968-   TAYLOR OF GRYFE B(L)
  1982-   TAYLOR OF HADFIELD
              B(L)
  1966-   TAYLOR OF MANSFIELD
              B(L)

  See also: Suenson-Taylor
Taylour
  1766-   BECTIVE E(I)
  1760-   HEADFORT B(I)
  1762-   HEADFORT V(I)
  1800-   HEADFORT M(I)
  1831-   KENLIS B
TAYSIDE
  B(L) 1967-1975X Urquhart
TEDDER
  B   1946-   Tedder
Tedder
  1946-   TEDDER B
TEIGNMOUTH
  B(I) 1797-1981X Shore
TEMAIR: See ABERDEEN & TEMAIR
Tempest: See Vane-Tempest-Stewart
TEMPLE
  E   1749-1889X Temple
TEMPLE OF STOWE
  E   1799-1822M Nugent-Temple-
                  Grenville
Temple
  1714-   COBHAM OF KENT B
  1718-   COBHAM OF KENT V
  1722-1865X PALMERSTON V(I)
  1749-1889X TEMPLE E
  See also: Cowper-Temple
            Hamilton-Temple-
            Blackwood
TEMPLEMAN * See Addenda

154

TEMPLETOWN
B(I) 1776-1981X Upton
V(I) 1806-1981X Upton
TEMPLEWOOD
V   1944-1959X Hoare
TENBY
V   1957-   Lloyd George
Tennant
1911-   GLENCONNER B
TENNYSON
B   1884-   Tennyson
Tennyson
1884-   TENNYSON B
TENTERDEN
B   1827-1939X Abbott
TERRINGTON
B   1918-   Woodhouse
TEVIOT
L(S) 1661-1724A Rutherford
V(S) 1685-1694X Spencer
V(S) 1696-1711X Livingston
B   1940-   Kerr
TEVIOTDALE   *
D   1799-1799M Guelph
TEWKESBURY
B   1831-   Fitz-Clarence
TEYNHAM
B   1616-   Roper
THAME
V   1620-1623X Norris
THANET
E   1628-1849X Tufton
THANKERTON
B(L) 1929-1948X Watson
Thellusson
1806-   RENDLESHAM B(I)
Thesiger
1858-   CHELMSFORD B
1921-   CHELMSFORD V
THETFORD
V   1672-1936A FitzRoy
THIRLESTANE & BOULTON
L(S) 1624-   Maitland
THOMAS
B(L) 1971-   Thomas
THOMAS OF SWYNNERTON
B(L) 1981-   Thomas
Thomas
1956-1960X CILCENNIN V
1912-1927X PONTYPRIDD B

    *See also Addenda

Thomas (Cont'd)
1916-1918X RHONDDA B
1918-1958X RHONDDA V
1971-   THOMAS B(L)
1981-   THOMAS OF SWYNNERTON B(L)
1983-   TONYPANDY V
See also: Freeman-Thomas
THOMOND
E(I) 1540-1741D O'Brien
E(I) 1756-1774X O'Brien
M(I) 1800-1855X O'Brien
B   1801-1808X O'Bryen
Thompson
1696-1745X HAVERSHAM B
1839-1852P WENLOCK B
See also: Mersey-Thompson
THOMSON
B   1924-1930X Thomson
THOMSON OF FLEET
B   1964-   Thomson
THOMSON OF MONIFIETH
B(L) 1977-   Thomson
Thomson
1892-1907X KELVIN B
1840-1841X SYDENHAM B
1924-1930X THOMSON B
1964-   THOMSON OF FLEET B
1977-   THOMSON OF MONIFIETH B(L)
1970-1978X TWEEDSMUIR OF BELHELVIE
            Bss(L)
See also: Courtauld-Thomson
          Mitchell-Thomson
THORNEYCROFT
B(L) 1967-   Thorneycroft
Thorneycroft
1967-   THORNEYCROFT B(L)
THORPE
B   1309-....X Thorpe, De
B   1381-1390X Thorpe, De
Thorpe, De
1309-....X THORPE B
1381-1390X THORPE B
THORTHORWALD: See NITH, THORTHORWALD
& ROSS
THRING
B   1886-1907X Thring
Thring
1886-1907X THRING B
THROWLEY
B   1676-1709X Sondes

155

THROWLEY (Cont'd)
B   1714-1746X Watson
V   1880-   Milles
THURLES
V(I) 1535-   Butler
THURLOW
B   1778-1806X Thurlow
B   1792-   Thurlow
Thurlow
1778-1806X THURLOW B
1792-   THURLOW B
THURSO
V   1952-   Sinclair
THWENG
B   1294-1374A Thweng, De
Thweng, De
1294-1374A THWENG B
THYNNE
B   1682-   Thynne
Thynne
1789-   BATH M
1784-1849X CARTERET B
1682-   THYNNE B
1682-   WEYMOUTH V
TIBBERS
V(S) 1706-1778P Douglas
TIBETOT or TIPTOFT
B   1308-1372A Tibetot, De
B   1426-1485A Tibetot, De
Tibetot, De or Tiptoft, De
1308-1372A TIBETOT B
1426-1485A TIBETOT B
Tichborne
1715-1731X FERRARD B(I)
TINDALE
B   1154/80-1189/99X Tindale, De
Tindale, De
1154/80-1189/99X TINDALE B
TINMOUTH
E   1687-1695F Fitzjames
TIPPERARY
E   1801-1904X Guelph
TIPTOFT: See TIBETOT
Tiptoft
1449-1485F WORCESTER E
See also: Tibetot, De
TIRY: See INVERARAY, MULL, MORVERN
& TIRY
TITCHFIELD
M   1716-   Bentinck

TIVERTON
V   1898-   Giffard
TODD
B(L) 1962-   Todd
Todd
1962-   TODD B(L)
TODENI
B   1066/87-1087/1100X Todeni, De
Todeni, De
1066/87-1087/1100X TODENI B
Toler
1827-   GLANDINE V(I)
1800-   NORBURY B(I)
1827-   NORBURY E(I)
1797-   NORWOOD B(I)
TOLLEMACHE
B   1876-   Tollemache
TOMLIN
B(L) 1929-1935X Tomlin
Tomlin
1929-1935X TOMLIN B(L)
TONI
B   1066/87-1272/1307X Toni, De
B   1299-1311X Toni, De
Toni, De
1066/87-1272/1307X TONI B
1299-1311X TONI, B
Tonson
1783-1861X RIVERSDALE B
TONYPANDY
V   1983-   Thomas
TORBOLTON
L(S) 1581-1672X Stuart
TORBOULTON
L(S) 1675-   Lennox
TORDOFF
B(L) 1981-   Tordoff
Tordoff
1981-   TORDOFF B(L)
TORPHICHEN
L(S) 1564-   Sandilands
TORRINGTON
E   1660-1688X Monck
E   1689-1716X Herbert
B   1716-1719X Newport
V   1721-   Byng
TORTHORWALD
V(S) 1681-   Douglas
TOTNESS
E   1626-1629X Carew
V   1675-1680X Fitzcharles

156

```
Tottenham                                   TREDEGAR
   1794-      ELY E(I)                          B    1859-1962X Morgan
   1801-      ELY M(I)                          V    1905-1913X Morgan
   1785-      LOFTUS B(I)                       V    1926-1949X Morgan
   1789-      LOFTUS V(I)                    TREFGARNE
   1801-      LOFTUS B                          B    1947-      Trefgarne
TOUCHET                                      Trefgarne
   B    1299-1322F Touchet                      1947-      TREFGARNE B
Touchet                                      TREGOZ
   1405-1631F AUDLEY B                          B    1299-1300A Tregoz
   1616-1777X CASTLEHAVEN E(I)                  B    1305-1335A Tregoz
   1299-1322F TOUCHET B                         B    1318-....X Tregoz
TOVEY                                        TREGOZ OF HIGHWORTH
   B    1946-1971X Tovey                        B    1626-1629X St John
Tovey                                        Tregoz
   1946-1971X                                   1299-1300A TREGOZ B
TOWNSHEND                                      1305-1335A TREGOZ B
   B    1661-      Townshend                    1318-....X TREGOZ B
   V    1682-      Townshend                 TREMATON
   M    1787-      Townshend                    V    1726-1765X Guelph
Townshend                                      V    1917-1957X Cambridge
   1810-1866X BEAUCHAMP B                    TRENCH
   1751-1855A FERRERS OF CHARTLEY B             B    1815-      Trench
   1767-1794X GREENWICH Bss                  Trench
   1784-1855X LEICESTER E                       1793-      KILCONNEL B(I)
   1723-      LYNN B                            1800-      ASHTOWN B(I)
   1682-      RAYNHAM V                         1803-      CLANCARTY E(I)
   1783-1890X SYDNEY B                          1823-      CLANCARTY V
   1789-1890X SYDNEY V                          1801-      DUNLO V(I)
   1874-1890X SYDNEY E                          1815-      TRENCH B
   1661-      TOWNSHEND B                    TRENCHARD
   1682-      TOWNSHEND V                       B    1930-      Trenchard
   1787-      TOWNSHEND M                       V    1936-      Trenchard
TRACI                                        Trenchard
   B    1135/54-1199/1216P Traci, De           1930-      TRENCHARD B
Traci, De                                      1936-      TRENCHARD V
   1135/54-1199/1216P TRACI B               TREND
TRACTON                                         B(L) 1974-      Trend
   B(I) 1780-1782X Dennis                   Trend
TRACY                                           1974-      TREND B(L)
   V(I) 1642-1797D Tracy                    TRENT
Tracy                                           B    1929-1956X Boot
   1642-1797D TRACY V(I)                    TRENTHAM
   See also: Hanbury-Tracy                      V    1746-      Leveson-Gower
TRANENT: See SETON & TRANENT                 TREOWEN
TRANMIRE                                        B    1917-1933X Herbert
   B(L) 1974-      Turton                    TREVELYAN
TRAPRAIN                                        B(L) 1968-      Trevelyan
   V    1922-      Balfour                   TREVETHIN
TRAQUAIR                                        B    1921-      Lawrence
   E    1633-1861D Stuart
```
157

TREVOR
  B(I) 1662-1706X Trevor
  B   1711-1824X Trevor
  B   1880-   Hill-Trevor
Trevor
  1819-1851A DACRE B
  1661-1706X DUNGANNON V(I)
  1765-1862X DUNGANNON V(I)
  1776-1824X HAMPDEN B
  1662-1706X TREVOR B(I)
  1711-1824X TREVOR B
TREVOR-ROPER
  B(L) 1979-   Trevor-Roper
Trevor-Roper
  1979-   TREVOR-ROPER B(L)
TRIM
  B(I) 1715-1731X Wharton
TRIMLESTOWN
  B(I) 1461-   Barnewall
Trollope
  1868-1915X KESTEVEN B
TRUMPINGTON
  Bss(L) 1980-   Barker
TRURO
  B   1850-1899X Wilde
TRUSBUT
  B   1100/35-....X Trusbut, De
Trusbut, De
  1100/35-....X TRUSBUT B
TRUSSEL
  B   1342-....X Trussel
Trussel
  1342-....X TRUSSEL B
TRYON
  B   1940-   Tryon
Tryon
  1940-   TRYON B
TUCKER
  B(L) 1950-1975X Tucker
Tucker
  1950-1975X TUCKER B(L)
Tudor
  1485-1495X BEDFORD D
  1452-1461F PEMBROKE E
  1485-1495X PEMBROKE E
  1452-1485M RICHMOND E
  1496-1499X SOMERSET D
  1494-1509M YORK D
TUFTON
  B   1626-1849X Tufton

Tufton
  1881-   HOTHFIELD B
  1628-1849X THANET E
  1626-1849X TUFTON B
TULLAMORE
  B(I) 1797-   Bury
TULLIBARDINE
  E(S) 1606-   Murray
  M(S) 1703-   Murray
TULLOUGH
  V(I) 1693-1759X Butler
TUNBRIDGE
  V   1624-1659X Burgh
  V   1695-1830X Nassau
Turner
  1959-   NETHERTHORPE B
TURNHAM
  B   1154/89-1189/99X Turnham, De
Turnham, De
  1154/89-1189/99X TURNHAM B
TURNOUR
  V(I) 1766-   Turnour
  B   1952-1962X Turnour
Turnour
  1766-   TURNOUR V(I)
  1952-1962X TURNOUR B
  1761-   WINTERTON B(I)
  1766-   WINTERTON E(I)
Turton
  1974-   TRANMIRE B(L)
TURVEY
  B(I) 1646-1833D Barnewall
TWEEDDALE
  E(S) 1646-   Hay
  M(S) 1694-   Hay
  B   1881-   Hay
TWEEDMOUTH
  B   1881-1935X Marjoribanks
TWEEDSMUIR
  B   1935-   Buchan
TWEEDSMUIR OF BELHELVIE
  Bss(L) 1970-1978X Thomson
TWINING
  B(L) 1958-1967X Twining
Twining
  1958-1967X TWINING B(L)
TYAQUIN
  B(I) 1687-1691X Burke
TYES
  B   1299-1321D Tyes,De

158

TYES or TEYES
B   1299-1324X Tyes, De
Tyes, De
B   1299-1321D TYES
B   1299-1324X TYES or TEYES B
TYLNEY
E(I) 1731-1784X Child
TYNDALE
B   1688-1716F Radcliffe
TYNEDALE
B   1663-   Scott
TYRAWLEY
B(I) 1797-1821X Cuffe
TYRAWLY
B(I) 1706-1774X O'Hara
TYRCONNEL
V(I) 1718-1754X Brownlow
E(I) 1761-1853X Carpenter
TYRCONNELL
E(I) 1603-1642X O'Donnell
B(I) 1622-1691F Talbot
E(I) 1663-1667X Fitzwilliam
E(I) 1685-1691F Talbot
M(I) 1689-1691F Talbot
D(I) 1689-1691F Talbot
TYRELL OF AVON
B   1929-1947X Tyrell
Tyrell
1929-1947X TYRELL OF AVON
TYRONE
E(I) 1542-1608F O'Neill
E(I) 1673-1704X Le Poer
V(I) 1720-   Beresford
E(I) 1746-   Beresford
B   1786-   Beresford
Tyrwhitt
1871-   BERNERS B

(TITLES are in CAPITALS
Surnames in smalls)

UFFINGTON
V   1801-   Craven
UFFORD
B   1308-1381A Ufford
B   1360-1361X Ufford
Ufford
1337-1382X SUFFOLK E
1308-1381A UFFORD B
1360-1361X UFFORD B
UGHTRED
B   1343-1365D Ughtred
Ughtred
1343-1365D UGHTRED B
ULLSWATER
V   1921-   Lowther
ULSTER
E(I) 1181-1204X Courcy, De
E(I) 1205-1242P Laci, De
E(I) 1243-1352P Burgh, De
E(I) 1352-1461M Plantagenet
E(I) 1368-1461M Mortimer
E(I) 1659-1685M Stuart
E(I) 1716-1728X Guelph
E(I) 1760-1767X Guelph
E(I) 1784-1827X Guelph
E   1866-1900X Guelph
E   1928-   Windsor
UMFREVILLE
B   1066/87-1216/72P Umfreville,
                         De
B   1295-1381D Umfreville, De
Umfraville
1297-1381X ANGUS E(S)
Umfreville, De
1066/87-1216/72P UMFREVILLE B
1295-1381D UMFREVILLE B
UNDERHILL
B(L) 1979-   Underhill
Underhill
1979-   UNDERHILL B(L)
Underwood
1840-1873X INVERNESS Dss
UPJOHN
B(L) 1963-1971X Upjohn
Upjohn
1963-1971X UPJOHN B(L)
UPPER OSSORY
B(I) 1541-1697S Patrick
E(I) 1751-1818X Fitzpatrick
B   1794-1818X Fitzpatrick

159

Upton
  1776-1981X TEMPLETOWN B(I)
  1806-1981X TEMPLETOWN V(I)
Ure
  1917-1928X STRATHCLYDE B
Urquhart
  1967-1975X TAYSIDE B(L)
UTHWATT
  B(L) 1946-1949X Uthwatt
Uthwatt
  1946-1949X UTHWATT B(L)
UVEDALE
  B   1332-1336X Uvedale
UVEDALE OF NORTH END
  B   1946-1974X Woodall
Uvedale
  1332-1336X UVEDALE B
UXBRIDGE
  E   1714-1769X Paget
  E   1784-   Paget

VAIZEY
  B(L) 1976-1984X Vaizey
Vaizey
  1976-1984X VAIZEY B(L)
VAL, DE LA
  B   1154/89-1272/1307X Val, De La
Val, De La
  1154/89-1272/1307X VAL, DE LA B
VALENCE
  B   1299-1323X Valence
Valence
  1247-1323X PEMBROKE E
  1299-1323X VALENCE B
VALENTIA
  B(I) 1556-1597R M'Carthy
  V(I) 1620-1642X Power
  V(I) 1622-   Annesley
VALLETORT
  B   1135/54-1272/1307X Valletort,
                              De
  V   1781-1789M Edgcumbe
  See also MOUNT EDGCUMBE & VALLETORT
Valletort, De
  1135/54-1272/1307X VALLETORT B
VALOINES
  B   1066/87-1216/72X Valoines, De
Valoines, De
  1066/87-1216/72X VALOINES B
Valonis, De
  1180-1219X PANMURE L(S)
Vanden-Bempde-Johnson
  1881-   DERWENT B
VANE
  E   1823-   Stewart
VANE OF DUNGANNON
  B(I) 1720-1789X Vane
  V(I) 1720-1789X Vane
Vane
  1698-   BARNARD B
  1754-   BARNARD V
  1827-1891X CLEVELAND M
  1833-1891X CLEVELAND D
  1833-1891X RABY B
  1720-1789X VANE OF DUNGANNON B(I)
  1720-1789X VANE OF DUNGANNON V(I)
  See also: Fletcher-Vane
Vane-Tempest-Stewart
  1795-   CASTLEREAGH V(I)
  1789-   LONDONDERRY B(I)
  1796-   LONDONDERRY E(I)
  1816-   LONDONDERRY M(I)

160

Vane-Tempest-Stewart (Cont'd)
1823-   SEAHAM V
1814-   STEWART B
1823-   VANE E
Vanneck
1796-   HUNTINGFIELD B
VANSITTART
B   1941-1957X Vansittart
Vansittart
1823-1851X BEXLEY B
1941-1957X VANSITTART B
VAUGHAN
B(I) 1621-1712X Vaughan
B   1643-1713X Vaughan
V(I) 1695-   Vaughan
Vaughan
1628-1712X CARBERY E(I)
1695-   FETHARD B(I)
1695-   LISBURNE V(I)
1776-   LISBURNE E(I)
1621-1712X VAUGHAN B(I)
1643-1713X VAUGHAN B
1695-   VAUGHAN V(I)
Vaughan-Davies
1921-1935X YSTWYTH B
Vaughan-Morgan
1970-   REIGATE B(L)
VAUX OF HARROWDEN
B   1523-   Vaux
See also: BROUGHAM & VAUX
Vaux
1523-   VAUX OF HARROWDEN B
VAVASOUR
B   1299-1313X Vavasour
Vavasour
1299-1313X VAVASOUR B
VEEL
B   1342-1342X Veel, Le
Veel, Le
1342-1342X VEEL B
Venables-Vernon
1762-   VERNON B
VENTRY
B(I) 1800-   Mullins
VERDON
B   1295-1316A Verdon
B   1332-1342X Verdon
Verdon
1295-1316A VERDON B
1332-1342X VERDON B

VERE
B   1066/87-1154/89X Vere, De
B   1299-....X Vere, De
VERE OF HANWORTH
B   1750-   Beauclerk
VERE OF TILBURY
B   1625-1635X Vere
Vere
1385-   DUBLIN M
1386-1388F IRELAND D(I)
1155-1338F OXFORD E
1392-1461F OXFORD E
1464-1702X OXFORD E
1625-1635X VERE OF TILBURY B
Vere, De
1205-....X CAMBRIDGE E
1066/87-1154/89X VERE B
1299-....X VERE B
Vereker
1816-   GORT V(I)
1946-1946X GORT V
VERNEY
E(I) 1742-1791X Verney
Verney
1703-1791X FERMANAGH V(I)
1792-1810X FERMANAGH Bss(I)
1742-1791X VERNEY E(I)
VERNON
B   1762-   Venables-Vernon
Vernon
1859-   LYVEDEN B
1762-1783X ORWELL B(I)
1762-1783X SHIPBROOKE E(I)
VERULAM
B   1618-1626X Bacon
V(I) 1719-   Grimston
B   1790-   Grimston
E   1815-   Grimston
VESCI
B   1066/87-1216/72P Vesci, De
B   1264-1297X Vesci, De
B   1449-1468X Bromflete
VESCI, DE
V(I) 1776-   Vesey
B   1884-1903X Vesey
Vesci, De
1066/87-1216/72P VESCI B
1313-1315X VESCI B
VESEY: See FITZGERALD & VESEY

161

Vesey
1776-   VESCI, DE V(I)
1884-1903X VESCI, DE B
1750-   KNAPTON B(I)
VESTEY
  B   1922-   Vestey
Vestey
  1922-   VESTEY B
VICKERS
  Bss(L) 1974-   Vickers
Vickers
  1974-   VICKERS Bss(L)
VICOUNT
  B   1154/89-1216/72X Vicount, Le
Vicount, Le
  1154/89-1216/72X VICOUNT B
VILLIERS
  V   1616-1687X Villiers
  B   1623-1659X Villiers
  B   1691-   Villiers
  V   1691-   Villiers
  V(I) 1767-1800X Villiers
VILLIERS OF STOKE
  B   1619-1687X Villiers
VILLIERS, DE
  B   1910-   Villiers, De
Villiers
  1623-1659X ANGLESEY E
  1616-1687X BLETCHLEY B
  1616-1687X BUCKINGHAM E
  1618-1632X BUCKINGHAM Css
  1618-1687X BUCKINGHAM M
  1623-1687X BUCKINGHAM D
  1776-   CLARENDON E
  1670-1709X CLEVELAND Dss
  1623-1687X COVENTRY E
  1620-1630 GRANDISON V(I)
  1721-1800X GRANDISON E(I)
  1746-1809X GRANDISON Vss(I)
  1766-1809X GRANDISON Css(I)
  1691-1691M HOO B
  1756-   HYDE B
  1679-1774X NONSUCH Bss
  1619-1657X PURBECK V
  1670-1774X SOUTHAMPTON Css
  1616-1687X VILLIERS V
  1623-1659X VILLIERS B
  1691-   VILLIERS B
  1691-   VILLIERS V
  1767-1800X VILLIERS V(I)

Villiers (Cont'd)
  1619-1687X VILLIERS OF STOKE B
  1616-1687X WHADDON B
Villiers, De
  1910-   VILLIERS, DE B
Villiers-Stuart
  1839-1874X STUART DE DECIES B
Vincent
  1914-1941X D'ABERNON B
  1926-1941X D'ABERNON V
VINSON
  B(L) 1985-   Vinson
Vinson
  1985-   VINSON B(L)
VIPONT
  B   1199/1216-1216/72? Vipont, De
Vipont, De
  1199/1216-1216/72? VIPONT B
VIVIAN
  B   1841-   Vivian
Vivian
  1893-   SWANSEA B
  1841-   VIVIAN B
  See also: Colborne-Vivian
Vosper
  1964-1968X RUNCORN B(L)

(TITLES are in CAPITALS
 Surnames in smalls)

162

WADE
B(L) 1964-   Wade
Wade
1964-   WADE B(L)
WAHULL
B   1297-....D Wahull, De
Wahull, De
1297-....D WAHULL B
WAKE
B   1295-1407A Wake
Wake
1295-1407A WAKE B
WAKEFIELD
B   1930-1941X Wakefield
V   1934-1941X Wakefield
WAKEFIELD OF KENDAL
B   1963-1983X Wakefield
Wakefield
1930-1941X WAKEFIELD B
1934-1941X WAKEFIELD V
1963-1983X WAKEFIELD OF KENDAL B
WAKEHURST
B   1934-   Loder
WALBERTON
V   1956-   Marquis
Walcher
1075-1080R NORTHUMBERLAND E
WALDEGRAVE
B   1686-   Waldegrave
E   1689-   Waldegrave
Waldegrave
1729-   CHEWTON V
1800-1953X RADSTOCK B
1686-   WALDEGRAVE B
1689-   WALDEGRAVE E
WALDEN
V(S) 1694-   Hay
WALERAN
B   1905-1966X Walrond
WALEYS
B   1321-....X Waleys
Waleys
1321-....X WALEYS B
WALKDEN
B   1945-   Walkden
Walkden
1945-   WALKDEN B
Walker
1919-1933X WAVERTREE B
See also: Gordon Walker

Walker-Smith
1983-   BROXBOURNE B(L)
WALL
B(L) 1976-   Wall
Wall
1976-   WALL B(L)
WALLACE
B   1828-1844X Wallace
WALLACE OF CAMPSIE
B(L) 1974-   Wallace
WALLACE OF COSLANY
B(L) 1974-   Wallace
Wallace
1828-1844X WALLACE B
1974-   WALLACE OF CAMPSIE B(L)
1974-   WALLACE OF COSLANY B(L)
WALLINGFORD
V   1616-1632D Knollys
WALLOP
B   1720-   Wallop
Wallop
1720-   LYMINGTON V
1743-   PORTSMOUTH E
1720-   WALLOP B
WALLSCOURT
B(I) 1800-1920X Blake
Walmoden
1740-1765X YARMOUTH Bss(L)
1740-1765X YARMOUTH Css(L)
WALPOLE
B   1723-   Walpole
WALPOLE OF HOUGHTON
B   1742-1797X Walpole
WALPOLE OF WOLTERTON
B   1756-   Walpole
Walpole
1742-1797X HOUGHTON B
1742-1797X ORFORD E
1806-1931X ORFORD E
1723-   WALPOLE B
1742-1797X WALPOLE OF HOUGHTON
1756-   WALPOLE OF WOLTERTON
Walrond
1905-1966X WALERAN B
Walsh
1868-1984X ORMATHWAITE B
WALSINGHAM
Css 1722-1778X Schulenburg
B   1780-   Grey, De

163

WALSTON
  B(L) 1961-   Walston
Walston
  1961-   WALSTON B(L)
WALTER
  B   1154/89-1199/1216X **Walter**
Walter
  1154/89-1199/1216X WALTER B
WALTHAM
  B(I) 1762-1787X Olmius
Waltheof
  1072-1076F NORTHUMBERLAND E
WANDESFORD
  B(I) 1706-1784X Wandesford
  E(I) 1758-1784X Wandesford
Wandesford
  1706-1784X CASTLECOMER V(I)
  1706-1784X WANDESFORD B(I)
  1758-1784X WANDESFORD E(I)
WANDSWORTH
  B   1895-1912X Stern
WANTAGE
  B   1885-1901X Loyd-Lindsay
WARD
  B   1644-   Ward
  V   1763-1833X Ward
WARD OF NORTH TYNESIDE
  Bss(L) 1974-   Ward
WARD OF WITLEY
  V   1960-   Ward
Ward
  1770-   BANGOR B(I)
  1781-   BANGOR V(I)
  1644-1757A DUDLEY B
  1860-   DUDLEY V
  1860-   DUDLEY E
  1763-1833X DUDLEY & WARD V
  1827-1833X DUDLEY OF DUDLEY
           CASTLE E
  1827-1833X EDNAM V
  1860-   EDNAM V
  1644-   WARD B
  1763-1833X WARD V
  1974-   WARD OF NORTH TYNE-
           SIDE Bss(L)
  1960-   WARD OF WITLEY V
WARDE, DE LA
  B   1299-1334X Delawarde
WARDINGTON
  B   1936-   Pease

WARGRAVE
  B   1922-1936X Goulding
WARING
  B   1922-1940X Waring
Waring
  1922-1940X WARING B
WARKWORTH
  B   1749-   Seymour   *
WARR, DE LA
  B   1299-1426P Warr, La
  B   1570-   West
  E   1761-   West
Warr, La
  1299-1426P WARR, DE LA B
WARREN
  E   1087/1100-1397X Warenne, De
  B   1154/89-1189/99X Warren, De
  E   1451-1475X Mowbray
  E   1477-1483X Plantagenet
Warenne, De
  1088-1148P SURREY E
  1087/1100-1397X WARREN E
Warren, De
  1154/89-1189/99X WARREN B
Warrender
  1942-   BRUNTISFIELD B
WARRINGTON
  E   1690-1758X Booth
  E   1796-1883X Grey
WARRINGTON OF CLYFFE
  B   1926-1937X Warrington
Warrington
  1926-1937X WARRINGTON OF CLYFFE B
WARWICK
  E   1066-1242C Newburgh
  E   1246-1268P Plessets
  E   1268-1445X Beauchamp
  D   1444-1445X Beauchamp
  Css 1445-1449X Beauchamp
  E   1449-1471F Nevill
  E   1472-1477F Plantagenet
  E   1561-1589X Dudley
  E   1618-1759X Rich
  E   1759-   Greville
WATERFORD
  E(I) 1446-   Talbot
  M(I) 1789-   Beresford
WATERPARK
  B(I) 1792-   Cavendish

164   *See Addenda

WATEVYLL
B   1326-1326X Watevyll, De
Watevyll, De
1326-1326X WATEVYLL B
WATH
B   1734-1782X Wentworth
WATKINS
B(L) 1972-   Watkins
Watkins
1972-   WATKINS B(L)
WATKINSON
V   1964-   Watkinson
Watkinson
1964-   WATKINSON V
WATSON
B(L) 1880-1899X Watson
Watson
1922-   MANTON B
1645-1782X ROCKINGHAM B
1714-1782X ROCKINGHAM V
1746-1782X ROCKINGHAM M
1760-   SONDES B
1929-1948X THANKERTON B(L)
1714-1746X THROWLEY B
1880-1899X WATSON B(L)
Watson-Armstrong
1903-   ARMSTRONG B
Watson-Wentworth
1725-1782X MALTON B
1734-1782X MALTON E
Watt: See Gibson-Watt
WAVELL
V   1943-1954X Wavell
E   1947-1954X Wavell
Wavell
1947-1954X KEREN V
1943-1954X WAVELL V
1947-1954X WAVELL E
WAVENEY
B   1873-1886X Adair
WAVERLEY
V   1952-   Anderson
WAVERTREE
B   1919-1933X Walker
Wayher
1066-....F NORFOLK E
WEARDALE
B   1906-1923X Stanhope
Webb
1929-1947X PASSFIELD B

WEBB-JOHNSON
B   1945-1958X Webb-Johnson
Webb-Johnson
1945-1958X WEBB-JOHNSON
Webster
1900-1915X ALVERSTONE B
1913-1915X ALVERSTONE V
WEDDERBURN OF CHARLTON
B(L) 1977-   Wedderburn
Wedderburn
1780-1805X LOUGHBOROUGH B
1795-   LOUGHBOROUGH B
1801-   ROSSLYN E
1977-   WEDDERBURN OF CHARLTON
             B(L)
WEDGWOOD
B   1942-   Wedgwood
Wedgwood
1942-   WEDGWOOD B
WEEKS
B   1956-1960X Weeks
Weeks
1956-1960X WEEKS B
WEICK: See GLENORCHY, BENEDARALOCH,
ORMELIE & WEICK
WEIDENFELD
B(L) 1976-   Weidenfeld
Weidenfeld
1976-   WEIDENFELD B(L)
WEINSTOCK
B(L) 1980-   Weinstock
Weinstock
1980-   WEINSTOCK B(L)
WEIR
B   1918-   Weir
V   1938-   Weir
Weir
1919-   INVERFORTH B
1918-   WEIR B
1938-   WEIR V
WELBY
B   1894-1915X Welby
Welby
1894-1915X WELBY B
Weld-Forester
1821-   FORESTER B
WELLES
B   1299-1461F Welles
B   1468-1503X Hastings
B   1487-1498X Welles
B(I) 1781-   Knox

165

Welles
1299-1461F WELLES B
1487-1498X WELLES B
WELLESLEY
V(I) 1760-   Wesley
B   1797-1842X Wellesley
M(I) 1799-1842X Wellesley
Wellesley
1857-   COWLEY E
1828-   COWLEY OF WELLESLEY B
1857-   DANGAN V
1809-   DOURO B
1814-   DOURO M
1821-1863X MARYBOROUGH B(I)
1797-1842X WELLESLEY B
1799-1842X WELLESLEY M(I)
1812-   WELLINGTON E
1812-   WELLINGTON M
1814-   WELLINGTON D
1809-   WELLINGTON OF TALAVERA
             & WELLINGTON V
WELLINGTON
E   1812-   Wellesley
M   1812-   Wellesley
D   1814-   Wellesley
WELLINGTON OF TALAVERA & WELLINGTON
V   1809-   Wellesley
WELLS-PESTELL
B(L) 1965-   Wells-Pestell
Wells-Pestell
1965-   WELLS-PESTELL B(L)
WEMYSS
E(S) 1633-   Wemyss
B   1821-   Charteris
WEMYSS OF ELCHO
L(S) 1628-   Wemyss
Wemyss
1672-1685X BURNTISLAND L(S)
1633-   ELCHO & METHEL L(S)
1814-   NIEDPATH B
1633-   WEMYSS E(S)
1628-   WEMYSS OF ELCHO L(S)
1919-1933X WESTER WEMYSS B
WENDOVER
V   1895-1928X Wynn-Carrington
WENLOCK
B   1461-1471X Wenlock
B   1831-1834X Lawley
B   1839-1852P Thompson
B   1852-1932X Lawley

Wenlock
1461-1471X WENLOCK B
WENMAN
B(I) 1628-1800X Wenman
V(I) 1628-1800X Wenman
Bss 1834-1870X Wykeham
Wenman
1628-1800X WENMAN B(I)
1628-1800X WENMAN V(I)
WENSLEYDALE
B   1856-1868X Parke
B   1900-   Ridley
WENTWORTH
B   1529-   Wentworth
V   1762-1815X Wentworth
WENTWORTH OF WENTWORTH WOODHOUSE
B   1628-1695X Wentworth
V   1628-1799X Wentworth
Wentworth
1626-1667X CLEVELAND E
1734-1782X HIGHAM V
1750-1782X MALTON B(I)
1750-1782X MALTON E(I)
1628-1695X NEWMARSH B
1628-1695X OVERSLEY B
1640-1799X RABY B
1640-1641F STRAFFORD E
1662-1695X STRAFFORD E
1711-1799X STRAFFORD E
1529-   WENTWORTH B
1762-1815X WENTWORTH V
1628-1695X WENTWORTH OF
             WENTWORTH WOODHOUSE B
1628-1799X WENTWORTH OF
             WENTWORTH WOODHOUSE V
Wesley
1760-   WELLESLEY V(I)
WEST
B   1342-   West
West
1761-   CANTELUPE V
1958-1984X GRANVILLE-WEST B(L)
1570-   WARR, DE LA B
1761-   WARR, DE LA E
1342-   WEST B
WESTBURY
B   1861-   Bethell
WESTCOTE
B(I) 1776-   Lyttelton
Westenra
1838-   ROSSMORE B

166

WESTERN
B   1833-1844X Western
Western
  1833-1844X WESTERN B
WESTER WEMYSS
B   1919-1933X Wemyss
WESTMEATH
  E(I) 1621-   Nugent
  M   1822-1871X Nugent
WESTMINSTER
  M   1831-   Grosvenor
  D   1874-   Grosvenor
WESTMORLAND
  E   1397-1570F Nevill
  E   1624-   Fane
WESTON
B   1628-1688X Weston
Weston
  1633-1688X PORTLAND E
  1628-1688X WESTON B
WESTON-SUPER-MARE
  B   1963-1965X Alexander
WESTPORT
  V(I) 1768-   Browne
WESTWOOD
B   1944-   Westwood
Westwood
  1944-   WESTWOOD B
WEXFORD
  E(I) 1446-   Talbot
WEYMOUTH
  V   1682-   Thynne
WHADDON
  B   1616-1687X Villiers
  B(L) 1978-   Page
WHARNCLIFFE
  B   1826-   Stuart-Wortley-
                     Mackenzie
  E   1876-   Stuart-Wortley-
                     Mackenzie
WHARTON
  B   1545-1974A Wharton
  E   1706-1728F Wharton
  M   1715-1728F Wharton
  D   1718-1728F Wharton
Wharton
  1714-1728F CATHERCLOUGH M(I)
  1715-1731X MALMESBURY M
  1715-1731X RATHFARNHAM E(I)
  1715-1731X TRIM B(I)
  1545-1974A WHARTON B

Wharton (Cont'd)
  1706-1728F WHARTON E
  1715-1728F WHARTON M
  1718-1728F WHARTON D
  1706-1731X WINCHENDON V
WHEATLEY
  B(L) 1970-   Wheatley
Wheatley
  1970-   WHEATLEY B(L)
WHITBURGH
B   1912-1967X Borthwick
WHITE
  Bss(L) 1970-   White
White
  1863-   ANNALY B(I)
  1797-1891X BANTRY B
  1800-1891X BANTRY V
  1816-1891X BANTRY E
  1893-1908X OVERTOUN B
  1970-   WHITE Bss(L)
WHITELAW OF PENRITH
  V   1983-   Whitelaw
Whitelaw
  1983-   WHITELAW OF PENRITH V
Whiteley
  1908-   MARCHAMLEY B
Whitfield
  1951-   KENSWOOD B
WHITTINGTON
  B   1297-1297X Whittington
Whittington
  1297-1297X WHITTINGTON B
WHITWORTH
  V   1813-1825X Whitworth
  E   1815-1825X Whitworth
WHITWORTH OF GALWAY
  B(I) 1720-1725X Whitworth
WHITWORTH OF NEWPORT-PRATT
  B(I) 1800-1825X Whitworth
Whitworth
  1815-1825X ADBASTON B
  1813-1825X WHITWORTH V
  1815-1825X WHITWORTH E
  1720-1725X WHITWORTH OF GALWAY B(I)
  1800-1825X WHITWORTH OF NEWPORT-
                     PRATT B(I)
WICKLOW
  V(I) 1785-1978X Forward-Howard
  E(I) 1793-1978X Forward-Howard
WIDDRINGTON
  B   1643-1716F Widdrington

167

Widrington
1643-1716F WIDRINGTON B
WIDGERY
B(L) 1971-   Widgery
Widgery
1971-   WIDGERY B(L)
Widvile
1448-1491X RIVERS B
1466-1491X RIVERS E
1462-1473A SCALES B
WIGAN
B   1826-   Lindsay
WIGRAM
B   1935-   Wigram
Wigram
1935-   WIGRAM B
WIGG
B(L) 1967-1983X Wigg
Wigg
1967-1983X WIGG B(L)
WIGODER
B(L) 1974-   Wigoder
Wigoder
1974-   WIGODER B(L)
WIGTON
E(S) 1341-1371X Fleming
E(S) 1606-1747L Fleming
WILBERFORCE
B(L) 1964-   Wilberforce
Wilberforce
1964-   WILBERFORCE B(L)
Wilbraham: See Bootle-Wilbraham
Wilde
1869-1899X PENZANCE B
1850-1899X TRURO B
Willey
1922-1982X BARNBY B
William, Prince of Scotland
1152-1157X NORTHUMBERLAND E
WILLIAMS
B   1948-1966X Williams
WILLIAMS OF BARNBURGH
B(L) 1961-1967X Williams
WILLIAMS OF THAME
B   1554-1559A Williams
Williams
1455-   BERNERS Bss
1962-1970X FRANCIS-WILLIAMS B(L)
1948-1966X WILLIAMS B
1961-1967X WILLIAMS OF BARNBURGH
                B(L)

Williams (Cont'd)
1554-1559A WILLIAMS OF THAME B
See also: Rees-Williams
WILLIAMSON
B(L) 1962-1983X Williamson
Williamson
1895-1930X ASHTON B
1922-   FORBES B
1962-1983X WILLIAMSON B(L)
WILLINGDON
B   1910-   Freeman-Thomas
V   1924-   Freeman-Thomas
M   1936-1979X Freeman-Thomas
WILLINGTON
B   1329-1396X Willington
Willington
1329-1396X WILLINGTON B
WILLIS
B(L) 1963-   Willis
Willis
1963-   WILLIS B(L)
WILLOUGHBY OF PARHAM
B   1547-1779X
WILLOUGHBY DE BROKE
B   1491-   Willoughby
WILLOUGHBY DE ERESBY
B   1313-   Willoughby
Willoughby
1711-   MIDDLETON B
1547-1779X WILLOUGHBY OF PARHAM B
1491-   WILLOUGHBY DE BROKE B
1313-   WILLOUGHBY DE ERESBY B
See also: Heathcote-Drummond-
    Willoughby
Wills
1929-   DULVERTON B
1906-1911X WINTERSTOKE B
WILMINGTON
B   1728-1743X Compton
E   1730-1743X Compton
B   1812-   Compton
WILMOT
V(I) 1621-1681X Wilmot
B   1643-1681X Wilmot
WILMOT OF SELMESTON
B   1950-1964X Wilmot
Wilmot
1620-1681X ATHLONE V(I)
1652-1681X ROCHESTER E
1621-1681X WILMOT V(I)

Wilmot (Cont'd)
  1643-1681X WILMOT B
  1950-1964X WILMOT OF SELMESTON B
WILSON
  B   1946-   Wilson
WILSON OF HIGH WRAY
  B(L) 1976-   Wilson
WILSON OF LANGSIDE
  B(L) 1967-   Wilson
WILSON OF RADCLIFFE
  B(L) 1974-1983X Wilson
WILSON OF RIEVAULX
  B(L) 1983-
Wilson
  1832-1871P BERNERS B
  1943-   MORAN B
  1906-   NUNBURNHOLME B
  1946-   WILSON B
  1976-   WILSON OF HIGH WRAY
             B(L)
  1967-   WILSON OF LANGSIDE
             B(L)
  1974-1983X WILSON OF RADCLIFFE
             B(L)
  1983-   WILSON OF RIEVAULX
             B(L)
Wilson-Patten
  1874-1892X WINMARLEIGH B
WILTON
  E   1801-   Egerton
  V   1714-1789X Brydges
WILTSHIRE
  E   1397-1399F Scrope
  E   1449-1461X Butler
  E   1470-1499X Stafford
  E   1509-1523X Stafford
  E   1529-1533X Boleyn
  E   1550-   Paulet
WIMBLEDON
  V   1626-1638X Cecil
WIMBORNE
  B   1880-   Guest
  V   1918-   Guest
WINCHENDON
  V   1706-1731X Wharton
WINCHESTER
  E   1207-1264X Quincy
  E   1322-1326X Despencer
  E   1472-1499S Bruges
  M   1551-   Paulet

WINCHILSEA
  E   1628-   Finch
WINDLESHAM
  B   1937-   Hennessy
WINDSOR
  B   1529-   Windsor
  V(I) 1699-1758X Windsor
  E   1796-   Stuart
  V   1905-   Windsor-Clive
  D   1937-1972X Windsor
Windsor   *
  1958-   CARRICK E(S)
  1958-   CHESTER E
  (1874-1943X CONNAUGHT & STRATHEARN D)
  1952-   CORNWALL D
  1928-   CULLODEN B
  1934-   DOWNPATRICK B
  1928-   GLOUCESTER D
  1920-1936M INVERNESS E
  1934-   KENT D
  1920-1936M KILLARNEY B
  1711-1758X MONTJOY OF THE ISLE OF
             WIGHT B
  1682-1843X PLYMOUTH E
  1934-   ST ANDREWS E
  1928-   ULSTER E
  1529-   WINDSOR B
  1699-1758X WINDSOR V(I)
  1937-1972X WINDSOR D
  1920-1936M YORK D
Windsor-Clive
  1905-   PLYMOUTH E
  1905-   WINDSOR V
WINDSORE
  E   1381-1384X Windsore
Windsore
  1381-1384X WINDSORE E
WINGFIELD
  B(I) 1743-   Wingfield
Wingfield
  1618-1634X POWERSCOURT V(I)
  1665-1718X POWERSCOURT V(I)
  1743-   POWERSCOURT V(I)
  1885-   POWERSCOURT B
  1743-   WINGFIELD B(I)
WINMARLEIGH
  B   1874-1892X Wilson-Patten
Winn
  1797-   ALLANSON & WINN B(I)
  1885-   ST OSWALD B

169   * See also Addenda

WINSTANLEY
   B(L) 1975-   Winstanley
Winstanley
   1975-   WINSTANLEY B(L)
WINSTER
   B   1942-1961X Fletcher
WINTERBOTTOM
   B(L) 1965-   Winterbottom
Winterbottom
   1965-   WINTERBOTTOM B(L)
WINTERSTOKE
   B   1906-1911X Wills
WINTERTON
   B(I) 1761-   Turnour
   E(I) 1766-   Turnour
WINTON
   E   1859-   Montgomerie
   See also: EGLINTON & WINTON
WINTOUN
   E(S) 1600-1716F Seton
WISE
   B   1951-   Wise
Wise
   1951-   WISE B
WITTENHAM
   B   1918-1931X Faber
WODEHOUSE
   B   1797-   Wodehouse
Wodehouse
   1797-   KIMBERLEY B
   1866-   KIMBERLEY B
   1797-   WODEHOUSE B
WOKINGHAM
   B.   1689-1708X Denmark, Prince
                      of
Wolfe
   1795-1830X KILWARDEN B(I)
   1798-1830X KILWARDEN B
   1800-1830X KILWARDEN V(I)
WOLFENDEN
   B(L) 1974-1985X Wolfenden
Wolfenden
   1974-1985X WOLFENDEN B(L)
WOLMER
   V   1882-   Palmer
WOLSELEY
   B   1882-1913X Wolseley
   V   1885-1936X Wolseley
Wolseley
   1882-1913X WOLSELEY B
   1885-1936X WOLSELEY V

WOLVERTON
   B   1100/35-1272/1307X Wolverton,
                      De
   B   1869-   Glyn
Wolverton, De
   1100/35-1272/1307X WOLVERTON B
Wood
   1866-   HALIFAX V
   1944-   HALIFAX E
   1868-1881X HATHERLEY B
   1925-   IRWIN B
   1979-   HOLDERNESS B(L)
Woodall
   1946-1974X UVEDALE OF NORTH END B
WOODBRIDGE
   B   1932-1949X Churchman
Woodhouse
   1918-   TERRINGTON B
WOODSTOCK
   B   1320-1407A Holland
   B   1320-   Plantagenet
   V   1689-   Bentinck
WOOLAVINGTON
   B   1922-1935X Buchanan
WOOLLEY
   B(L) 1967-   Woolley
Woolley
   1967-   WOOLLEY B(L)
WOOLTON
   B   1939-   Marquis
   V   1953-   Marquis
   E   1956-   Marquis
WOOTTON OF ABINGER
   Bss(L) 1958-   Wootton
Wootton
   1958-   WOOTTON OF ABINGER Bss(L)
WORCESTER
   E   1135/54-1166X Bellomont, De
   E   1397-1404X Percy
   E   1420-1431 Beauchamp
   E   1449-1485F Tiptoft
   E   1514-   Somerset
   M   1642-   Somerset
WORLINGHAM
   B   1835-   Acheson
Worms, De
   1895-1903X PIRBRIGHT B
WORSLEY
   B   1837-   Anderson-Pelham
Wortley: See Stuart-Wortley
                Stuart-Wortley-Mackenzie

WOTTON
B   1603-1630X Wotton
B   1650-1683X Kirckhoven
Wotton
    1680-1683X BELLOMONT E(I)
    1660-1667X CHESTERFIELD Css
    1603-1630X WOTTON B
WOTTON-BASSET
B   1681-1753X Hyde
WRAXALL
B   1928-   Gibbs
WRENBURY
B   1915-   Buckley
WRIGHT
B(L) 1932-1964X Wright
WRIGHT OF ASHTON UNDER LYNE
B(L) 1968-1974X Wright
Wright
    1932-1964X WRIGHT B(L)
    1968-1974X WRIGHT OF ASHTON UNDER
            LYNE B(L)
WRIOTHESLEY
B   1544-1667X Wriothesley
Wriothesley
    1653-1667X CHICHESTER E
    1547-1667X SOUTHAMPTON E
    1544-1667X WRIOTHESLEY B
WROTTESLEY
B   1838-   Wrottesley
Wrottesley
    1838-   WROTTESLEY B
WYCOMBE
B   1760-   Petty-Fitzmaurice
E   1784-   Petty-Fitzmaurice
WYFOLD
B   1919-   Hermon-Hodge
Wykeham
    1834-1870X WENMAN Bss
WYNDHAM
B(I) 1731-1845X Wyndham
Wyndham
    1749-1845X EGREMONT E
    1963-   EGREMONT B
    1859-   LECONFIELD B
    1731-1845X WYNDHAM B(I)
Wyndham-O'Brien
    1543-1774X IBRACKAN B(I)
Wyndham-Quin
    1866-1926X KENRY B
WYNFORD
B   1829-   Best

Wynn
    1776-   NEWBOROUGH B(I)
Wynn-Carrington
    1895-1928X CARRINGTON E
    1895-1928X LINCOLNSHIRE E
    1912-1928X LINCOLNSHIRE M
    1895-1928X WENDOVER V
WYNNE-JONES
B(L) 1964-1982X Wynne-Jones
Wynne-Jones
    1964-1982X WYNNE-JONES B(L)

(TITLES are in CAPITALS
Surnames in smalls)

171

YARBOROUGH
  B   1794-   Anderson-Pelham
  E   1837-   Anderson-Pelham
Yarburgh-Bateson, De
  1885-   DERAMORE B
Yarde-Buller
  1888-   CHURSTON B
YARMOUTH
  V   1673-1732X Paston
  E   1679-1732X Paston
  Bss(L) 1740-1765X Walmoden
  Css(L) 1740-1765X Walmoden
  E   1793-   Seymour
YELVERTON
  B(I) 1795-1910D Yelverton
Yelverton
  1795-1910D AVONMORE B(I)
  1800-1910D AVONMORE V(I)
  1643-1799P GREY DE RUTHYN B
  1690-1799X LONGUEVILLE V
  1717-1799X SUSSEX E
  1795-1910D YELVERTON B(I)
Yerburgh
  1929-   ALVINGHAM B
YORK
  D   1385-1461M Plantagenet
  D   1474-1483X Plantagenet
  D   1494-1509M Tudor
  D   1605-1625M Stuart
  D   1643-1685M Stuart
  D   1716-1728X Guelph
  D   1760-1767X Guelph
  D   1784-1827X Guelph
  D   1892-1910M Guelph
  D   1920-1936M Windsor
Yorke
  1788-1792X DOVER B
  1733-   HARDWICKE B
  1754-   HARDWICKE E
  1754-   ROYSTON V
YOUNG
  Bss(L) 1971-   Young
  B(L) 1984-   Young
YOUNG OF DARTINGTON
  B(L) 1978-   Young
Young
  1935-   KENNET B
  1870-1876X LISGAR B
  1971-   YOUNG Bss(L)
  1984-   YOUNG B(L)

Young (Cont'd)
  1978-   YOUNG OF DARTINGTON B(L)
  See also: Hughes-Young
YOUNGER OF LECKIE
  V   1923-   Younger
Younger
  1923-1946X BLANESBURGH B(L)
  1923-   YOUNGER OF LECKIE V
YPRES
  E   1922-   French
Ysondon
  1199/1216-1216/72X EWE B
YSTWYTH
  B   1921-1935X Vaughan-Davies

ZETLAND
  E   1838-   Dundas
  M   1892-   Dundas
ZOUCHE OF HARYNGWORTH
  B   1272/1307-....P Zouche, La
  B   1308-1485F Zouche, La
  B   1495-1625A Zouche, La
  Bss 1829-   Curzon
ZOUCHE OF ASHBY
  B   1299-1314A Zouche, La
ZOUCHE OF MORTIMER
  B   1323-1406X Zouche, La
Zouche, La
  1272/1307-....P ZOUCHE OF HARYNGWORTH B
  1308-1485F ZOUCHE OF HARYNGWORTH B
  1495-1625A ZOUCHE OF HARYNGWORTH B
  1299-1314A ZOUCHE OF ASHBY B
  1323-1406X ZOUCHE OF MORTIMER B
ZUCKERMAN
  B(L) 1971-   Zuckerman
Zuckerman
  1971-   ZUCKERMAN B(L)

ADDENDA

AIREY OF ABINGDON
  Bss(L) 1979-   Neave
ALDBOROUGH
  Bss 1722-1778X Schulenburg
ALDERNEY
  B   1726-1765X Guelph
BARNETT
  B(L) 1983-   Barnett
Barnett
  1983-   BARNETT B(L)
BLANCH
  B(L)   Blanch
Blanch
  1983-   BLANCH B(L)
BOTTOMLEY
  B(L) 1984-   Bottomley
Bottomley
  1984-   BOTTOMLEY B(L)
BRANDON OF OAKBROOK
  B(L) 1981-   Brandon
Brandon
  1981-   BRANDON OF OAKBROOK B(L)
Braye
  1529-   BRAYE B
BRIGHTMAN
  B(L) 1982-   Brightman
Brightman
  1982-   BRIGHTMAN B(L)
Browne
  1841-1853X KENMARE B
BROXBOURNE
  B(L) 1983-   Walker-Smith
BRUCE-GARDYNE
  B(L) 1983-   Bruce-Gardyne
Bruce-Gardyne
  1983-   BRUCE-GARDYNE B(L)
CAMERON OF LOCHBROOM
  B(L) 1984-   Cameron
Cameron
  1984-   CAMERON OF LOCHBROOM
            B(L)
CAMPDEN
  V   1628-1629X Hicks
CARMICHAEL OF KELVINGROVE
  B(L) 1983-   Carmichael
Carmichael
  1983-   CARMICHAEL OF KELVIN-
          GROVE B(L)

CARRICK
  E(I) 1315-1321X Butler
CHAPPLE OF HOXTON
  B(L) 1985-   Chapple
Chapple
  1985-   CHAPPLE OF HOXTON B(L)
CHESTER *
  E   1398-   Plantagenet
CORNWALL *
  D   1399-   Plantagenet
Courtenay
  1553-   DEVON E
DEVON
  E   1553-   Courtenay
Drummond
  1685-1902D MELFORT V(S)
EVERSLEY OF HECKFIELD
  V   1857-1888X Shaw-Lefevre
FANSHAWE OF RICHMOND
  B(L) 1983-   Royle
Fitzalan
  1397-1556P MALTRAVERS B
Gibbs
  1923-   HUNSDON B
GLENAWLEY
  B(I) 1701-1814X Howe
GRAHAM OF EDMONTON
  B(L) 1983-   Graham
GRAY OF CONTIN
  B(L) 1983-   Gray
Gray
  1983-   GRAY OF CONTIN B(L)
Guelph
  1726-1765X ALDERNEY B
  1874-1943X CONNAUGHT & STRATHEARN D
  1892-1910M INVERNESS E
  1726-1765X KENNINGTON E
  1892-1910M KILLARNEY B
  1892-1910M YORK D
HENDERSON OF BROMPTON
  B(L) 1984-   Henderson
Henderson
  1984-   HENDERSON OF BROMPTON B(L)
Hogg: See McGarel Hogg
INVERNESS
  E   1892-1910M Guelph
Jenkinson
  1786-1851X HAWKESBURY B

* Special creation as hereditary title of heir to throne

173

```
KENNINGTON
  E    1726-1765X Guelph
KILLARNEY
  B    1892-1910M Guelph
King
  1764-      KINGSTON B(I)
  1766-      KINGSTON V(I)
  1768-      KINGSTON E(I)
LANE
  B(L) 1979-      Lane
Lane
  1979-      LANE B(L)
MALTRAVERS
  B    1397-1556P Fitzalan
MONTAGU
  M    1461-1477F Nevill
  B    1533-1539F Pole
MURRAY
  B(L) 1985-      Murray
Murray
  1985-      MURRAY B(L)
Plantagenet
  1398-      CHESTER E
  1399-      CORNWALL D
Pole
  1444-1503F SUFFOLK M
ROSKILL
  B(L) 1980-      Roskill
Roskill
  1980-      ROSKILL B(L)
SANDHURST
  B    1871-      Mansfield
Schulenburg
  1722-1778X ALDBOROUGH Bss
TEMPLEMAN
  B(L) 1982-      Templeman
Templeman
  1982-      TEMPLEMAN B(L)
TEVIOTDALE: See CUMBERLAND &
                TEVIOTDALE
TEYES: See TYES
WARNOCK
  Bss(L) 1985-      Warnock
Warnock
  1985-      WARNOCK Bss(L)
Windsor
  1952-      ROTHESAY D(S)
  1958-      THE ISLES L(S)
```

(TITLES are in CAPITALS
 Surnames in smalls)